CW00919472

Jan Tschichold
Designer
The Penguin Years

Jan Tschichold Designer

The Penguin Years

Richard B. Doubleday

Oak Knoll Press

Lund Humphries

2006

Published in 2006 by
Oak Knoll Press
310 Delaware Street
New Castle, Delaware, USA
www.oakknoll.com

&

Lund Humphries
Gower House
Croft Road
Aldershot
Hampshire GU11 3HR
United Kingdom

Lund Humphries is part of Ashgate Publishing

www.lundhumphries.com

ISBN: 1-58456-178-5 (Oak Knoll Press)
ISBN: 0 85331 946 4 (Lund Humphries)

Title: Jan Tschichold, Designer: The Penguin Years
Author: Richard B. Doubleday
Copy Editor: Donna Giordano
Typographer & Designer: Geoffrey E. Matheson
Dust Jacket Design: Geoffrey E. Matheson
Publishing Director: J. Lewis von Hoelle

The British CIP Record for this book is available from
The British Library, London, UK

Library of Congress Cataloging-in-Publication Data:
Available from Publisher

This work was printed and bound in China on archival, acid-free paper meeting the requirements of the American Standard for Permanence of Paper for Printed Library Materials.

Table of Contents

For Elizabeth Doubleday

Acknowledgements

At Oak Knoll Press, I would like to extend my thanks to John L. von Hoelle, Publishing Director, and Geoffrey E. Matheson for his elegant design of the book. At Lund Humphries, I would like to extend my thanks to Lucy Myers, Managing Director, and particularly, Lucy Clark, Commissioning Editor, whose comments, suggestions, and guidance were invaluable during the tenuous moments. I am also indebted to Helen Fraser, Managing Director of the Penguin Group (UK), for giving me permission to access the Penguin Books archive and Ms. Hannah Lowery, Nicholas Lee, and Michael Richardson, Archivists, Special Collections, Arts and Social Sciences Library at Bristol University, who offered me assistance and guided me through the many boxes comprising the Penguin archive. Also to Dr. Graham Hogg, Rare Book Collections, National Library of Scotland, Edinburg, for his patience and assistance with the Ruari McLean archive.

Over the last several years, Professor Alston Purvis and Professor Bob Burns have been trustworthy colleagues providing encouragement, with intellectual and illuminating conversation, and I am eternally grateful.

My many thanks are due to Ruari McLean, whose writing on Tschichold was the catalyst for me to pursue this project and who unselfishly provided me with essential primary sources for the book. I would also like to acknowledge the helpful suggestions by Fianach Lawry.

I am also indebted to Alan Fletcher for his poignant introductory note concerning Jan Tschichold. I have the greatest admiration for Fletcher's sumptuous work, inspirational and thought provoking books, and those rare moments when he has graciously invited my graphic design students into his extraordinary studio in Notting Hill Gate.

I would also like to acknowledge the late Rudolf Hostettler for the expanded bibliography. Prior to his death Jan Tschichold modified the bibliography and appeared in *Typographische Monatsblätter*, vol. 9, 287-322 (St. Gall, 1972). This newly edited version was designed for the purpose of the work on Jan Tschichold published in 1976 by Verlag der Kunst of Dresden.

And lastly, my love, admiration and sincere thanks go to my wife, Elizabeth.

The typeface, Sabon, used in this text was designed by Jan Tschichold. As an added tribute to this internationally famous book designer, most of the formatting and typographical conventions used in this work are those recommended by this master typographer.

Foreword by Alston W. Purvis

Alston W. Purvis is Associate Professor of Graphic Design at Boston University. During his career, he has worked as an instructor at The Cooper Union and at the Royal Academy of Fine Arts at the Hague. He is author of *Dutch Graphic Design, 1918-1945*; and *H. N. Werkman*; and co-author of *Graphic Design 20th Century, A Century of Posters*; and *Wendingen: A Journal of Arts 1918-1932*; and co-author of *Meggs' History of Graphic Design, Fourth Edition*.

In 1935, perhaps referring to his own career, F. Scott Fitzgerald wrote "*there are no second acts in American life.*" This statement is applicable to other places, times, and professions — Jan Tschichold not only experienced a "second act" but a glorious third act as well. Through his ability to re-invent himself, Tschichold's life followed a complete circle beginning with tradition, then embracing neue typographie, and finally returning to classical book design.

As the son of a designer and sign painter in Leipzig, Tschichold acquired an early enthusiasm and love for traditional calligraphy and classical letterforms, and his studies at the Leipzig Academy and his work as a calligrapher at Insel Verlag helped to deepen and solidify this passion. This was augmented by his extensive examination of the type specimen book collection at the Master Printers Federation in Leipzig. Then, in 1924 he began to fervently incorporate the design concepts of the Bauhaus and the Russian constructivists into his work. Whatever path Tschichold chose to follow was invariably pursued without compromise or deviation, and he soon became the paladin of the neue typographie in Europe. With this abrupt and radical transformation he discarded outright what he then considered to be the "degenerate typefaces and arrangements" of the past, and through asymmetrical typography he seized upon a new means to express his vision of the contemporary "Zeitgeist." He was now convinced that an active force should permeate typographic arrangement and that type should appear to be in motion rather than stationary. For him symmetrical typography was erroneous because it did nothing to interpret the content of the message. In addition, he felt that typefaces should be elementary in form without embellishment, and in his eyes sans serif types satisfied this requirement.

Working mainly as a book designer after moving to Basel in 1934, Tschichold gradually commenced to refute the maxims of neue typographie and began to incorporate roman, Egyptian, script, and decorative ornaments as part of his design repertoire. Although he wrote in 1946 that a principal reason for his abandonment of neue typographie was because its "impatient attitude" conformed to "the German bent for the absolute," there was perhaps a more fundamental rationale for this transformation. Could Tschichold have then sensed that he had arrived at a stage where the development of neue typographie could go no further, that he had pushed this form to its logical conclusion? In his 1937 poster for the constructivist exhibition in Basil there are clear signs that he had reached the culmination of what he had begun in 1924.

Even with his abrupt transformation in 1924, Tschichold was never far from his roots. Many of his maxims for asymmetrical typography could be equally applied to the symmetrical phase as well. The later work is similarly concerned with balance, hierarchy, and visual contrast. For Tschichold the objective of good typography would always be to deliver the content in the most terse and effective way possible. With both asymmetrical and symmetrical typography, white space intervals were used as important design devices and played an important fundamental role, and typographic rules and bars were often employed as structural tools. In addition, the diverse methodologies both stressed clarity as well as beauty.

Most importantly, Tschichold was a humanist, and he became increasingly convinced that typographers should maintain a traditional heritage and draw upon the wisdom of past typographic achievements. Although he continued to believe that the neue typographie could be appropriate for advertising and industrial purposes, as well as for publications concerning contemporary art, he ultimately considered it nonsensical to apply it to books such as Shakespeare's plays or even modern literature. Legibility was an additional factor, and he later said that reading lengthy amounts of sans serif texts was "genuine torture." It is noteworthy, though, that he continued to use a sans serif type for many of the Penguin covers, although his choice was Gill Sans which had calligraphic origins.

Through his typography for Penguin Books, Tschichold helped to generate a resurgence of traditional typography. Even though in most of his later work he resolutely stressed symmetry and serif typefaces, Tschichold would continue to vigorously defend freedom of artistic and intellectual thought. His contribution to a rebirth of classical typography helped to reestablish a humanist approach to book design, and with this he made yet another permanent contribution to our graphic design heritage.

Alston W. Purvis

Foreword by Alan Fletcher

Member of the now legendary design consultancy Fletcher, Forbes, Gill and a founding partner of the international design group Pentagram. He is currently a consultant art director to Phaidon Press.

I never met Jan Tschichold. He was at Penguin books in London between 1947 and 1949. I had my first acquaintance with the world of design in 1949 when I first attended art school. Certainly, as a naïve nineteen-year-old, I'd never even heard of the word Typography. However, when I moved to the Central School of Art in 1950, under the tutelage of Anthony Froshaug and Herbert Spencer, Tschichold soon became a star in my firmament. I confess I never quite understood the passion, almost ecclesiastic, behind the debate on the virtues and vices of asymmetric and symmetric, or those between serif and non-serif. But what I did learn was that typographers, like medieval stonemasons, had attitude.

Tschichold had attitude and a clear perception of how things should be. He had high standards and meticulous concern for the smallest details. His sojourn at Penguin during the late 1940's has had a profound influence ever since as this book sets out.

Some decades later, after a memorable lunch with John McConnell in New York, we ended up at the Reinhold Brown Gallery on East 78th Street. There, on the wall was the celebrated Jan Tschichold poster *Der Berufsphotograph*. He did it in 1938. I was mesmerised. It now hangs in my studio.

Jan Tschichold will always remain a typographic conundrum in himself.

Alan Fletcher

Preface

This book is a result of my initial and ongoing admiration concerning Tschichold's typographic work and his writings on typography and its magnificent history. My desire to learn more about Tschichold, the designers, typographers, calligraphers, and printers who influenced and shaped his thinking, has been a natural and underlying motivation to look back on the historical development of the book and the graphic arts.

My fascination and typographic love affair with Tschichold began during my graphic arts education, particularly my introduction to the history of graphic design. I was immediately drawn to Tschichold's wide-range of work– masterful juxtoposition of asymmetric layout, the practice of centered typography, exquisite Calligraphy, and revival of Classic book design.

After carefully studying Tschichold's career, it became clearer to me that although Tschichold had pulled away from "The New Typography" and the "functional" principles of the Bauhaus while designing books in Switzerland, his classical typographic roots had been firmly established 19 years earlier and would for many years later inform his approach to book design, particularly at Penguin. Most of us are familiar with Tschichold's Bauhaus period or asymmetric typography and layout and certainly less familiar with his symmetrical book designs, particularly his classical book design and wide-ranging body of work for Penguin Books.

Ruari McLean's chapter pertaining to Penguin Books 1947-49 in his book *Jan Tschichold: typographer* (David Godine, Publisher, 1975) was the impetus and paramount influence to write a thorough chronicle of Tschichold's innovative design practices at Penguin.

I was surprised to learn at present that there had yet to be a book on Jan Tschichold's reign at Penguin and his adherence to the tenets of classical typography and it's application to the mass production of books. I felt it was not only critical, but fitting to write a detailed account and abundantly illustrated book on Jan Tschichold's prolific redesign of Penguin Books.

This account of Tschichold's 32 fruitful months as typographer at Penguin Books is an attempt to illustrate Tschichold's undertaking, innovative design practices, and masterful typographic accomplishments.

Introduction: The Flowering of the Printed Book

"I find it consoling, in these days when civilization appears to be tottering, to think that the great tradition of European book-printing has been revived by a few faithful men and is now in our hands, to carry on and, even in the changed conditions of modern mass-production, to improve, if we go to our task with enough seriousness and sense of responsibility. Where could such qualities be more desirable than in the work of passing on the wisdom of the great poets and thinkers by means of books available to Everyman?" —Jan Tschichold

Between 1947 and 1949 Penguin Books hired Jan Tschichold to standardize Composition Rules and redesign the entire series of paperback and hardback books that could be applied to mass production. Tschichold established the standard for successful book design in Britain, revolutionized typographic principles, and initiated a rebirth of classical book design. He was the first typographer to effectively supervise and design, on such a comprehensive spectrum, well over 500 mass-produced books for a publishing firm.

Jan Tschichold is heir to a rich and long history of typographic design and evolution of the printed book. Graphic and typographic design was made possible in the third century A.D., with the Chinese invention and development of relief printing from woodblocks. From the third to the fifteenth century A.D, illustrated, handwritten, and illuminated manuscripts—Greek, Roman, early Christian, Celtic, Spanish Christian, Romanesque, Gothic, Judaic, Islamic, and late medieval evolved into an opulent design vocabulary comprising complex, geometric patterns, exquisite page designs, various initial letterforms, and gold leaf applied to book design. These dynamic, luminescent scholarly texts exhibited elaborate graphic art by way of the written word. China's invention of paper and printing dispersed slowly toward the West, arriving in Italy in the fourteenth century. Because visual language and early writing systems—hieroglyphs, cuneiform, and Chinese calligraphy—were difficult to learn, Europeans eventually replaced these pictographs, signs, and symbols with the twenty fundamental signs comprising the Greek and Latin alphabets.

The next major printing discovery was movable typographic printing by Johann Gensfleisch zum Gutenberg (circa 1390s-1468). The availability of paper, emerging literate middle class, and subsequent demand for books, were all factors that made typography attainable in Europe during the fifteenth century. Printers in Europe sought a system of book production by exploring the medium and concept of movable type. Gutenberg devised a two-part type mold for casting individual letters of type. His efforts led to the first typographic book, the *Gutenberg Bible*, 1450-55. This two column, forty-two-line Bible, one of the foremost examples of a printer's craft using movable type, displaced handwriting as a means of book makeup and marked the introduction of efficient methods of book production and the mass-production of books.

Another significant printing development occurred 21 years later in England when William Caxton (c. 1422-c. 1491), established the first English printing press in Westminster. Upon his return from Cologne to study the art of printing, he printed the earliest dated book in England, *The Dictes or Sayings of the Philosophers*. Caxton's greatest contribution was his introduction of printing to England, and the impact of his printed works which synthesized the English language throughout the United Kingdom.

German graphic artists and printers created a long standing cultural practice of woodcut illustrated books and textura typography, an early gothic black-letter style whose characteristic was the broken character of its lines, also referred to as Fraktur type. This new medium of communication spread throughout Europe in the sixteenth century. A cultural revival period in the fourteenth and fifteenth centuries in Italy, marking the transition from the medieval to the modern world, revived classical Greek and Roman literature and brought a new approach to book design. The book continued to be a collaboration between a typographic printer and the illuminator who added decorated letters to the beginning of each chapter and decorative ornaments and borders. Three noteworthy Italian renaissance master calligrapher's were Lodovico Arrighi (d.c. 1527), Giovanni Antonio Tagliente (d. 1527), and Giovanni Battista Palatino (c. 1515-c. 1575). All three Italian writing masters produced magnificent specimens of italic handwriting styles and also how to teach the celleresca script. In 1540, Palatino published a popular printer's manual on writing, *Libro nuovo d'imparare a scrivere tutte sorte lettere* (New book to learn to write), that included various handwriting styles, cipher alphabets, exquisite chancery scripts, as well as a voluminous compendium, *Compendio del gran volume* (Compendium of the great volume, 1566).

The sixteenth century in France became known as "The Golden Age of French Typography," as printing and graphic design experienced remarkable growth and benefited from the influence of the Italian Renaissance as well as King Francis I's (1494-1547) promotion of education and the arts. Additionally, two outstanding French graphic artists, Geoffroy Tory (1480-1533) and Claude Garamond (1480-1561), developed an affection for woodcut borders, calligraphy, Roman typefaces, and efflorescent initials designed with such perfection. What was particularly unique about French book design was the geometric shape of type on each page, woodcut borders, unique illustrations, ornaments, lucent gracefulness, and clarity of each page. These skilled artists established a definitive French character of book production and influenced future generations of book designers.

Printing arrived in North America in 1639, with the printing of *The Whole Book of Psalmes*. Although this first effort at printing was a painstaking effort and lacked aesthetic quality, the arrival of printing, coupled with imposed taxes on all legal documents and censorship, nudged the American colonies toward revolution and struggle for independence.

The Rococo era of the eighteenth century brought a period of impressive typographic innovation. In France, Pierre Simon le Jeune (1712-1768), maintained an independent type design and foundry. His type measurement standards, florid type specimens, typographic innovation, and masterful expertise of rococo form had a significant impact on graphic design. In England, William Caslon (1692-1766), worked in a tradition of old style Roman typography. One of his earliest consignments was an Arabic font cast for the Society for Promoting Christian Knowledge. In addition, he designed the graceful Caslon Old Style font that was popular among English printers and solidified his reputation. The tradition of Old Style Roman typographic design continued within England with the innovations of the bookmaker John Baskerville (1706-75). His immersion in the bookmaking practice—setting and casting type, experimenting with printing methods, and wide-ranging lettering styles—helped to improve and transform English printing and type founding. His exquisite serif type designs were the crowning point of the transitional style and bridged the gap of Old Style Roman typographic design and modern typographic design.

England became the center for development and growth during the Industrial Revolution of the eighteenth and nineteenth centuries. As urban populations and technological improvements rapidly grew, the supply and demand for graphics played an important role in marketing and mass-communication. The construction of cast-iron and steam-powered printing presses for high-speed factory operation revolutionized printing. As a result, hand presses were soon replaced as Ottmar Mergenthaler's (1854-99) Linotype text type setting machine replaced hand-type-setters. These rapid changes ushered in a new period of mass communication.

In the second half of the Victorian era, punch-cutters cut their designs in soft metal and stamped the type into a brass matrix. This process of mechanical punch-cutting, in an intensifying and tempestuous graphic-arts market, increased the number of Victorian display faces. With the proliferation of American and English type foundries such as MacKellar, Smith & Jordan (c1866), Herman Ihlenburg (1843-1905), John F. Cumming (1852-1937), and Dickinson Type Foundry (c1839), many Victorian type catalogs and elaborate type specimen books became available in the early 19th century, from which metal-type foundries and letterpress printers could choose from a number of typefaces. A growing need for a more individualized profession of typographer materialized, someone with special talents who studied the history and design of letterforms and could carefully choose the most suitable font for a specific text or printed material to be set in type. As the nineteenth century moved forward, the English publisher William Pickering (1796-1854), collaborated with Charles Whittingham (1795-1876), to establish the Chiswick Press and led the revival of Roman types, Gothic ornament, and liturgical books that penetrated the last decades of the nineteenth century.

Graphic designer and Kelmscott Press founder William Morris (1834-96), bridged the Arts & Crafts movement to the fluid line characteristics of Art Nouveau through exceptional printing and book design. He reclaimed the exquisiteness of incunabula books (books printed before 1501) with hand-made paper, initials, typefaces revived from the fifteenth century, woodcut decorations, woodcut borders, and hand-printing. The Kelmscott Press treated the book as an art form and influenced a new generation of book designers. At the end of the nineteenth century, photographic methods of plate- and block-making put wood engravers out of business. Printing had become a decidedly machine-driven industry.

The revitalization of typographic design as an independent profession was nourished by the influence of the Arts & Crafts movement and the energy of the American book designer Bruce Rogers (1870-1956), American typeface designer Frederick W. Goudy (1865-1947), and American book designer William Addison Dwiggins (1880-1956). Rogers, Goudy, and Dwiggins were influenced by the Kelmscott Press and actualized their affection of letterforms and book design through extraordinary craftsmanship and exhausting work, and applied the design decision-making process to commercial production. In fact, "*During the 1920s Dwiggins first used the term graphic designer to describe his professional activities.*"[1] The two designers working in England's publishing industry who applied the modern art movement's new approach to everyday printing, design problems, and the mass-production of books were Stanley Morison (1889-1967) and Jan Tschichold (1902-1974).

Morison was a self-educated typographer who had a great understanding of letterforms and the history of type design. Among Morison's many contributions to British typography and printing, was his design supervision of *The Times of London* and his design of the typeface Times New Roman, which he used to redesign the newspaper and which became one of the most widely used typefaces throughout England in the twentieth century. In addition, Morison firmly established his design legacy as typographic advisor to both the Cambridge University Press and The British Monotype Corporation, where he was responsible for the growth of its type library from 1920 until after the Second World War. The typefaces he designed were based on historical models—Caslon Old Face, Bembo, Bell, Baskerville, Garamond, Pastonchi, Scotch Roman, Lutetia, and Walbaum—designed explicitly for the Monotype casting system. In particular his efforts as "typographic consultant" at the British Monotype Corporation firmly established an intrical link to Tschichold's efforts at Penguin, where he adopted Morison's distinguished Monotype typefaces. Thanks to the availability of Morison's revived classical typefaces for machine composition, Tschichold chose fonts that reflected the distinguishing characteristics and personality of each Penguin book.

---

[1] Philip B. Meggs, *A History of Graphic Design* (New York: Wiley & Sons, Inc., 1998), p. 175

In 1930, Morison designed a series of distinct yellow book jackets for the publishing firm Victor Gollancz. The whimsical cover designs utilized a mixture of black and magenta typefaces in various sizes and words combined with design to intrigue and invoke the reader.

By the time Jan Tschichold arrived at Penguin Books in 1947, he had already firmly established himself as an exceptional typographer and prolific author with uncommon principles and noteworthy problem-solving ideas on typographic rules, composition, and design of books.

Jan Tschichold's three-year reorganization of all typographic design titles at Penguin Books, during which he designed or prepped for press 500 elegant books—often one per day—was a notable chapter in his design career and led to a revolution in traditional typographic conventions applied to the mass production of books. Tschichold's efforts at Penguin led to the creation of a conventional formulaic style and helped bring typographic communication for the twentieth century to fruitful and successful results. Of all the early authorities of "contemporary typography," Tschichold stood apart from his contemporaries due to his early training in written letters and calligraphic writing, and his study of roman alphabets, old type specimens, and of Italian Renaissance writing masters.

Tschichold was the first designer at Penguin to separate the profession of graphic designer from production editor. Tschichold's prudent planning, inflexible control, and painstaking and exhaustive instructions to the machine compositors and printers permitted outstanding craftsmanship and superior quality of book production. Tschichold tried to achieve a balance between extraordinary handicraft and the restraints, preconditions, and demands of mass-produced books. Tschichold cultivated a design philosophy based on craftsmanship of the past and attempted to apply his design attitudes to the mass-production of books. Comparisons can be traced between Tschichold and the Kelmscott Press. Both were committed to salvaging the gallantry, spirit, intricacy, and beautiful design of incunabula books—hand-made paper, hand-printing, woodcut embellishments, a variety of typefaces based on fifteenth century classical models, attention to the smallest details, faithful adherence to design specifications for printers and compositors, quality paper, decorative borders, and hand drawn lettering. Penguin books' flawless design standard established a supremacy of uniformity and improved the overall aesthetic of books throughout Britain.

The collection of Penguin Books, most of which are from 1947-1949, is my attempt to describe the nature of Tschichold's typographic accomplishment, international revival of traditional typography, and advancement of British book production.

Chapter 1
Tschichold's Graphic Design Foundation

Jan Tschichold (1902-74) was born in Leipzig, Germany, on April 2, 1902, the oldest son of Franz Tschichold and Maria neé Zapff. His father was a sign writer, and as a young child, Jan was exposed to a variety of painted lettering, and he acquired an early interest in typography. To appease his parents' concern for such a dubious future as a professional artist, Tschichold enrolled into the Teacher Training College at Grimma, to develop artistic skills and become an instructor of drawing.

In 1914, Tschichold visited the Internationale Exhibition of Graphic Arts (Internationale Ausstellung für Buchgewerbe und Graphik) at Leipzig, Germany. He was immediately attracted to an issue of the magazine der Zwiebelfisch, a 'Taste in Books and Other Things'. Tschichold spent time studying civilizations, typography, and the book arts in the Leipzig "Hall of Culture," at the age of twelve. It was during this period that Tschichold studied roman alphabets, calligraphy, ornate writing in illuminated manuscripts, the history and craftsmanship of written letters and old type specimens and thus shaped his educational foundation. Tschichold had witnessed for the first time the beautiful work of Italian, Spanish, German, Swiss, and Dutch writing masters such as Giovanni Battista Palatino (d. 1575), Lodovico Arrighi (d.c. 1527), Giovanni Antonio Tagliente (d. 1527), Francisco Lucas, Vespasiano Amphiareo (1501-63), Juan de Yçiar (1515-90), Johann Neudörffer (1497-1563), Urban Wyss, Pierre Simon Fournier le Jeune (1712-68), and Jan van de Velde (1568-1623). (Figure 1, 2, 3, 4)

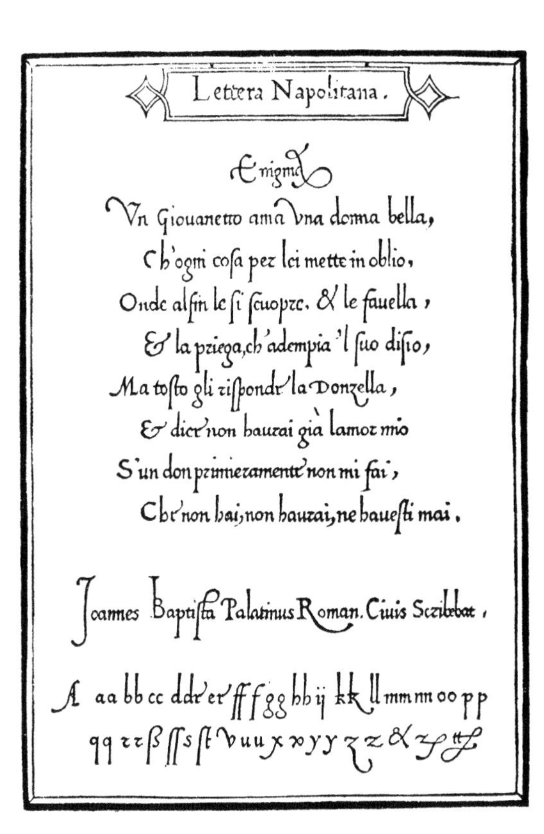

FIGURE 1

Giovani Battista Palatino (d. 1575). Libro di Giovani Battista Palatino nel quale s'insegna a scrivere ogni sorte lettera. Roma. Palatino's standards of letter writing. 1544.

Tschichold carefully studied the handwriting styles and sixteenth century writing manuals of Giovani Battista Palatino.

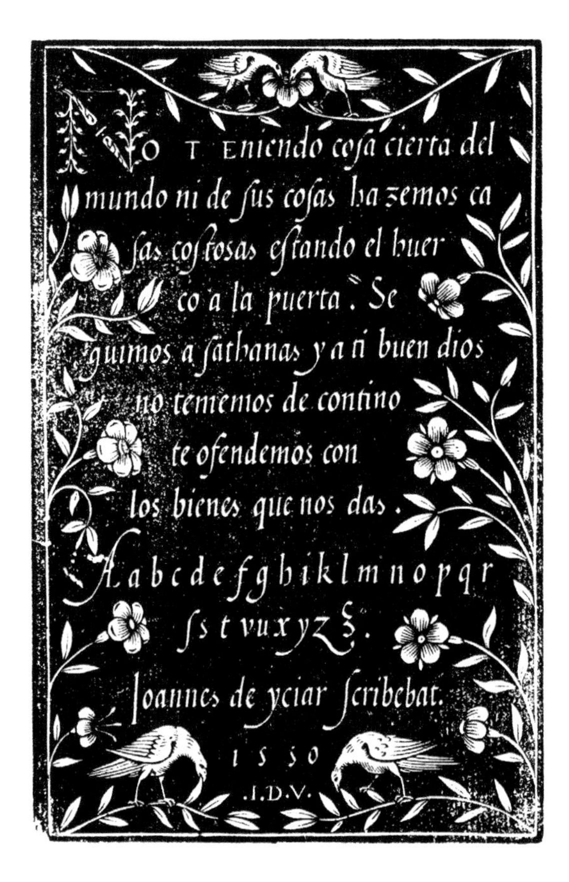

FIGURE 2

Juan de Yçiar (1515-90). Arte subtilissima, por la qual se ensena a escrevir perfectamente . . . por Juan de Yçiar vizcayno. From illustrations in L'Art pour tous. 1550.

Tschichold examined closely and translated cursive and derivatives of cursive by Juan de Yçiar into his own designs for Swiss publishers and Penguin.

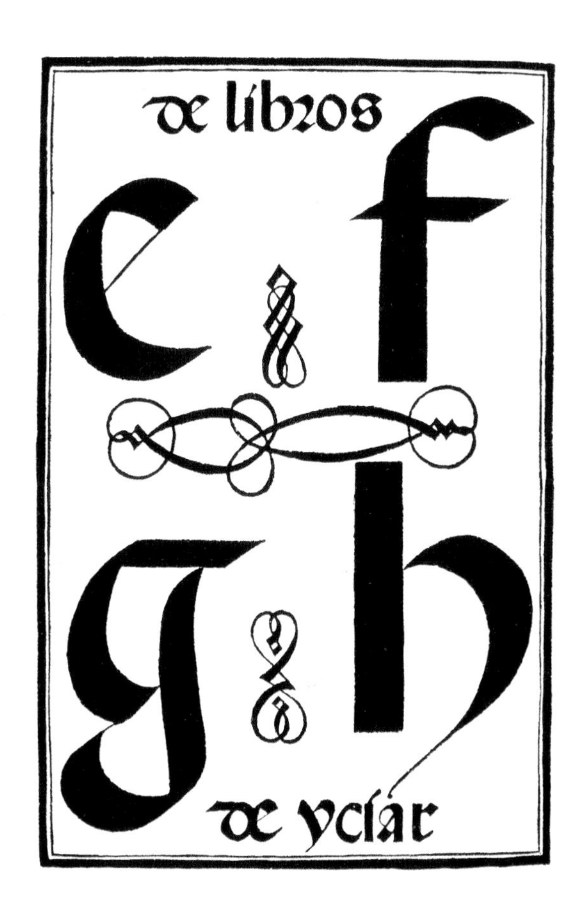

FIGURE 3

Juan de Yçiar (1515-90). From the Gothic period, the beautiful cursive-styled Spanish decorative alphabet, Redonda. 1550.

Another source of inspiration for Tschichold was this Spanish-style cursive example characterized by clear and florid forms and calligraphic ornaments.

FIGURE 4 (below)

Urban Wyss. Libellus valde doctus, elegans & utilis, multa & varia scribendarum literarum genera complectens. 1549.

The Swiss master calligrapher Urban Wyss developed a German hand script model, handsomely crafted with distinguishing features, particularly the graceful and exquisite border, an evident decorative treatment employed by Tschichold for many Penguin cover and title page designs.

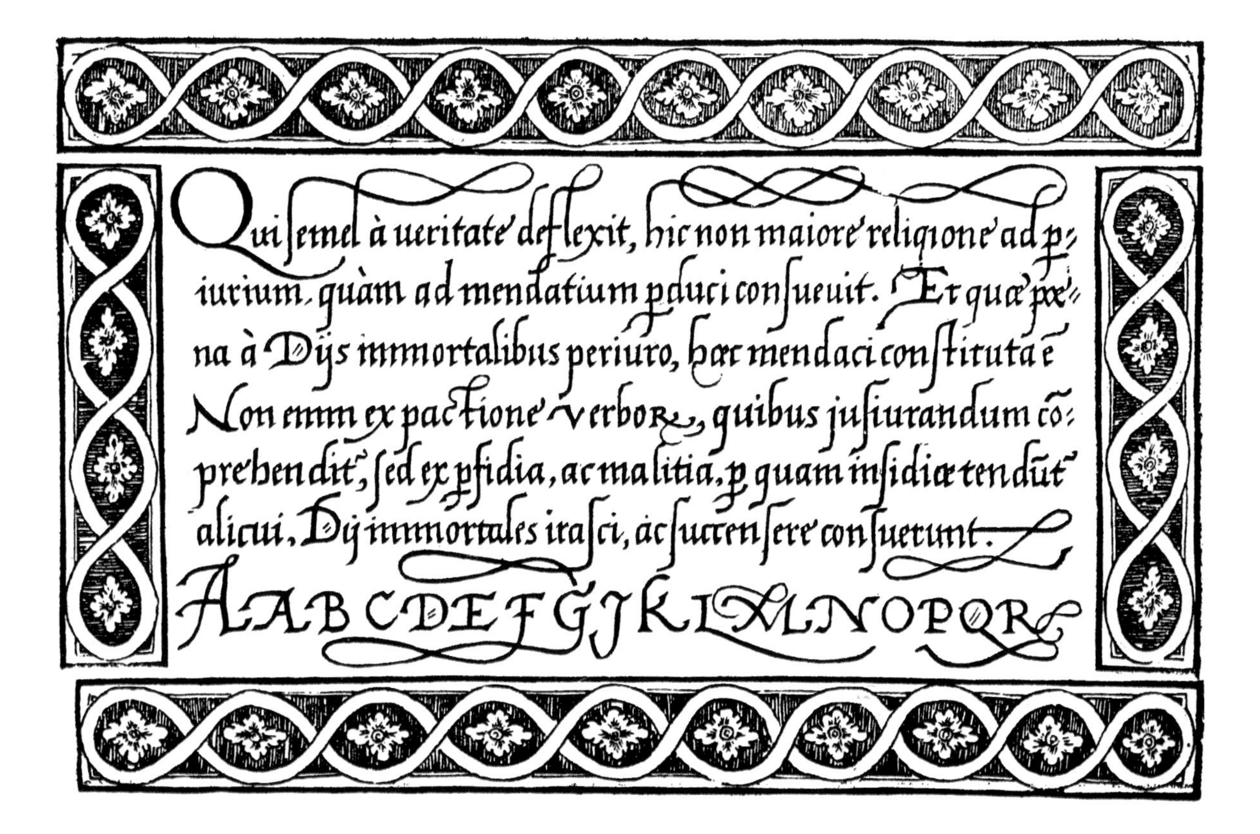

During his studies at the Teacher Training College at Grimma, Tschichold realized that he wanted to become a type designer and was given permission by his parents to enroll at the Academy for the Graphic Arts and the Book Production Trade in Leipzig learning book-binding, calligraphy, etching, and engraving. Tschichold taught himself lettering and calligraphy by hand, examining the lettering in Edward Johnston's (1872-1944) book *Writing and Illuminating, and Lettering* and Rudolf von Larisch's (1856-1934) *Unterricht in Ornamentaler Schrift* (Instruction in Ornamental Writing). These self taught calligraphy exercises increased Tschichold's knowledge and sensitivity to letter spacing, word spacing, and leading by assimilating the lettering of Johnston and von Larisch. Apart from his studies at the Academy for the Graphic Arts and the Book Production Trade, Tschichold enrolled for one year at the School of Arts and Crafts in Dresden and was mentored by the type designer and writing teacher Heinrich Wieynck (1874-1931). Wieynck was educated at the Teaching Institute, Royal Museum of arts and crafts in Berlin and further studies at the Urban College of arts and crafts in Charlottenburg. Tschichold was inspired by many of Wieynck's type designs – Mercedes Antiqua, Tranon, Woellmer Antiqua, Belvedere, and Kolumbus – that were based on the Italian Renaissance writing scripts. In addition, Wieynck designed a family of fraktur's including Wieynck Gotisch, Wienck Fraktur, and Wienck Kanzlei.

In 1921, he returned to the Academy for the Graphic Arts and the Book Production Trade at Leipzig and was appointed assistant of evening lettering classes under the guidance of Professor Hermann Delitsch (1869-1937) and Walter Tiemann (1876-1951). He began to look at the gothic revival lettering of Rudolph Koch's German scripts and embraced the handwriting style in his own type designs. During this time, he spent many hours studying the great type specimen book collection at the Master Printers Federation Library in Leipzig. The Italian Renaissance writing masters and reading room books and resources impressed Tschichold, and firmly established his classical typographical roots. They would, many years later, inform his approach to book design, particularly at Penguin Books. One notable Italian

Renaissance writing master who had an impact on Tschichold was Lodovico Arrighi (d.c. 1527). In 1522, he produced a small manual on writing, the first to be published, *Le Operina da imparare di scrivere littera cancellaresca* (The first writing manual of the chancery hand), that included brilliant examples on how to teach celleresca script. The second part of *Le Operina* was a similar, popular writing manual, *Il Modo de temperare le penne*, which demonstrated a number of italic handwriting styles that were punch cut onto woodblocks by Lautizio de Bartolomeo dei Rotelli. Tschichold also aquired typesetting skills while working for a brief period at Poeschel and Trepte, skillful printers who worked for Insel-Verlag, and later, produced hand-drawn advertisements for the printing firm of Fischer and Wittig in Leipzig. (Figure 5, 6)

Figure 5

Cover drawn by Tschichold for a Leipzig printer's New Year Card, 1922

Originally in Blue, Green, Red, Yellow color. Based on Tschichold's examination of the writing manuals of Lodovico Arrighi and Giovanni Antonio Tagliente, the two Italian Renaissance writing masters of Scripts and Chancery Cursive. This design represents Tchichold's carefully centered placement of exquisitely hand drawn calligraphy, delicate symmetry of the flower motif, and inverted uppercase letters within the frame. This early design treatment, arrangement of calligraphy, framing, and subtle decorative elements were similar to Tschichold's cover designs many years later at Penguin.

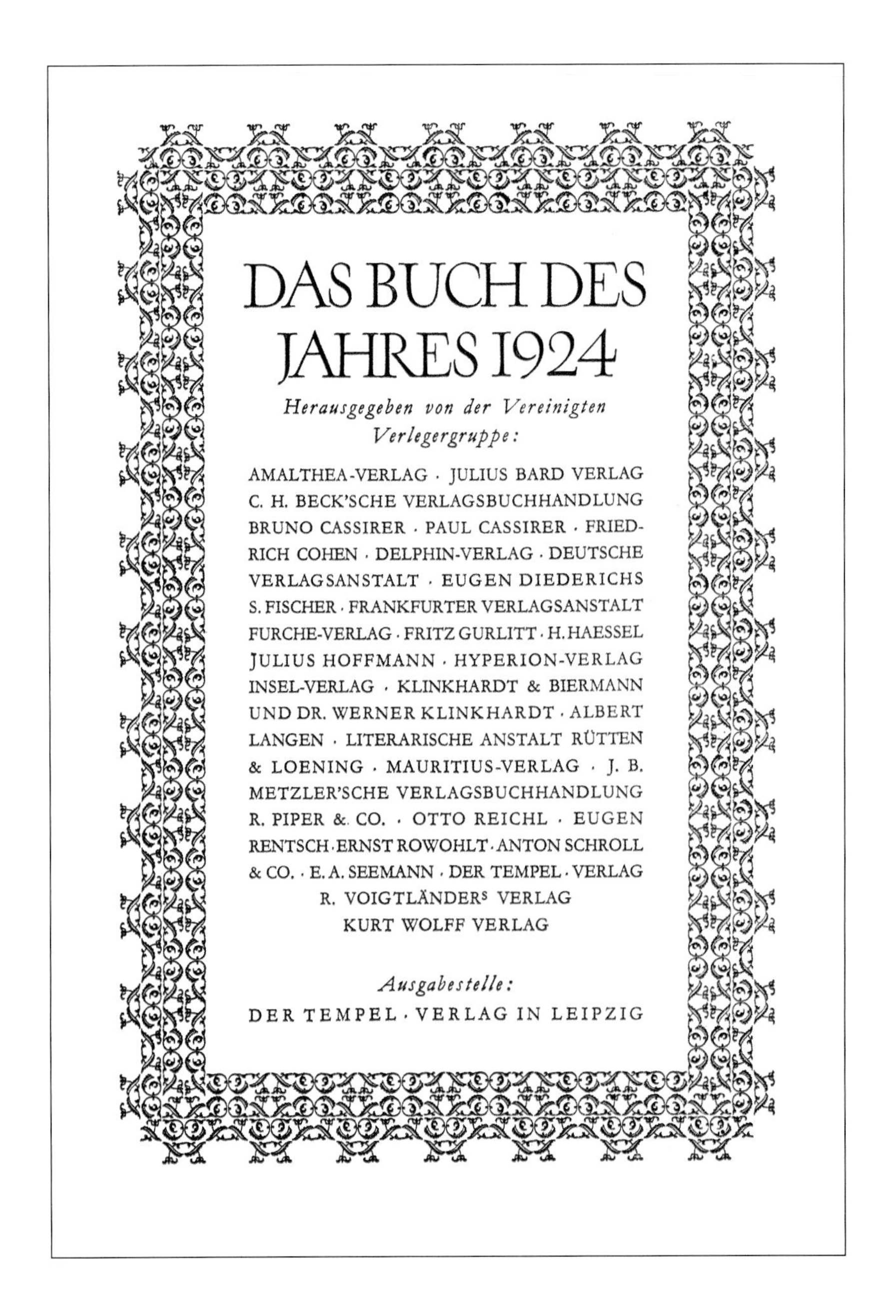
DAS BUCH DES JAHRES 1924

Herausgegeben von der Vereinigten Verlegergruppe:

AMALTHEA-VERLAG · JULIUS BARD VERLAG
C. H. BECK'SCHE VERLAGSBUCHHANDLUNG
BRUNO CASSIRER · PAUL CASSIRER · FRIEDRICH COHEN · DELPHIN-VERLAG · DEUTSCHE VERLAGSANSTALT · EUGEN DIEDERICHS
S. FISCHER · FRANKFURTER VERLAGSANSTALT
FURCHE-VERLAG · FRITZ GURLITT · H. HAESSEL
JULIUS HOFFMANN · HYPERION-VERLAG
INSEL-VERLAG · KLINKHARDT & BIERMANN UND DR. WERNER KLINKHARDT · ALBERT LANGEN · LITERARISCHE ANSTALT RÜTTEN & LOENING · MAURITIUS-VERLAG · J. B. METZLER'SCHE VERLAGSBUCHHANDLUNG
R. PIPER & CO. · OTTO REICHL · EUGEN RENTSCH · ERNST ROWOHLT · ANTON SCHROLL & CO. · E. A. SEEMANN · DER TEMPEL · VERLAG
R. VOIGTLÄNDERS VERLAG
KURT WOLFF VERLAG

Ausgabestelle:

DER TEMPEL · VERLAG IN LEIPZIG

FIGURE 6

Das Buch Des Jahres 1924 Der Tempal, Verlag in Leipzig 1924

The delicate and exquisitely tapered arrangement of typography and ornate detailed framing were comparable to Tschichold's title page designs and book covers many years later at Penguin. The decorative border technique that frames the typography was a forerunner to many of the Penguin covers and title pages, particularly the decorative border for the Penguin Poets series. The elegant and restrained typographic composition is based on Tschichold's study of Roman alphabets and ornate writing in illuminated manuscripts.

The Impact of the Bauhaus

In August 1923, at the age of twenty-one, Tschichold attended the first Weimar Bauhaus Exhibition. He had seen for the first time the graphic design of Josef Albers (1888-1976), Alfred Arndt (1898-1976), Herbert Bayer (1900-85), Marcel Breuer (1902-81), Lyonel Feininger (1871-1956), Walter Gropius (1883-1969), Johannes Itten (1888-1967), Wassily Kandinsky (1866-1944), Paul Klee (1879-1940), Gerhard Marcks (1889-1981), Laszlo Moholy-Nagy (1895-1946), Hannes Meyer (1889-1954), Georg Muche (1895-1987), Hinnerk Scheper (1897-1957), Oskar Schlemmer (1888-1943), Joost Schmidt (1893-1948), Lothar Schreyer (1886-1966), and Gunter Stadler-Stolzl (1897-1983).

The Bauhaus was the logical consequence of a German concern for upgrading design in an industrial society that began in the early 20th century. Prior to the Bauhaus Manifesto, the Deutsche Werkbund (German Association of Craftsman) attempted to elevate standards of design, attracting artists and critics to its class. The group also attempted to unify artist and craftsman with manufacturer to bring aesthetic qualities to mass production. The Bauhaus' link with the wider field of Constructivist designers El Lissitsky (1890-1941) from the Soviet Union and Laslo Moholy-Nagy from Hungary; De Stijl designers Piet Zwart (1885-1977) and Theo van Doesburg (1883-1931) from the Netherlands; Dadaist/Surrealist designers Kurt Schwitters (1887-1948) and John Heartfield (1991-1968) from Germany; and Man Ray (1890-1976) from America, reflected its international ambitions.

The Bauhaus Manifesto, endorsed the ideology of the newly formed school:

"The complete building is the ultimate aim of all the visual arts. Once the noblest function of the fine arts was to embellish buildings; they were indispensable components of great architecture. Today the arts exist in isolation, from which they all can be rescued only through the conscious, cooperative effort of all craftsmen. Architects, painters, and sculptors must learn anew the composite character of the building as an entity...The artist is an exalted craftsman. In rare moments of inspiration, transcending his

conscious will, the grace of heaven may cause his work to blossom into art. But proficiency in his craft is essential to every artist. Therein lies the prime source of creative imagination.

Let us therefore create a new guild of craftsmen without the class-distinctions that raise an arrogant barrier between craftsmen and artists! Let us desire, conceive, and create the new building of the future together. It will combine architecture, sculpture, and painting in a single form, and will one day rise towards the heavens from the hands of a million workers as the crystalline symbol of a new and coming faith." [1A]

The Bauhaus' central purpose and teachings were to release students' creative abilities in order to develop an appreciation for the physical nature of materials such as charcoal for rendering, with emphasis on new design language as well as to teach the fundamental principles of design as a foundation for all visual arts.

Two innovative designers from the Bauhaus school who greatly influenced Jan Tschichold's work were the Hungarian constructivist Laszlo Moholy-Nagy and Herbert Bayer, a student there from 1921 to 1923; both were concerned with pushing for a new unity of art and technology. Laszlo Moholy-Nagy submitted notable comments about typography and graphic design, saying:

"a tool of communication. It must be communicated in its most intense form. The emphasis must be on absolute clarity ... Legibility—communication must never be impaired by a prior esthetics. Letters must never be forced into a preconceived framework, for instance a square." [2]

"an uninhibited use of all linear directions (therefore not only horizontal articulation)." We use all typefaces, type sizes, geometric forms, colors, etc. We want to create a new language of typography whose elasticity, variability, and freshness, of typographical composition [are] exclusively dictated by the inner laws of expression and the optical effect." [3]

[1A] *Bauhaus Journal.* (Munchen: Kraus Reprint, 1977), p. 280.

[2] Philip B. Meggs, *A History of Graphic Design* (New York: Wiley & Sons, Inc.,1998), p. 280.

[3] Meggs, p. 280.

Moholy-Nagy's love for typography present in his interior catalogue layout for the 1923 exhibit, *Staatliches Bauhaus in Weimer, 1919-1923*, inspired Tschichold's interest in visual communication and stylistic devices, and led to his experiments with integrating typography and images. For the design of the interior catalogue, Moholy-Nagy created unconventional spatial arrangements and strong figure ground relationships. He also used smooth right angles, bold red color for hierarchy, contrast of texture and pattern, and juxtoposition of san serif typography. This resulted in a unity of proportion and balance with a mimimal amount of type. Moholy-Nagy's typography treatments encouraged Tschichold to utilize a composition's "white space" with carefully placed typography within that space for balance and hierarchy, and to seek exact interpretation of the contents for clear and precise communication. (Figure 7, 8)

Another important appointed master who greatly influenced Tschichold's work was Herbert Bayer, who had become professor of typography and graphic design at the Bauhaus in 1925. His typographic experimentations helped Functionalism and Constructivism to flourish at the Bauhaus. He used only sans serif fonts and designed a single-case type, Universal, constructed of simple curves and geometrically constructed forms. The Universal alphabet, commonly associated with the Bauhaus school, was a logical approach to creating a typeface for practical use and as an appealing alternative to the preferred heavy, gothic style fonts and broken scripts, known as frakturs, that were traditionally used in German printing. Bayer quoted Dr. Walter Porstmann, a German government specialist in measurement systems, regarding his single-case type:

"There is no large and small alphabet. It is not necessary for one sound to have a large and small sign. The simultaneous use of two characters of completely different alphabets is illogical and unharmonious. We would recommend that the restriction to one alphabet would mean a saving of time and materials (one thinks of the typewriter)." [4]

---

4 Jeremy Aynsley, *Graphic Design in Germany 1890-1945* (Los Angeles: University of California Press, 2000), p.109. This statement was first published as a contribution to a special issue on the new typography edited by Jan Tschichold and entitled 'elementare typographie', *Typographische Mitteilungen*, Leipzig, Year 22, No. 10, October 1925, p. 198.

A distinguishing feature of Bayer's Bauhaus period was extreme contrasts of type size and weight, used to establish a hierarchy and emphasis determined by the most important to the least important of supporting information. In addition, aggressive vertical and horizontal arrangements of typography and images accomplished a well balanced and energetic composition.

The impact of Russian Constructivism

Tschichold met Lissitzky shortly after the Weimer Bauhaus Exhibition in 1923. Tschichold was deeply influenced by the work of Lissitzky, who resided in Germany throughout most of the Weimer Republic and Third Reich. He began to apply Lissitzky's treatment of typography as concrete and abstract contrasting shapes to his own work, including summarizing his observations of sans-serif typography and asymmetrical layouts in his 1925 manifesto, *Typographische Mitteilungen,* and titled 'Elementare Typographie' (The Principles of Typography). He advocated the new typography as unwavering for clear communication of content. Legibility, distinctness, and basic elements of typography, lettering, asymmetry and san-serif type were, in his opinion, the only qualities capable of expressing new-age ideas. Tschichold had embodied the Bauhaus and Russian Constructivists' modernistic design concepts into his own design and developed a new approach to his work.

Work and Teaching in Munich

Shortly thereafter in 1926, Paul Renner (1878-1956) from the German Masters Printers School in Munich appointed Tschichold to teach master printer and trade courses in calligraphy and typography. During this eight-year period at the Munich School he designed film posters for the Munich, 'Phoebus Palace,' which later became classics. These film posters reflected his current ideas of asymmetrical layout and san-serif typography and were endangered by the growing Nazi movement's dislike for the "New Typography," which they labeled as self-indulgent, compared to their preferred, more "German" black-letter typography (based on contemporary calligraphy) in their printed propaganda material. The Nazis German Art

Association considered avant-garde artists who rejected the black-letter style, including Tschichold, to be "Kultur-Bolshvismus." In fact, in defiance to the Nazis, Tschichold would often sign his designs "Ivan Tschichold."

Lenhard: Mensch unterm Hammer
Mensch unterm Hammer
Roman von Josef Lenhard
Die sonderbare Geschichte des sonderbaren Proleten Kilian Narr aus der katholischen bayerischen Pfalz. Unbändiger Freiheits- und Wissensdrang bringt ihn unaufhörlich in Widerstreit mit allen möglichen Obrigkeiten. Dieser Kilian Narr ist zur guten Hälfte Josef Lenhard selbst, der in diesen seinem Erstlingsroman voll bittern Humors Gericht über sich selbst hält.
In Ganzleinen 4.30 RM

FIGURE 7

Des Luigi Da Porto Geschichte Von Romeo und Julia. Paper Cover of a title in the 'Sammlung Birkhauser' Series. Cover designed by Tschichold, 1944.

Tschichold designed this paper cover three years before his arrival at Penguin Books Ltd. The florid and intricate patterned paper cover may have derived from Tschichold's study of the French Rococo era, as well as the modern geometric stylings of Giovani Battista Palatino. This charming and rhythmic standardization would become an important recurring theme for many of the Penguin Book series. The small rectangular title plate is similar to Tschichold's standardization of the King Penguin series and patterned paper technique for the Penguin Music Scores.

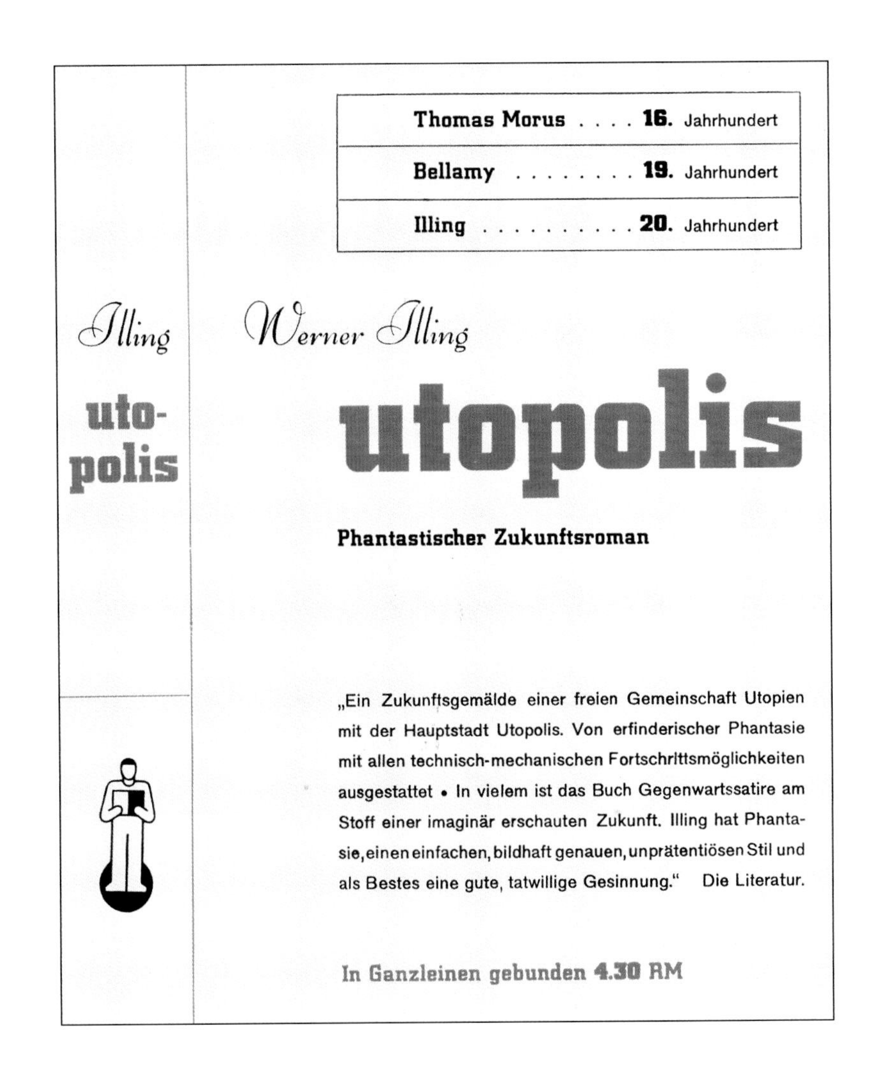

Thomas Morus . . . . 16. Jahrhundert
Bellamy . . . . 19. Jahrhundert
Illing . . . . 20. Jahrhundert
Illing
uto-
polis
Werner Illing
utopolis
Phantastischer Zukunftsroman
„Ein Zukunftsgemälde einer freien Gemeinschaft Utopien mit der Hauptstadt Utopolis. Von erfinderischer Phantasie mit allen technisch-mechanischen Fortschrittsmöglichkeiten ausgestattet • In vielem ist das Buch Gegenwartssatire am Stoff einer imaginär erschauten Zukunft. Illing hat Phantasie, einen einfachen, bildhaft genauen, unprätentiösen Stil und als Bestes eine gute, tatwillige Gesinnung." Die Literatur.
In Ganzleinen gebunden 4.30 RM

FIGURE 8

Utopolis by Werner Illing, Book Jacket designed by Tschichold, 1931.

Although this book cover reflects Tschichold's application of the New Typography, comparisons can be drawn to Tschichold's design direction at Penguin. Tschichold retained sans serif typography (Gill Sans) for the Penguin fiction titles and assymetric layout for *The Artist at Work*, Penguin Planning, Design, and Art Books Series. An underlying element in Tschichold's typography during the Bauhaus period, which he never abandoned through the Penguin period, was the use of Scripts and Calligraphy. The elegant and refined qualities of these scripts complimented the heavier sans and slab serif fonts on this book jacket and the classic serif fonts used on the Penguin jacket, cover, and title pages.

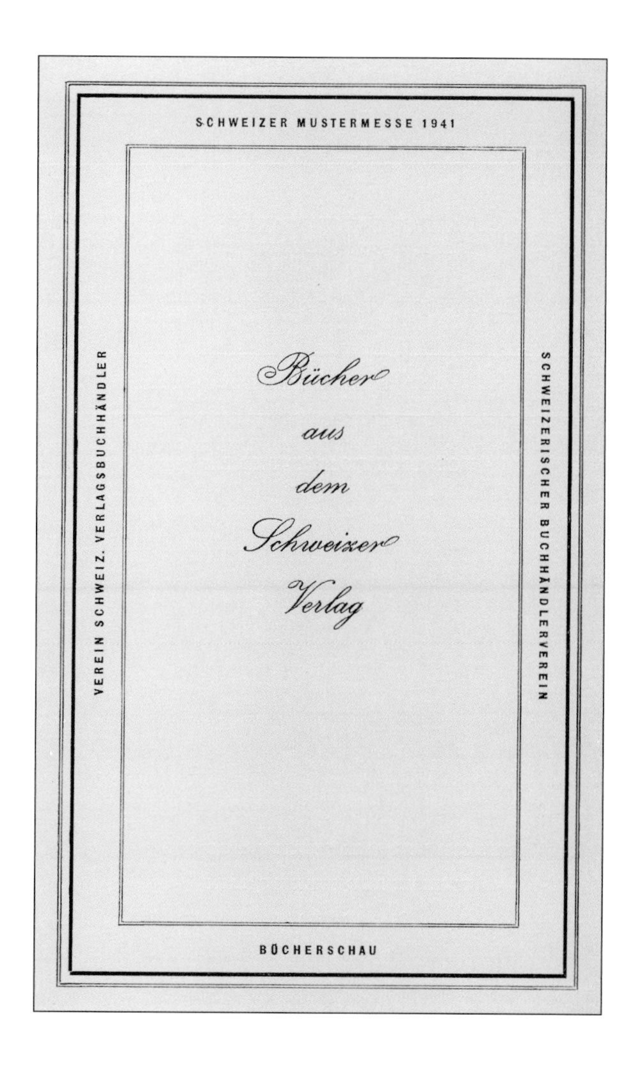

FIGURE 9

Bücher aus dem Schweizer Verlag. Cover for a Catalogue designed by Tschichold 1941

This cover, designed by Tschichold six years before his tenure at Penguin Books, reflects his approach to typographic treatments, for example, all upper case sans serif type inside the ruled border and exquisite script font for the title. Tschichold's knowledge and study of calligraphy was often present in his choice of fonts. This particular script is similar to the dynamic and rhythmical lettering of the Dutchman Jan van den Velde (1568-1623), and the flowing and charming cursive scripts of the Englishman George Bickham (d. 1769).

The fundamental design structure and careful placement of typography is comparable to the redesign of the Pelican Book series and informed Tschichold's design approach at Penguin, particularly the central placement of type, one color and framing method (scotch rules), the Italian Renaissance technique of composing a cover or title page with typography.

FIGURE 10

Julius Casar, Antonius und Cleopatra, Coriolanus. Shakespeare works in the 'Birkhauser-Klassiker' Series, Birkhauser Basel. Cover Series designed by Tschichold 1943

Tschichold's knowledge and study of scripts was often present in his choice of fonts. The title is in broken script (Fraktur), the German manuscript hand writing style, was invented by Leonard Wagner. In addition, Tschichold was influenced by the German hands and various cursive script masters who developed their own personal styles, Johann Neudörffer (1497-1563), Urban Wyss, Caspar Neff, and Wolffgang Frugger. This cover, designed by Tschichold four years prior to his arrival at Penguin Books, has a classical appearance due to the broken script (Fraktur), complimentary Roman serif lettering, centered placements, and meticulously composed illuminating floral decorative border. The floral border technique is a precursor to Tschichold's styling of the Penguin Poets series. Tschichold used a similar broken script for the title page of *A Book of Scripts* by Alfred Fairbank, A King Penguin Book.

Immigration to Switzerland

In March of 1933, Tschichold, along with his wife, Edith, were arrested in Munich and placed into protective custody by armed Nazis. Edith Tschichold was immediately released but Tschichold was held for six weeks. With the help of Dr. Hermann Kienzle (1876-1946), Director of the Basle School of Arts and Crafts, Tschichold, his wife, Edith, and their four-year old son, emigrated to Riehen, Switzerland. While in Switzerland, Tschichold worked for a Basle publishing and printing firm, Benno Schwabe, where he instituted fourteen fundamental typographic house rules to overcome the bad design that pervaded in-house. These house rules helped guide both hand and machine compositors on how to set type precisely and to the same guidelines, while underscoring faultless spacing. "The first three of his new rules may be quoted here:

1. All display lines in jobbing and advertising work, and the text in books and other higher quality work, must be spaced with thick spaces. Especially in hand composition, optically even word spacing is to be aimed at, especially after punctuation and in the change between roman and italic.

2. After full points, use only the normal word space of the line. Only in long lines may a larger space be used. In long lines, a space in front of commas and hyphens may also be used. Between a word and its parenthesis mark, a space should be inserted, except after a full point and in very short lines.

3. Display lines and lines on a title-page should be set without full points."[5]

These rudimentary house rules, highlighting thorough spacing as the foundation for superior typesetting, were a precursor and foundation for composition rules that would help overcome inconsistency and bad design at Penguin Books, thirteen years later.

---

[5] Ruari McLean, *Jan Tschichold: Typographer* (Boston: David R. Godine, Publisher, Inc., 1975), p. 57.

FIGURE 11

Des Luigi Da Porto Geschichte Von Romeo und Julia. Paper Cover of a title in the 'Sammlung Birkhauser' Series. Cover designed by Tschichold 1944

Tschichold designed this paper cover three years before his arrival at Penguin Books Ltd. The florid and intricate patterned paper cover may have derived from Tschichold's study of the French Rococo era as well as the modern geometric stylings of Giovani Battista Palatino This charming and rhythmic standardization would become an important recurring theme for many of the Penguin Book series. The small rectangular title plate is similar to Tschichold's standardization of the King Penguin series and patterned paper technique for the Penguin Music Scores.

Tschichold had begun to pull away from "The New Typography" and the "functional" principles of the Bauhaus while designing books in Switzerland between 1933-46. (Figure 9, 10)

He then realized that symmetrical and asymmetrical typographic treatments could equally accomplish the requirements of successful book design and that asymmetrical composition was less appropriate for the type of books he was designing as well as the desires of rigid Swiss publishing clients. Tschichold had been a strong advocate of modern functional design and changed his position based on a more realistic assessment of the requirements of book design for these publishers. He felt that a practising book designer must serve and respect the given text. As he stated in a 1959 lecture at The Type Director's Club, New York City: "Obeying good rules of composition and book design in the manner of traditional typography is not 'putting the clock back;' but an eccentric style of setting is almost always debatable."[6] In April 1935, Tschichold's change of design direction became public. His article *"The Design of Centred Typography,"* (Vom richtigen Satz auf Mittelachse) in *Typographische Monatsblätter No. 4,* stated that centered typography was acceptable, and typographic design is subject to the technical and aesthetic requirements and demands of book design. Title pages with short lines of text are aesthetically more appealing when centered and symmetrical settings were easier and more feasible for compositors, for example. Tschichold took great concern with title pages, having felt that they lacked any typographic feeling and had become a neglected area within books. In addition, the title page sets the tone and first impression for the reader and must depict the style of the book. He had fervently studied examples of title pages and centered typography from M. Brun's Manuel Pratique de la typographie française, Paris, 1825, and Henri Fournier's Traité de la typographie, Paris, 1825. These practical typographic handbooks covered the fine details and nuances of composition

---

6 Ruari McLean, *Jan Tschichold: Typographer,* Appendix 3: Belief and Reality, Schweizer *Graphische Mitteilungen,* (June 1946).
(Boston: David R. Godine, Publisher, Inc., 1975), p. 136.

and presswork and were principle French typographic reference books for virtually all of the nineteenth century.

Tschichold's work at Benno Schwabe in Switzerland in the early 1930s foreshadowed his work at Penguin. The standard house rules Tschichold established and enforced there, which addressed word and letter spacing, leading, punctuation, and spelling, were a foundation for the composition rules at Penguin. Likewise, the practical, symmetric house style Tschichold set for Birkhäuser Classics (Birkhäuser Verlag, Basle) was similar to his design approach at Penguin as well. These pocket volumes included 12 volumes of the Works of Johann Wolfgang von Goethe; Fairy Tales, Short Stories, and Poems. Although produced for a mass market, Birkhäuser titles were lavished with high production values, such as patterned paper and covers made of linen or sometimes in leather. His work for Sammlung Birkhäuser Collection, (Figure 11) the publisher's series of classic editions, established a house style using black and one color on unbleached paper, ornate patterns, and all upper-case typography on three or four lines with a thin rule separating the title from the publisher's name—elements that would be seen in titles produced later at Penguin.

Chapter 2
Penguin Books 1935-1946

The gradual evolution and development of the paperback book in England came about by a group of British publishers' concern for inexpensive pocket editions and reprints. Penguin books published their first ten titles in 1935 and quickly became a success. They were not the first successful paperback publishers that descended from a remarkable ancestery of English paperback publishers; British Poets Series, Diamond Classics, Family Library, Joseph Malaby Dent's Everyman Library, Miscellany, the Railway Library, the Run and Read Library, the Shilling Series, Sixpennie and Seven Penny Novels, Standard Novels, the Travellers' Library, Victor Gollancz, and Albatross (London branch).

Each recognized that the concept and purpose of inexpensive pocket editions was to attract a mass audience and that paperbacks could be produced economically and displayed easily in stores. Paperbacks were inexpensive, could fit in one's pocket, and could contain a great depth of interesting text. The paperback's historical beginnings can be traced back to the year 1501 and to the adeptness and pioneering presswork of Aldus Manutius.

Inexpensive pocket editions of the major works of classical writings from Greek and Roman cultures had been published 500 years earlier by the esteemed scholar of the Italian Renaissance, Aldus Manutius (1450-1515). Manutius established the Aldine Press in Venice in 1494, which was known for its publishing of scholarly Aldine editions.

In 1501, Manutius published a small, more cost-effective model of the "pocket book," *Virgil's Opera* (Works). This edition had a 7.7 by 15.4-centimeter page size and was set in the very first italic type font, closely modeled on the cancelleresca script, an oblique handwriting style popular among scholars due to its dexterity and writing speed.

An important member of the Aldine Press was the exceptional typeface designer and punch cutter Francesco da Bologna, surnamed Griffo (1450-1518). He cut Greek, Hebrew, and italic types for Aldine editions. His initial project was a Roman typeface for Pietro Bembo's (1470-1547) *De Aetna* in 1495. Griffo analyzed pre-Caroline scripts (Uncial: from Latin "uncia," "inch-high." A formal, majuscule bookhand used especially in Greek and Latin manuscripts from the fourth to the ninth centuries), to produce a Roman type as a model for the typeface Garamond in the sixteenth century, which serves as the prototype for two centuries of typographic design in Europe. In fact, Griffo's Roman typeface design endures today as the font Bembo.

Aldine Press books were masterpieces of graphic design. Their influence was still felt in the late 19th century by the Kelmscott Press, which led the renaissance of typographical design in the British commercial printing industry and influenced typographic designers on into the 20th Century. The Kelmscott Press was devoted to recapturing the beauty of incunabula books (books printed before 1501) such as Aldine Press books, with hand-made paper, initials, borders, and hand-printing. The Kelmscott Press treated the book as an art form and influenced a whole new generation of book designers, including Tschichold's classical approach to the redesign of Penguin books.

The Bodley Head, founded in 1887 as a partnership between Exeter bookseller Charles Elkin Mathews (1851-1921) and John Lane (1854-1925), was a reputable publishing house, well known for its publishing of Oscar Wilde (1854-1900) and Aubrey Beardsley (1872-1989). In 1934-35, managing director Allen Lane (1902-1970) faced with declining sales and in danger of bankruptcy, broke away from the traditional and often conservative mould of the family publishing firm and converted The Bodley Head into Penguin Books Ltd. as a personal venture with his two brothers. Penguin Books Ltd.

settled into an impromptu front office located on Great Portland Street and a warehouse in the crypt of Holy Trinity Church, Euston Road, London. Penguin's first books appeared in the summer of 1935 and quickly set a precedent by taking the lead in "The Paperback Revolution" in Britain, by providing a range of books–biography, novels, and crime–that were high quality, affordable, and sold in bookshops and unlikely places like railway stations and department stores. Woolworth's ordered 12 copies of each title for every store in England, for a total of 63,000 copies. Within twelve months Penguin had sold over 3 million paperbacks. Each book within the complete series of Penguin publications was catalogued beginning with a letter followed by the number 1; for example, Penguin Books, 1 through 1169; Pelican Books, A1 through A369; and the Buildings of England, BE 1 through BE11.

The first ten titles to appear were *Ariel* by André Maurois (1885-1967), *A Farewell to Arms* by Ernest Hemingway (1899-1961), *Poet's Pub* by Erik Linklater (1899-1974), *Madame Claire* by Susan Ertz (1894-1985), *The Unpleasantness at the Bellona Club* by Dorothy Sayers (1893-1967), *The Mysterious Affair at Styles* by Agatha Christie (1891-1976), *Twenty Five* by Beverly Nichols (1898-1983), *William* by E.H. Young, *Gone to Earth* by Mary Webb (1881-1927), and *Carnival* by Compton Mackenzie (1883-1972).

By publishing these titles Penguin books was attempting to take on the problems of applying mass-production to books and attract the reading public back to the bookshops:

"In making what amounted to the first serious attempt at introducing 'branded goods' to the book trade, we realized the cumulative publicity value of, first, a consistent and easily recognizable cover design, and, secondly, a good trade-mark that would be easy to say and easy to remember. Hunting about for a mascot, we hit on the Penguin—a lucky shot—and the cover almost designed itself once we knew what we wanted. It is composed, as everybody knows, of the simplest elements: a bright splash of flat colour with a white band running horizontally across the centre for displaying author and title in Gill Sans. Thus there is no difficulty in distinguishing

between the different titles, but at the same time the "brand" is unmistakable, even in the various colours used to indicate classification. Orange for fiction, green for detection, dark blue for biography, cerise for travel, red for plays, and light blue for pelicans." [7]

By 1936, Lane could claim that his Penguin series was a monumental success. Costing only six pence each, Penguin Books had captured the attention of a mass market of new readers. The Penguin slogan, "Good Books Cheap," reflected the differences between Penguin and their predecessors, as the Penguin motto had now become a reality:

"There are many who despair at what they regard as the low level of people's intelligence. We, however, believed in the existence. . . of a vast reading public for intelligent books at a low price and staked everything upon it." [8]

The American typographer, writer, and printing historian Beatrice Warde (1900-69) wrote:

"What sharply distinguished the first Penguin books from their predecessors was not any striving after decorative enrichment; on the contrary, they had the rather severe simplicity which in this machine age often ironically characterizes the better class commercial article from the kind of rose-garlanded, bead-trimmed object that the 'public' of the bargain basement is supposed to prefer. The typographic planning of these early Penguins was an exercise in discipline, good manners, and economic realism which would have reflected credit on the most mature designer . . ." [9]

Within three years of July, 30, 1935, Penguin "had ceased considering any figure less than 50,000 and that only as a first printing order."[10]

---

7 Allen Lane, *Penrose Annual,* A Review of the Graphic Arts. Volume 40, Penguins and Pelicans, 1938 (Lund Humphries & Co. Ltd., London, UK) p. 42.

8 Steve Hare. *Penguin Portrait, Allen Lane and the Penguin Editors* 1935-1970. (Harmondsworth, Middlesex, England: Penguin Books Ltd., 1995), p. 53

9 Lynton Lamb, *Penrose Annual, A Review of the Graphic Arts.* Volume 46, Penguin Books - Style and Mass Production, 1952 (Lund Humphries & Co. Ltd., London, UK) p. 40.

10 Penguin (Firm). *Penguins: A Retrospect:* 1935-1951. (Harmondsworth, Middlesex, England: Penguin Books Ltd., 1951), Pamphlet.

By 1937, Penguin Books Ltd. moved from their impromptu office on Euston Road to a contemporary building on Bath Road, Harmondsworth. The Pelican imprint was launched and was soon followed by the Penguin Specials, Penguin Classics, and King Penguins as well as Puffin Picture and Story Books for children. The Penguin Specials ran more than 160 titles and many sold a quarter million copies before rationing began. In the years just before the Second World War, Penguin Books Ltd was able to command an adequate paper supply as a result of the mammoth sales from the first ten published titles. By the end of the Second World War, more than a million books per month were being distributed in America. Paperbacks were available to purchase "everywhere":

"With such unquestionable attractions to offer it could hardly be disputed that Penguins are finding a new public and training that public to like the best of modern writing. And they are reaching this public through myriads of distribution channels, not merely through the bookshop proper, but through Woolworth's, the village shop, the small tobacconist, and the slot-machine." [11]

Competition began to emerge in the market in early 1944, when Alan Bott (1893-1952) launched Pan Books. At Penguin, Lane was able to stay ahead of this increased competition by publishing crime writing and biographies, followed by the Pelicans that included politics, economics, sociology, and history. No other publishing company could claim to provide such a variety of subject matter as Penguin.

By 1945, nearly 500 Penguin titles and 150 Pelican titles had materialized. With well over 650 titles to date, many new series were being introduced, including Editions Penguin, Penguin Handbooks, Periodical Publications, and Ptarmigan Books. Lane and his colleagues had many new ideas for new proposals.

By 1945, after achieving his goal of getting paperback books the recognition they deserved, and making money on them as a successfully thriving

[11] Steve Hare. *Penguin Portrait, Allen Lane and the Penguin Editors 1935-1970.* (Harmondsworth, Middlesex, England: Penguin Books Ltd., 1995), p. 12

business venture, Lane and his colleagues were once again restless and full of new ideas and new projects. They set their sights on the design of each series of books. The crop of covers was simple, yet striking, and the distinctive Penguin logo stood as a symbol of "Good Books Cheap," and bright colors provided distinction between genres. Penguin Books clearly stood out amongst the competition. Even so, Lane was determined to raise the level of branding, and he clearly understood the importance of design as an instrumental marketing tool in the current and continued success of the Penguin series. In addition, Lane recognized Albatross's effectiveness in using design to establish a brand identity in the marketplace, and he wanted Penguin to do the same. Lane often stated that he was trying to emulate the Albatross collection series (Figure 12), which set the standard for early paperback book design. The Albatross cover features included the elegant golden section proportions (111mm x 181mm), symmetry and centered type placements, color-coding by genre, san serif typographic covers, and a distinct and beautifully drawn albatross bird symbol incoprporated onto each edition. The pattern of birds as an identifying logo was commonly used by British publishers as they recognized the need to find a bird or animal as a mascot, something one could easily identify with and was recognizably linked to the Albatross Books mascot. In fact, a year after the successful launch of Penguin books and their Penguin logo was the introduction of another exotic bird, the Toucan, for the launching of the Toucan novels paperback series in 1936.

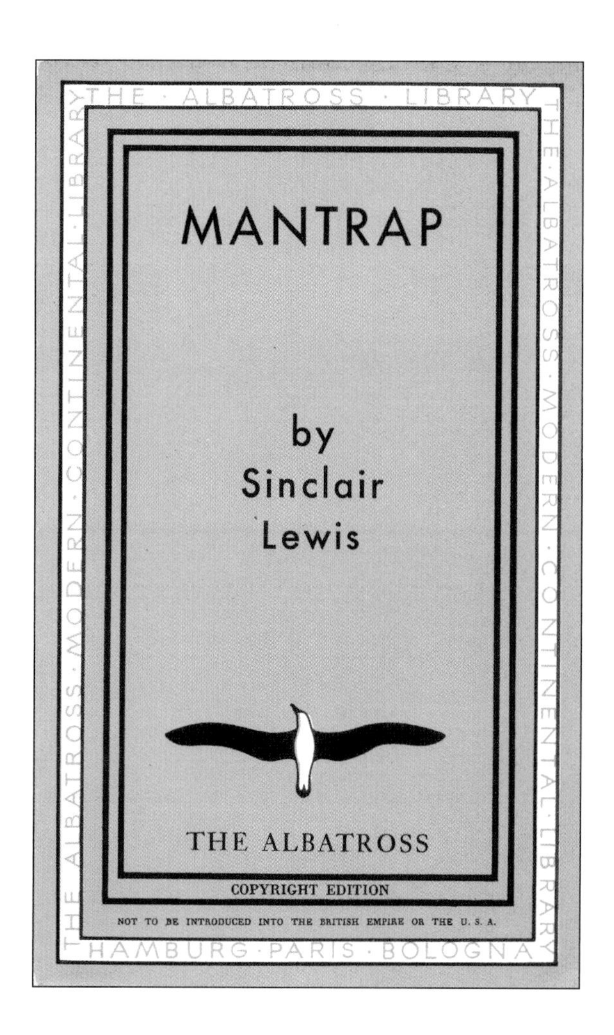

FIGURE 12

Book Cover *Mantrap*: Sinclair Lewis,
Book Cover Series Designed by Giovanni Mardersteig, 1935
4 3/8" x 7 1/8"

Giovanni Mardersteig (1892-1977), lead typographer at Albatross books, was the first designer within a publishing firm to establish house design rules and an elegant golden section format (111mm x 181mm), which allowed an elongated type page and proportions that could be placed into one's pocket. He also used better quality paper, a beautifully drawn depiction of an Albatross for the colophon, sans serif typography, color coding to distinguish the genre of each volume, a captivating standardized cover pattern. Allen Lane was determined to raise the level of branding, and he clearly understood the importance of design as an instrumental marketing tool in the continued success of the Penguin series.

Chapter 3
Penguin Books 1947-1949

In the years following World War II, book publishers like Penguin sought the best typographic talent in Europe and offered designers unparalleled artistic freedom. When Penguin Books publisher Allen Lane decided to bring in Tschichold, he may have been unaware that, over the course of the next three years, Tschichold would set the standard for successful book design in Britain. Tschichold's redesign of Penguin Books in the late 1940s revolutionized typographic conventions.

Tschichold's earlier commission and series styling of the Birkhäuser Classics, one of his greatest and most successful achievements during the early 1940s, provided the proof that Tschichold had the qualifications by producing 53 volumes with outstanding quality and touch of elegance for the mass market.

By the time Tschichold arrived at the company from Switzerland in March 1947, paperbacks had become a popular form of mass media, and Penguin Books, in particular provided the general public with a wide range of affordable, easily attainable, and exceptional literature. Penguin Books' design, however, fell far short of their literary reputation. Tschichold had aquired a wide-range of book series, each bearing its own design style, which reflected inconsistency of design, most noticeably on the covers. In addition, Penguin production was outsourced to numerous binders, printers, and compositors throughout the United Kingdom as Tschichold was faced with roundabout and lengthy delays regarding correspondence of page make-up and all other details associated with book production. Approximately 15 million books were being produced per year, with a breakdown of 15 to 20 titles per month and installments between 50,000 to 100,000 copies. As a result, there was a mass appeal and growing demand for Penguin paperbacks in the marketplace. Paperbacks were small in size, and thus could be produced economically and displayed easily in stores. British publishers soon realized the importance of a book's appearance for marketing purposes and thus, the demand for skilled designers increased.

Historically, symmetrical typography has applied to classical, "traditional" books, while asymmetrical typography applied to the experimental design and spirit of the "modern" 1920s. Breaking from adherence to asymmetrical design, Tschichold decided to set a practical look for Penguin that would suit a large number of books and achieve balance, consistency, and legibility. In his view, adherence to the tenets of classical typography—legibility, a balance of type styles, wide margins, exquisite contrast, simplicity, and integrated rules and ornaments—was integral to a book's function. For example, he preferred classical typefaces for long pages of text, noting that

"Good typography has to be perfectly legible and is, as such, the result of intelligent planning. The classical typefaces such as Garamond, Janson, Baskerville and Bell are undoubtedly the most legible." [12]

His work on the Birkhäuser Classics impressed Oliver Simon (1895-1956) in London, best known for his leadership and expansion of book production at the Curwen Press, Plaistow, London, and thus made a major contribution to British typography, and for the magazine, Signature. Simon recommended that his colleague, Lane, hire Tschichold to undertake the redesign of Penguin Books shortly after the Second World War. These Classic volumes were an important design standard template and precursor to this idea of centered style and practicality. These books proved to Simon, that Tschichold had the aptitude and skill of implementing superior typographical standards for an

---

[12] *Print*, XVIII, No. 1, New York, 1964.
Jan Tschichold lecture to The Type Director's Club, New York, April 18, 1959.

extensive Penguin readership and, thus, would be the perfect designer for the challenging task of redesigning Penguins.

In September 1946, Lane and Simon flew to Basle, Switzerland, and invited Tschichold to design, improve the typographic standards, and supervise the volume of its production. In the following year, March 1947, Tschichold arrived in England, having already accepted the invitation the previous year, but was unable to immediately give up his prior design commitments.

The challenging task at Penguin was a natural evolution and perfectly suited for Tschichold as a designer, particularly with the decline in standards and appearance of Penguin books during and after World War II. These wartime restrictions effected paper quality and encumbered printers and publishers, thus, having an accumulative effect on the entire British publishing industry. Designing for mass production was something Tschichold had considered his entire career, and now he had the opportunity to do so. The Penguin invitation presented an opportunity to develop a new set of typographic rules, raise the level of design, exercise his typographic theories, and apply his classic, historical knowledge of typography to the mass-production of books. Before Tschichold's arrival at Penguin Books, there were other designers working for British publishers, who had successfully accomplished the implementation of typographic house rules and designing for the mass-production of books; for example, Giovanni Mardersteig, (1892-1977) for The Albatross Library and Stanley Morison for Victor Gollancz's cheap paperback imprint, Mundanus Ltd., in the 1930s and 40s. Mardersteig's lead typographer at Albatross books, was one of the first designers within a publishing firm to establish house design rules and an elegant format which allowed an elongated type page and proportions that could be placed into one's pocket. He also used better quality paper, and originated the concept of color-coding to distinguish the genre of each volume, and to captivate standardized cover patterns. However, the task presented Tschichold with the far greater challenge of designing and managing for mass-production. He now had a wide range of books, editors, compositors, binders and printers to deal with.

Tschichold's own prolific design practice set the standards for the new approach and redesign of Penguin books. Before making the trip over to England, Tschichold had asked for every single piece of printed paper used by Penguins, as well as examples of all their books. Before Tschichold's arrival, composition rules and standards were virtually nonexistent at the company, as the production department depended on sample pages and different sets of house rules supplied by printers employed by Penguin. In addition, Old Style No. 2, Gill Sans and Times New Roman were the only fonts being utilized throughout all the series. Tschichold provided explanatory notes and criticisms and circulated them to the editorial and production staff before he arrived. He used this strategy to help employees unfamiliar with the design process as an educational introduction to typography.

The Penguin Composition Rules

Once at Penguin, Tschichold circulated written comments and criticisms about existing Penguin examples to the editorial staff. He then developed and implemented the "Penguin Composition Rules" (Figures 13, 14, 15, 16) in order to establish a more consistent system of layout and composition. These standardized formats and typographic specifications addressed word and letterspacing. As an example, Tschichold mandated that compositors avoid wide spacing for body text. Tschichold told compositors to use the thickness of the letter 'i' as a guideline for proper spacing. He recommended that spelling should follow the Oxford's *Rules for Compositors and Readers* and Collins's *Author's and Printers' Dictionary.* His house design rules also called for more attention to letterspacing for words and capitals, small capitals, running heads and contents pages; italics for titles of books, foreign words and phrases as well as emphasis; and the avoidance of mixing old-style text composition with modern faces. Tschichold also ordered that asterisks, daggers and doubledaggers be used for references in mathematical and scientific books and Arabic numerals for folios. He also decreased the point size of footnotes, used hanging identation and spaced small capitals for character names in printing of plays, and modified leading for all composition and spacing for the printing of poetry. He also created rules for the correct sequencing of preliminary pages, utilizing the same

Penguin Composition Rules

TEXT COMPOSITION

All text composition should be as closely word-spaced as possible. As a rule, the spacing should be about a middle space or the thickness of an 'i' in the type size used.

Wide spaces should be strictly avoided. Words may be freely broken whenever necessary to avoid wide spacing, as breaking words is less harmful to the appearance of the page than too much space between words.

All major punctuation marks – full point, colon, and semicolon – should be followed by the same spacing as is used throughout the rest of the line.

INDENTING OF PARAGRAPHS

The indent of the paragraph should be the em of the fount body.

Omit indents in the first line of the first paragraph of any text and at the beginning of a new section that comes under a subheading. It is not necessary to set the first word in small capitals, but if this is done for any reason, the word should be letter-spaced in the same way as the running title.

If a chapter is divided into several parts without headings, these parts should be divided not only by an additional space, but always by one or more asterisks of the fount body. As a rule, one asterisk is sufficient. Without them it is impossible to see whether a part ends at the bottom of a page or not. Even when the last line of such a part ends the page, there will always be space for an asterisk in the bottom margin.

PUNCTUATION MARKS AND SPELLING

If this can be done on the keyboard, put thin spaces before question marks, exclamation marks, colons, and semicolons.

Between initials and names, as in G. B. Shaw and after all abbreviations where a full point is used, use a smaller (fixed) space than between the other words in the line.

Instead of em rules without spaces, use en rules preceded and followed by the word space of the line, as in the third paragraph above.

Marks of omission should consist of three full points. These should be set without any spaces, but be preceded and followed by word spaces.

1

FIGURE 13

FIGURE 13, 14, 15, 16

Penguin Composition Rules devised by Tschichold, 1947.

Some designers among Tschichold's generation had accomplished the implementation of house design rules before he joined Penguin: Alvin Lustig (1915-55) at New Directions in the United States; in England, Stanley Morison (1889-1967) at Victor Gollancz and Giovanni Mardersteig (1892-1977) at Albatross Library. However, the standards they set were not as extensive in size, because of the vast amount of Penguin's existing and new series to manage.

Use full points sparingly, and omit after these abbreviations: Mr, Mrs, Messrs, Dr, St, WC2, 8vo, and others containing the last letter of the abbreviated word.

Use single quotes for a first quotation and double quotes for quotations within quotations. If there is still another quotation within the second, return to single quotes. Punctuation belonging to a quotation comes within the quotes, otherwise outside.

Opening quotes should be followed by a hairspace except before A and J. Closing quotes should be preceded by a hairspace except after a comma or a full point. If this cannot be done on the keyboard, omit these hairspaces, but try to get the necessary attachment.

When long extracts are set in small type do not use quotes.

Use parentheses ( ) for explanation and interpolations; brackets [ ] for notes.

For all other queries on spelling, consult the *Rules for Compositors and Readers at the University Press, Oxford,* or Collins's *Authors' and Printers' Dictionary.*

CAPITALS, SMALL CAPITALS, AND ITALICS

Words in capitals must always be letter-spaced. The spacing of the capitals in lines of importance should be very carefully optically equalized. The word spaces in lines either of capitals or small capitals should not exceed an en quad.

All display lines set in the same fount should be given the same spacing throughout the book.

Use small capitals for running headlines and in contents pages. They must always be slightly letter-spaced to make words legible.

Running headlines, unless otherwise stated, should consist of the title of the book on the left-hand page, and the contents of the chapter on the right.

Italics are to be used for emphasis, for foreign words and phrases, and for the titles of books, newspapers, and plays which appear in the text. In such cases the definite article 'The' should be printed in roman, unless it is part of the title itself.

In bibliographical and related matter, as a rule, authors' names should be given in small capitals with capitals, and the titles in italics.

FIGURES

Do not mix old style text composition with modern face figures. Either hanging or ranging figures may be used if they are cut in the fount used for the text.

In text matter, numbers under 100 should be composed in letters. Use figures when the matter consists of a sequence of stated

2

FIGURE 14

quantities, particulars of age, &c. In dates use the fewest possible figures, 1946–7, not 1946–1947. Divide by an en rule without spaces.

REFERENCES AND FOOTNOTES

The reference to a footnote may be given by an asterisk of the fount body, if there are only a few footnotes in the book, and not more than one per page. But if there are two or more footnotes per page, use superior fraction figures preceded by a thin space.

Do not use modern face fraction figures in any old style fount. Either hanging or ranging fraction figures may be used provided that they are in harmony with the face used for the text. For books composed in any old face letter, we recommend Monotype Superior Figures F627, to be cast on the size two points below the size of the face used.

Footnotes should be set two points smaller than the text. Indent the first line of these with the same number of points as the paragraphs in the text matter. Use equal leading between all lines of footnotes, use the same leading as in the text matter, and put 1–2 point lead underneath the last line in order to get register with the normal lines.

For the numbering of footnotes use normal figures followed by a full point and an en quad. These figures may run either throughout the chapter, or even through the whole book, according to the special instructions given by the typographer.

FOLIOS

These should, as a rule, be set in the same size and face as the text, and in arabic numerals.

Pagination should begin with the first leaf in the book, but the first folio actually appearing is that on the verso of the first page of the text.

When there is preliminary matter whose extent is unknown at the time of making up the text into pages, it is necessary to use lower-case roman numerals, numbered from the first page of the first sheet. The first actually appearing cannot be definitely stated, but may be on the acknowledgements page, or at latest on the second page of the preface. In this case, the first arabic folio to appear will be '2' on the verso of the first text page.

Folios for any text matter at the end of the book, such as index &c., should continue the arabic numbering of the text pages.

THE PRINTING OF PLAYS

The same rules should apply to the printing of plays as to the printing of prose. Names of characters should be set in capitals

3

FIGURE 15

and small capitals. The text following is indented. Stage directions should be in italics, enclosed in square brackets. The headline should include the number of the act and the scene.

THE PRINTING OF POETRY

For printing poetry use type of a smaller size than would be used for prose. All composition should be leaded and the words evenly spaced with middle spaces. The titles should be centred on the measure, not on the first line. The beginning of each poem may be treated as a chapter opening, with small capitals, &c.

Extra leading, especially between verses of irregular length, may often be misleading, as it is impossible to see whether the verse ends at the bottom of the page or not. The safest way of recognizing the poet's intention is to indent the first line of every new verse, after which leading is not really necessary. Therefore, the first line of the second and following verses should be indented, unless the poet has indicated a shape not allowing for indentations.

MAKE-UP

Books should, with certain exceptions, be made up in the following order:

I. Preliminary pages: 1, half title; 2, frontispiece; 3, title; 4, Imprint or date of publication; 5, dedication; 6, acknowledgements; 7, contents; 8, list of illustrations; 9, list of abbreviations; 10, preface; 11, introduction; 12, errata.

II. The text of the book.

III. Additional matter: 1. appendix; 2. author's notes; 3. glossary; 4. bibliography; 5. index.

The above should each begin on a right-hand page, imprint and frontispiece excepted. As a rule, chapter headings should be dropped a few lines.

The preliminary pages should be set in the same face and style as the book itself. Avoid bold faces.

The index should be set in two or more columns and in type two points smaller than the text. The first word of each letter of the alphabet should be set in small capitals with capitals.

Jan Tschichold

FIGURE 16

font face and style of the book and two or more columns setting for the index and make-up of all books.

The objective for Tschichold was to relay methodical instructions for machine and hand compositors when composing each book. Tschichold was particularly concerned with every nuance and subtlety related to the page layout, placement of type in a given space, choice of typeface, leading, and spacing. These composition rules emphasized close spacing, leading, and use of the en-dash and unified the design of all series while bringing improved legibility to text composition, harmony, and economy to its publishing program.

"The shortcomings of English compositors – whose apprenticeship lasts a full seven years – are in sharp contrast with the opportunities offered by the splendid range of type-faces which have been available on English composing machines for more than twenty years. Fine type-faces, bad composition and appalling hand composition, are the characteristics of the average English printing house of today. The difference between the best English printing (e.g. Oliver Simon at the Curwen Press) and the average is very great – far greater than in Switzerland or the USA. It would be wrong to draw any inference from the one to the other, but unfortunately this fallacy is often committed when one thinks of English typography. While I was in England, I learned to appreciate the value of our own Further Education Courses and Trade Training Schemes in Switzerland." [13]

Underlying the Penguin Composition Rules was the implementation of a grid system. The grids were unalterable instructions that set the foundation for the trimmed page area, width and height of each book, visual cover size, type area on cover and spine, position and style of the spine label, and lettering on labels for all the Penguin series. (Figure 17, 18)

The grid gave Tschichold the flexibility to create appropriate scale relationships between type and dimensions of each book, to initiate a maximum area and correct imposition for any King Penguin plate, and to

---

[13] Ruari McLean, *Jan Tschichold: typographer,*
Mein Reform der Penguin Books, *Schweizer Graphische Mitteilungen,* No. 6, 1950
(Boston: David R. Godine, Publisher, Inc., 1975), pp. 145-146.

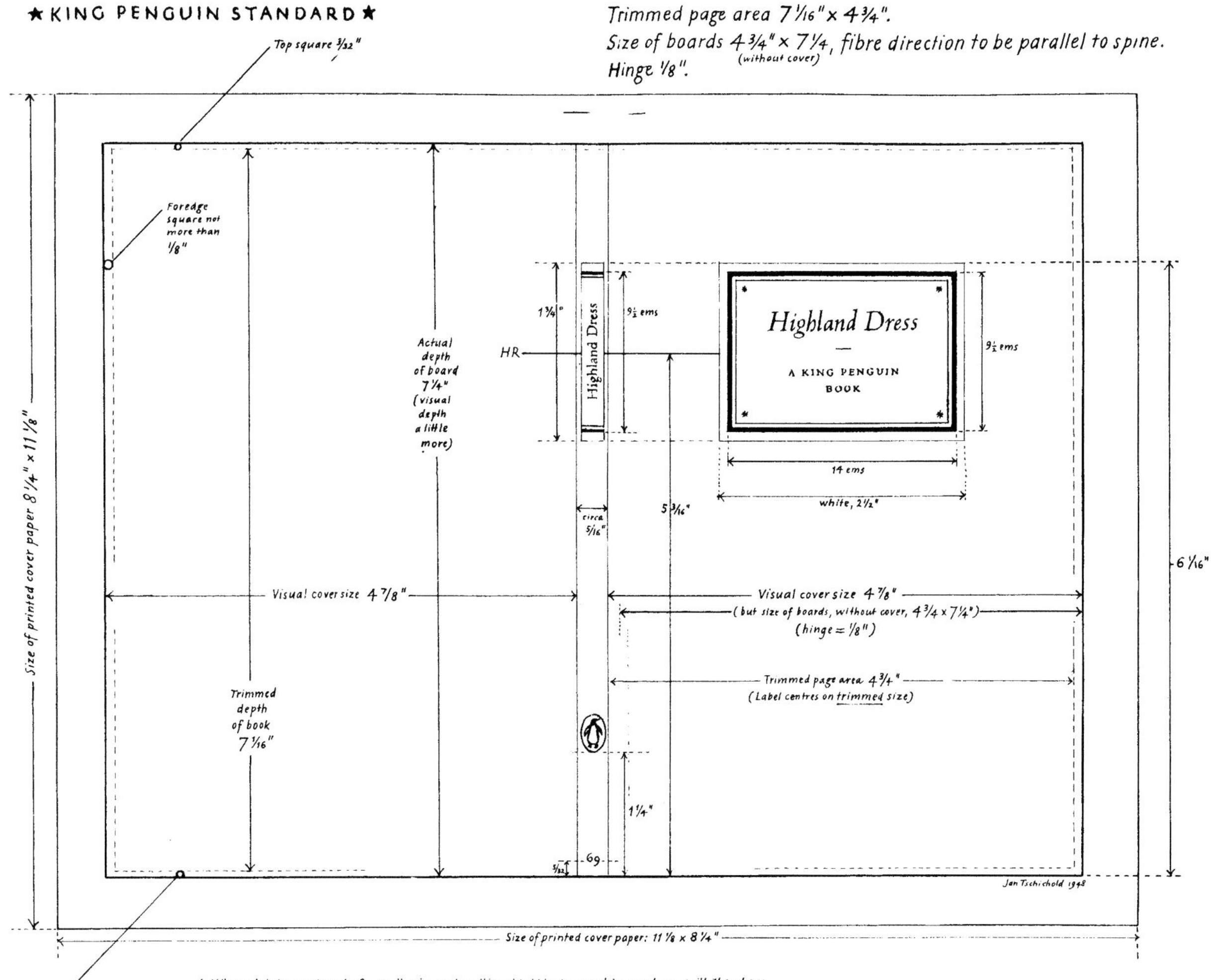

FIGURE 17

King Penguin Standard instructions or 'grid' for King Penguin Covers
Highland Dress: by John Piper
King Penguin Series Cover Drawn and Devised by Jan Tschichold
A King Penguin Book Number K 46, 1948
4 3/4" x 7 1/16"

King Penguin Standard Grid, 1948.

FIGURE 18

Highland Dress: by George F. Collie; R.R. McIan
King Penguin Series Cover Design by Jan Tschichold
A King Penguin Book Number K 46, August 1948
4 3/4" x 7 1/16"

The distinguishing typographic feature is the upbeat and clear-cut monotype Centaur.
This series was edited by Nikolaus Pevsner. Its format is the same as that of the Insel-Bücherei.

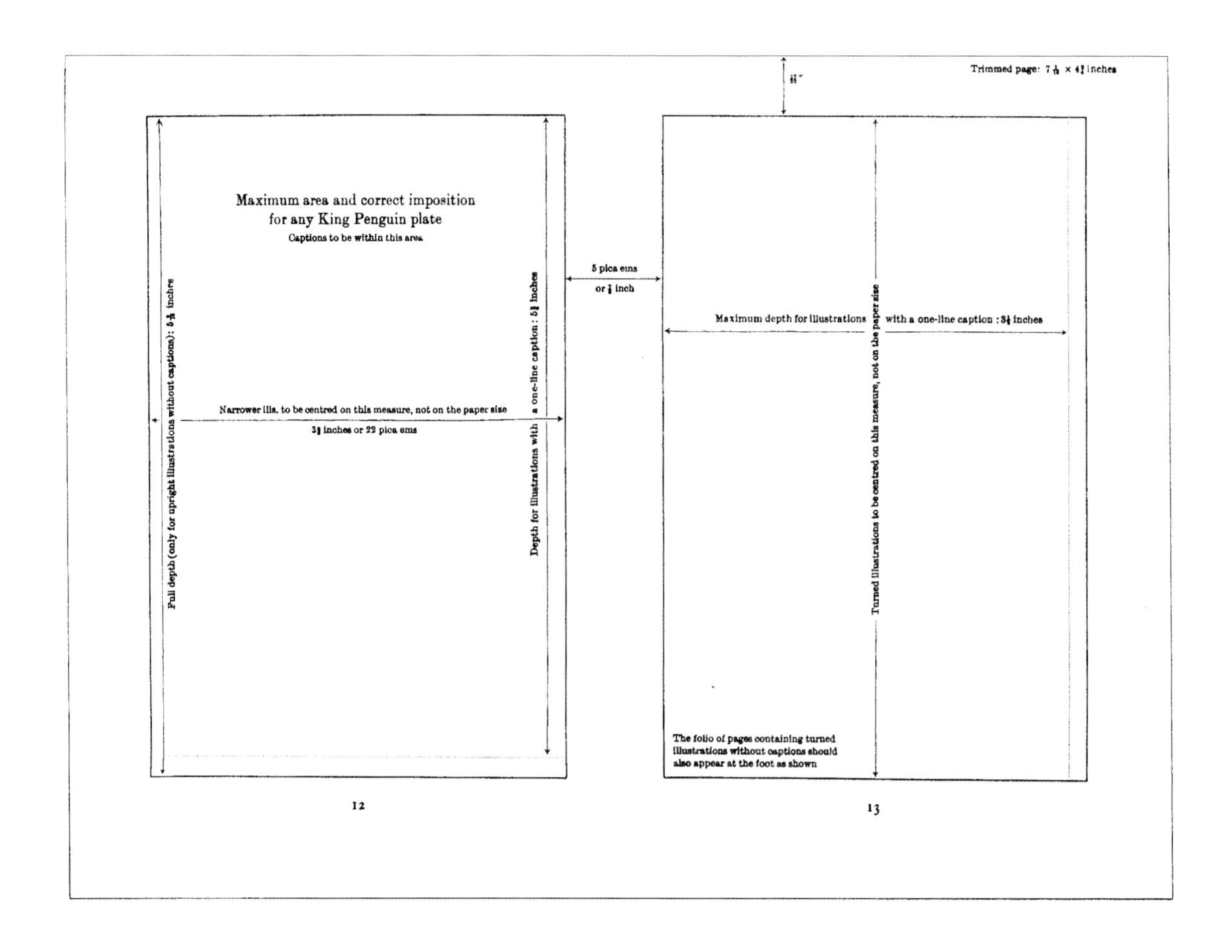

FIGURE 19

King Penguin Maximum Area and Correct Imposition for any King Penguin Plate, 1948.
4 3/4" x 7 1/16"

Plate 28. From *Arte Subtilissima* by Juan de Yciar. Saragossa, 1555. V. and A. M.

28

FIGURE 20

A Book of Scripts: by Alfred Fairbank
King Penguin Series Page Design by Jan Tschichold
A King Penguin Book, Number K 48, November 1949
4 3/4" x 7 1/16"

The following illustration from *Arte Subtilissima* by Juan de Yçiar Saragossa, clearly defines the maximum area and correct imposition based on the King Penguin plate devised by Tschichold. Its format is the same as that of the Insel-Bücherei.

designate the most appropriate typeface to accurately reflect the content of the book. (Figure 19,20)

Tschichold said, "*Very soon after my coming to England I had to design a maximum area for the King Penguins. Such a maximum area is important for the look of the plates as much as it is a guarantee for the harmony of ordinary text pages. In a book of such a small size as the King Penguins, certain compromises are unfortunately unavoidable.*" [14]

After establishing these design standards, Tschichold had the responsibility of explaining it to the large group of Penguin Books compositors and printers, many of whom were less than enthusiastic for the intensified level of scrutiny and involvement in their work. Tschichold demanded attention to detail, a strong belief in his principles, and consistent adherence to design standards he was introducing into the Penguin culture. Tschichold would often get terribly upset with the compositors and printers but rarely with his design assistant, Erik Ellegaard Frederiksen (1924-1997). Their relationship was one of mutual respect as well as levity. They relished their time together as two foreigners working in England. Tschichold left no detail unchecked, and his presence was clearly felt in the composing rooms, which he often visited to make arduous revisions to typographical arrangements and layouts. Tschichold stated,

"*They simply could not understand what I meant by 'capitals must be letter-spaced.' Because every day I had to wade through miles of corrections (often ten books daily) I had a rubber stamp made: 'Equalize letter-spaces according to their visual value.' It was totally ignored; the hand compositors continued to space out the capitals on title-pages (where optical spacing is essential) with spaces of equal thickness*" [15]

For many of the redesigned book covers and title pages, Tschichold typically used symmetrical and centered arrangements for the purpose of overcoming repeated mistakes by inexperienced compositors.

---

[14] Ruari McLean, *Jan Tschichold: typographer,* Jan Tschichold Letter to Alfred Fairbanks, (Boston: David R. Godine, Publisher, Inc., 1975), p. 152.

[15] Ruari McLean, *Jan Tschichold: Typographer,* Mein Reform der Penguin Books, *Schweizer Graphische Mitteilungen,* No. 6, 1950 (Boston: David R. Godine, Publisher, Inc., 1975), p. 145.

Tschichold explained, "*A centered typography, while certainly not suitable for all purposes, is comparatively simple, and even the inexperienced compositor without intelligent guidance cannot commit grave faults there.*" [16]

One of the major obstacles Tschichold faced was his awkwardness with the English language, which often made conversation and communication difficult. As a result, it had taken Tschichold four or five months to get to know the capabilities and specialties of various printers. In addition, Tschichold was faced with the distribution of Penguin production to bindery and printing houses throughout the United Kingdom. It was impossible for Tschichold and Frederiksen to make visits to the print houses particularly, with limited time constraints; therefore, the communication, rarely by telephone, was mostly done through letters, thus, thorough attention to detail and painstaking execution was critical to the success of each title. (Figure 21, 22, 23)

Tschichold demanded attention to detail and consistent adherence to the design standards he introduced. Many of the major printing firms throughout Britain which were employed by Penguin argued against Tschichold's inflexibility. Despite initial resistance, Tschichold persisted, and after about a year he began to see improvements. He told of his experience:

"*I saw how urgent it was to establish strict rules for composition. The printers who set the type either had no composition rules at all, or worked to nineteenth-century conventions, or followed one set or another of house rules. Luckily, even in England, the machine compositors can be directed and are ready to follow good composition rules: I had hardly any problems with them, and after about a year (the production of a single often takes as long, or longer) I could see the improvement in straightforward composition as a result of my Penguin Composition Rules, which ran to four printed pages.*" [17]

---

[16] *Print,* XVIII, No. 1, New York, 1964. Jan Tschichold lecture to The Type Director's Club, New York, April 18, 1959.

[17] Ruari McLean, *Jan Tschichold: typographer,* Mein Reform der Penguin Books, *Schweizer Graphische Mitteilungen,* No. 6, 1950 (Boston: David R. Godine, Publisher, Inc., 1975), pp. 144-145.

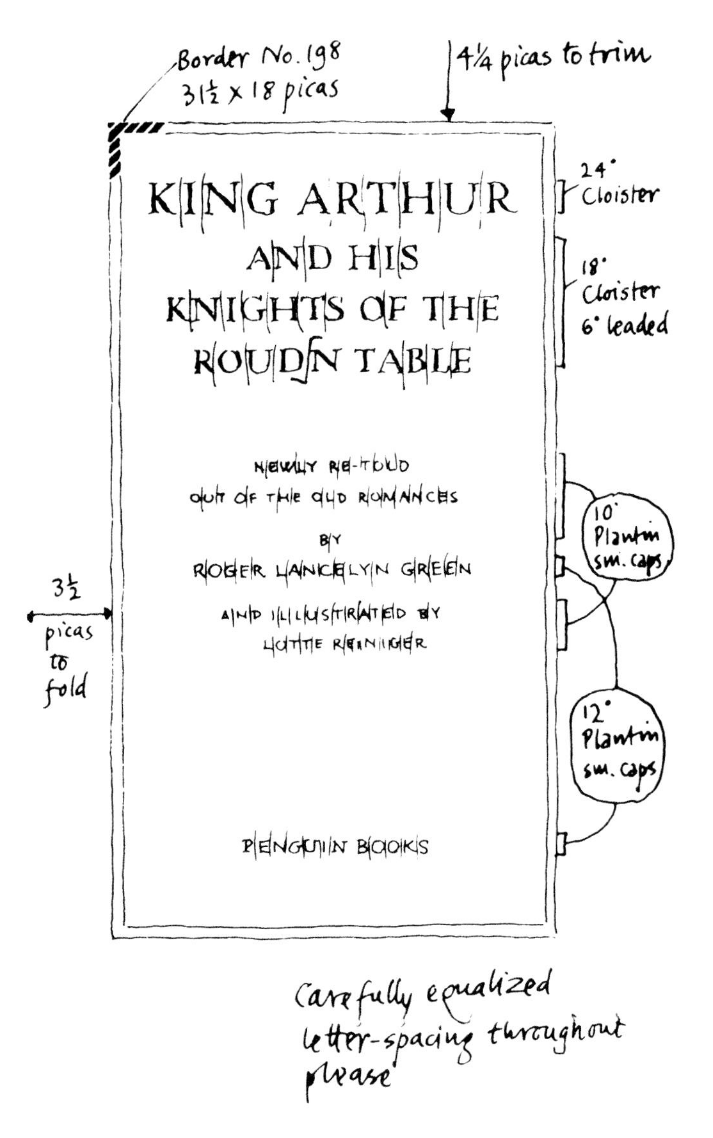

FIGURE 21, 22, 23

King Arthur and his Knights of the Round Table: Roger Lancelyn Green
Illustrations by Lotte Reiniger, Title-Page Instructions by Tschichold
A Puffin Story Book, Number PS 73, May 1953
4 3/8" x 7 1/8"

This hand drawn marked-up title page shows Tschichold's attention to detail, such as word and letterspacing, placements and preferences of fonts. Monotype Cloister is suggested for the title and Monotype Plantin Light is used for the smaller set type.

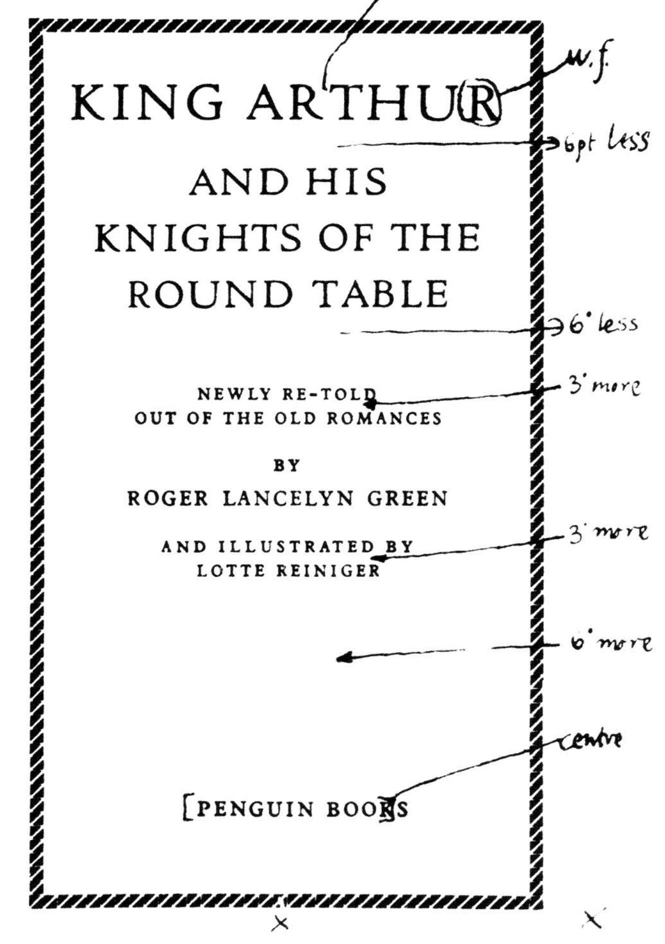

FIGURE 22

From hand sketch to typeset stage, Tschichold's annotations reflect concerns for additional letter-spacing and leading before the final stage. Monotype Cloister is composed for the title and Monotype Plantin Light for the smaller set type.

KING ARTHUR
AND HIS
KNIGHTS OF THE
ROUND TABLE

NEWLY RE-TOLD
OUT OF THE OLD ROMANCES
BY
ROGER LANCELYN GREEN
AND ILLUSTRATED BY
LOTTE REINIGER

PENGUIN BOOKS
LONDON
MELBOURNE • BALTIMORE

FIGURE 23

The final design incorporates Tschichold's final design modifications. Note the subtle difference in the frame from the previous revision, as it more closely resembles the geometric forms in the cover illustration.

FIGURE 24

Original hand drawn design template for Penguin Book Series by Tschichold
Penguin Books Series Design Template, Penguin Front Cover 1948
4 3/8" x 7 1/8"

This rough design was used as a template for Tschichold's redesign of the Penguin fiction titles. Tschichold also introduces his redesigned Penguin logo to symbolize a double volume. It was during this mock-up stage that subtle relationships such as scale, proportions, and placement were considered and tested.

FIGURE 25

When William Came: 'Saki' (H.H. Munro)
Penguin Books, Number 331, First Published, March 1941
4 3/8" x 7 1/8"

The original Penguin cover as Tschichold found it upon his arrival in 1947. This cover was designed by Edward Young, Penguin Books first production editor and thus created a distinctive brand among paperback book publishers.

Penguin books' impeccable design standard spread to printing firms all over Britain. The standards established a precedence of uniformity and improved the overall esthetic of books throughout Britain. Once he established the standardization rules and grid, Tschichold could then turn his full energies toward the actual design of the books.

Tschichold had to come to grips with a wide-range of poorly designed books that comprised all of the Penguin series. Each book lacked any individual distinguishing characteristics and it was difficult to determine one series from the other. The appearance of many of the covers designed between 1935-46, by the ensuing production managers Edward Young, Bob Maynard, and John Overton, was based on the initial Penguin series template or "Penguin look"—the recognizable color horizontal stripes. In addition, the typographic covers, appearing only in Old Style No. 2, Gill Sans, or Times New Roman, were badly composed with inexact letterspacing, excessive point sizes, and indiscreet type and image placements. Tschichold's chief objective, as was evidenced by many of his Penguin series designs or redesigns, was to synthesize all of the Penguin series with unprecedented quality, distinctiveness, and uniform styling, while at the same time, designating singular individuality and genuine features for each and every book.

The Penguin Series

One of Tschichold's first design tasks was to refine the Penguin series covers. (Figure 24) The elegant golden section proportions, 4 3/8" x 7 1/8" (111mm x 181mm), color-coding by genre, sans serif typographic covers, and bird logo were based on the German Albatross Books series, which set the standard for early paperback publishing by using design as an effective form of branding. Although Tschichold was prevented by his publisher to completely redesign the Penguin series due to brand loyalty, he did what he could to modify the existing "Penguin look"—the distinguishing orange horizontal stripes, developed by the imprint's first production editor, Edward Young (1913-2003). Tschichold had inherited a cover design whose elements, Penguin book label, typography, and logo, were all the incorrect sizes and did not correspond proportionally to one another. (Figure 25) In particular was the erroneous serif typeface for

FIGURE 26

Hotel Splendide: Ludwig Bemelmans, Penguin Books, Number 670
First Published, March 1941
4 3/8" x 7 1/8"

Tschichold's first revision of the Penguin cover with the original Penguin logo in 1948.

FIGURE 27

Strait is the Gate: André Gide, Penguin Books, Number 881
September 1952
4 3/8" x 7 1/8"

Tschichold's second revision of the Penguin cover with the new Penguin logo in 1948.

the label and the flawed sans serif typeface for the title and author, which was to tightly letterspaced, appearing condensed and difficult to read. In 1948, Tschichold's first revision (Figure 26) included the introduction of different weights of monotype Gill Sans for hierarchy and emphasis, meticulous letter and word spacing for both the title and author's name, and a warmer tone of the original orange color. Tschichold commented on his design strategy: "*I could only bring the earlier ugly proportions into a happier relationship.*" [18] For the second revision (Figure 27), Tschichold redesigned the Penguin logo at the bottom center of the front jacket. He also reduced the point size of the typography and introduced a four-point line between the title and author's name. What he did retain was Penguin's characteristic color-coding by genre—orange for fiction, green for crime, blue for biography, burgundy for travel, yellow for miscellaneous, and gray for current affairs—and avoidance of pictorial covers.

Tschichold's final revision (Figure 28) of the Penguin cover in 1949 was to modify the Penguin Books trademark. He improved the letter spacing and reduced its overall size for improved proportion. He decreased the line between the title and author's name to two points and also introduced two hairline border rules above and below the title and author's name. These final revisions firmly established a standardized format, which unified the Penguin series. (Figure 29, 30, 31)

Tschichold developed a variation on the cover design shortly after final revisions were made to the horizontal format. Tschichold modified the cover design by developing a strikingly new variation by rotating the horizontal bands in a vertical direction. This allowed Tschichold greater flexibility with the type placements, for example, increased leading to accommodate additional typography such as a book description, and the introduction of illustrations within the white panel. The new vertical format maintained the warm orange and the two vertical stripes have been decreased in width to allow for the illustrations. (Figure 32, 33) However, many books within the

---

[18] Letter to Ruari McLean, Esq. *British Printer, The international monthly printing publication.* (Maclean-Hunter Ltd, May 12, 1975), p.1.

series were void of illustrations and often carried typography only. In fact, the type cover designs were similar in type treatment to the new redesigned Pelicans, with a description of the book contents placed centrally on 10-12 lines of text. The typography was generally set in monotype Gill Sans with all uppercase styling. The Penguin logo was placed inside a white ellipse and centered on the right vertical orange stripe. The new vertical variation was used on a limited basis by Tschichold during his remaining time at Penguin Books. By 1955, the vertical format was used more consistently by Hans Schmoller.

Penguin Books was one of the largest publishing houses in England during Tschichold's tenure from March 1947 until December 1949. Tschichold was heavily engaged during this design period and many design variations would be executed and often times deserted before a final design resolution was decided on, which is often the norm in the design process.

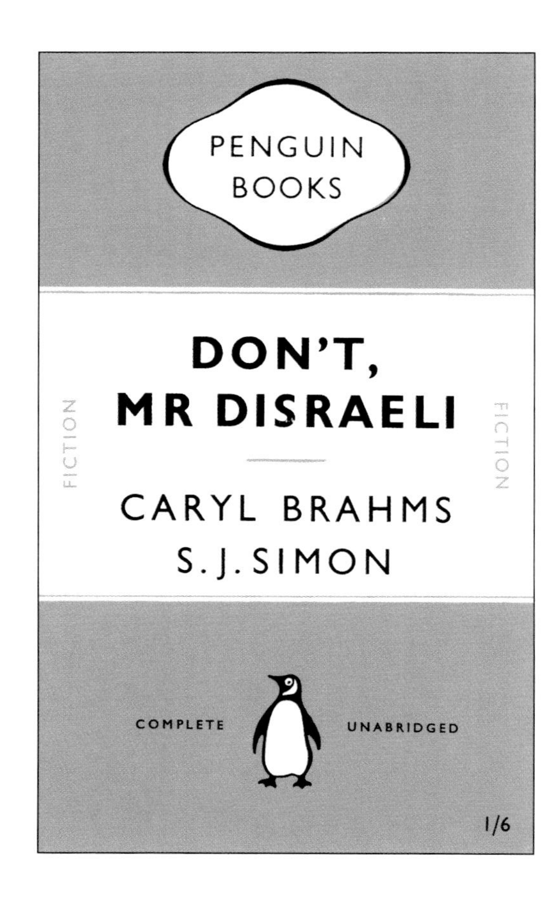

FIGURE 28

Don't, Mr Disraeli: Caryl Brahms and S.J. Simon
Penguin Books, Number 715, September 1949
4 3/8" x 7 1/8"

Tschichold's third revision of the Penguin cover in 1949.

FIGURE 29

The Great Gatsby: F. Scott Fitzgerald.
Penguin Number 746, January 1950.
4 3/8" x 7 1/8"

Tschichold's subtle variation of the Penguin cover. Modifications on the cover included a smaller point size for the author's name and the introduction of descriptive copy.

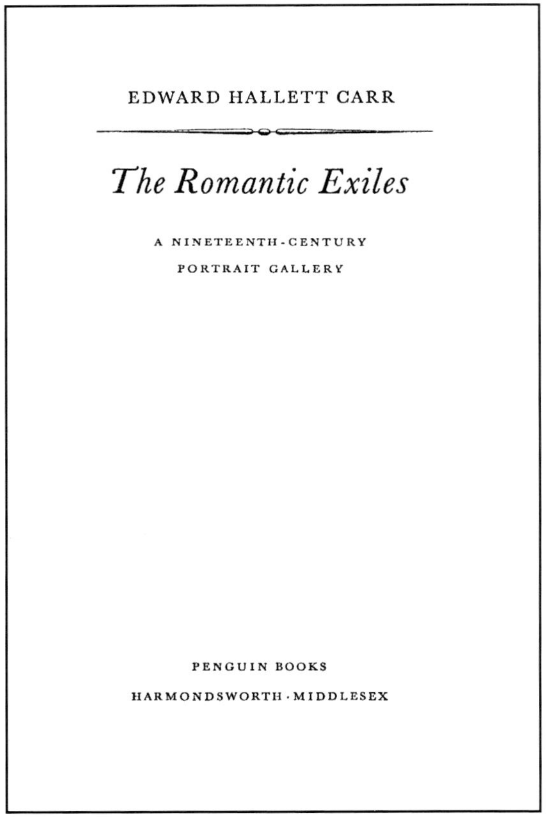

EDWARD HALLETT CARR

The Romantic Exiles

A NINETEENTH-CENTURY
PORTRAIT GALLERY

PENGUIN BOOKS
HARMONDSWORTH · MIDDLESEX

FIGURE 30

The Romantic Exiles: Edward Hallett Carr
Title Page Design by Tschichold
Penguin Book Number 707, May 1949
4 3/8" x 7 1/8"

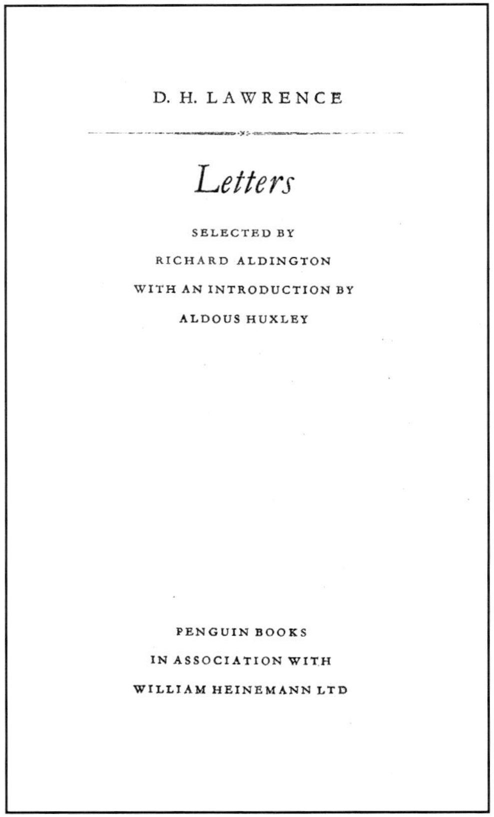

D. H. LAWRENCE

Letters

SELECTED BY
RICHARD ALDINGTON
WITH AN INTRODUCTION BY
ALDOUS HUXLEY

PENGUIN BOOKS
IN ASSOCIATION WITH
WILLIAM HEINEMANN LTD

FIGURE 31

Selected *Letters:* D.H. Lawrence
Tschichold's second revision of the Penguin Title Page
Penguin Number 759, March 1950
4 3/8" x 7 1/8"

FIGURE 32

Angel Pavement: J.B. Priestley
Penguin Number 650
July 1948
4 3/8" x 7 1/8"

Original hand drawn comp by Jan Tschichold.

(FIGURE 32, 33)

Tschichold developed a new variation of the Penguin Books series on a vertical format, which allowed greater flexibility for both typography and illustrations. This new format was used infrequently during Tschichold's tenure. However, the design was used more routinely by Hans Schmoller in the mid 1950s. The sans serif typography was designed to be set in Monotype Gill Sans.

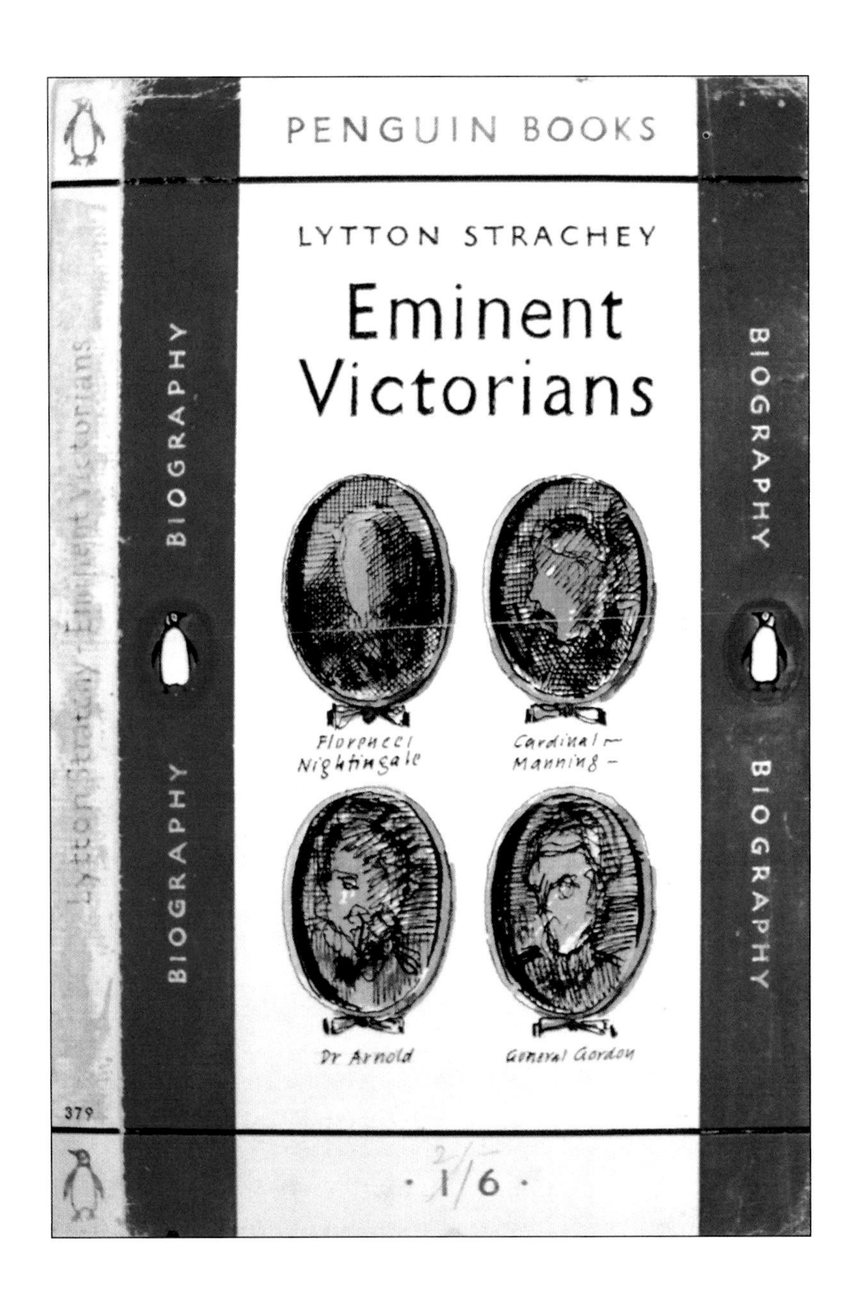

FIGURE 33

Eminent Victorians: Lytton Strachey
Penguin Cover, Penguin Number 649
July 1948
4 3/8" x 7 1/8"

Original hand drawn comp by Jan Tschichold.

Chapter 4
Pelican, King Penguin and Penguin Classics

A new bird, the Pelican imprint series, emerged as an educational counterpart to the Penguin fiction titles. This new development occurred as a result of Penguin's need to build on its earlier success of Penguin fiction titles by offering new original writing on expanded topics for expressly commissioned volumes.

The series was intended to provide Penguin's readership with a broader range of educational topics and scholarly interests. The series included such topics as Popular Science, Politics, Practical Economics, History, Physiology, Psychology, Genetics, and the Philosophy of Art. Some of the early Pelicans included *Essays in Popular Science* by Julian Huxley, *The Great Victorians* edited by H.J. and Hugh Massingham, and titles that Tschichold redesigned such as *The English Parliament* by Kenneth Mackenzie and *The Welsh* by Wyn Griffith.

Lane described the Pelican series as "*... at present heavily weighted on the side of History, Sociology, Politics and Economics, which together claim sixteen out of the twenty current titles. In addition there are two books on Archaeology, one on Art and one on Poetry. But plans exist for a whole series of books in every field of Art. So that the Pelican books bid fair to become the true everyman's library of the twentieth century, covering a whole range of the Arts and Sciences, and bringing the finest products of modern thought and art to the people.*" [19]

Tschichold began the design of the Pelicans by implementing a completely new look of the jackets and covers, thus, giving the series unique visual features to set them off from the current Penguin fiction series. (Figure 34, 35, 36, 37)

FIGURE 34

The Harp and the Oak: Hugh Massingham
Penguin Front Cover Jacket, Penguin Number 622, September 1948
4 3/8" x 7 1/8"

Original preliminary hand drawn comp by Jan Tschichold. This rough cover with colorful border could have influenced Tschichold's design direction for the Pelican series.

FIGURE 35

The Harp and the Oak: Hugh Massingham
Penguin Front Cover Jacket, Penguin Number 622, September 1948
4 3/8" x 7 1/8"

Original preliminary hand drawn comp by Jan Tschichold. This rough cover is based on figure 34 (left). One noteworthy element is the five lines of writing which appear in Danish. The cover may have been composed with the assistance of Erik Ellegaard Frederiksen, Tschichold's only design assistant.

FIGURE 36

Hotel Splendide: Ludwig Bemelmans
Penguin Front Cover, Penguin Number 670, December 1948
4 3/8" x 7 1/8"

Original hand drawn comp by Jan Tschichold. A strange personality graces the cover of this mock-up, a suitable pose for the characters in this memoir of the Hotel Splendide. The line illustration is a fitting style for Ludwig Bemelmans' own poignant cartoon style throughout the book. When the book was published the illustration was moved to the inside title page.

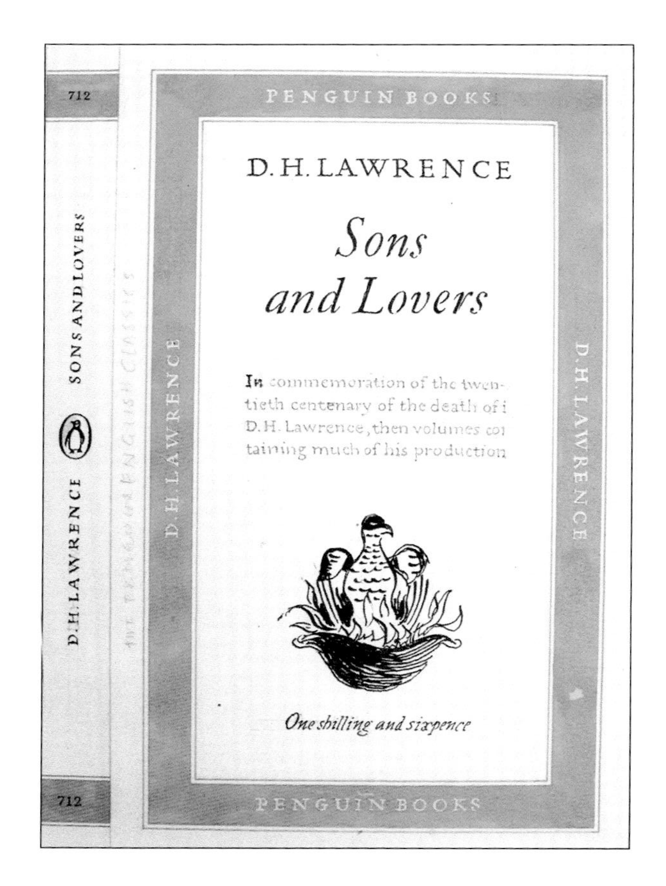

FIGURE 37

Sons and Lovers: D.H. Lawrence
Penguin Front Cover, Penguin Number 668, December 1948
4 3/8" x 7 1/8"

Original hand drawn comp by Jan Tschichold, for a commemorative of the twentieth centenary of the death of D.H. Lawrence. The hand drawing was for a proposed Penguin English Classics series according to the handwriting near the spine. The design is similar in styling to the Pelican series with its distinctive border frame. The light green and cream paper color coding and typographic treatment with italic styling for both the title and price is similar to the Penguin Poets series.

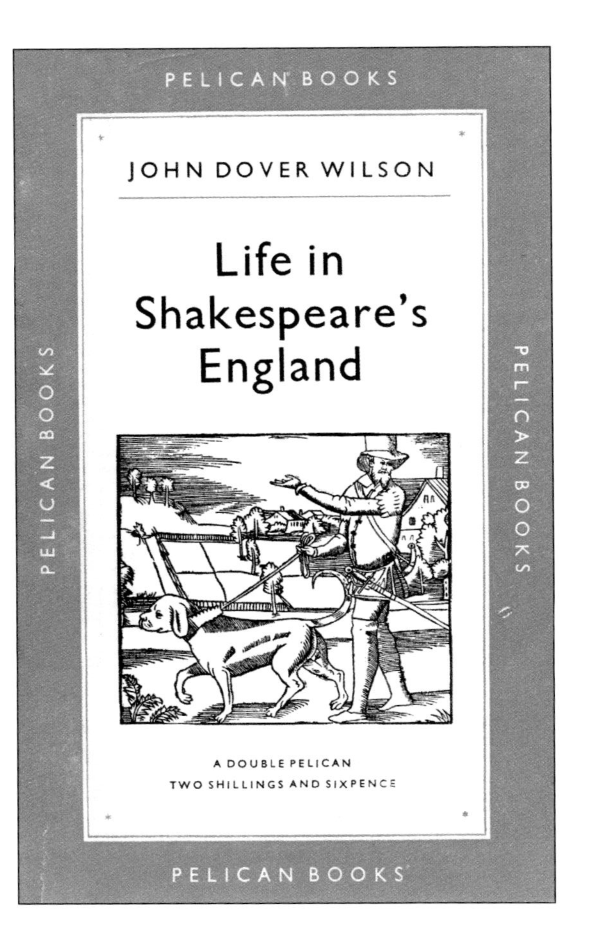

FIGURE 38

Life in Shakespeare's England: John Dover Wilson
Cover Series Redesigned for Pelican Books by Tschichold,
Pelican, Number A 143, August 1944
4 3/8" x 7 1/8"

The distinguishing typographic feature is the quirky and essentric monotype Gill Sans throughout. Tschichold devised a new look for the Pelican jackets with the introduction of a pale aqua blue frame and accompanying upper case typography inverted within the frame. This striking frame creates a dynamic contrast to the delicate centered typography within the white panel.

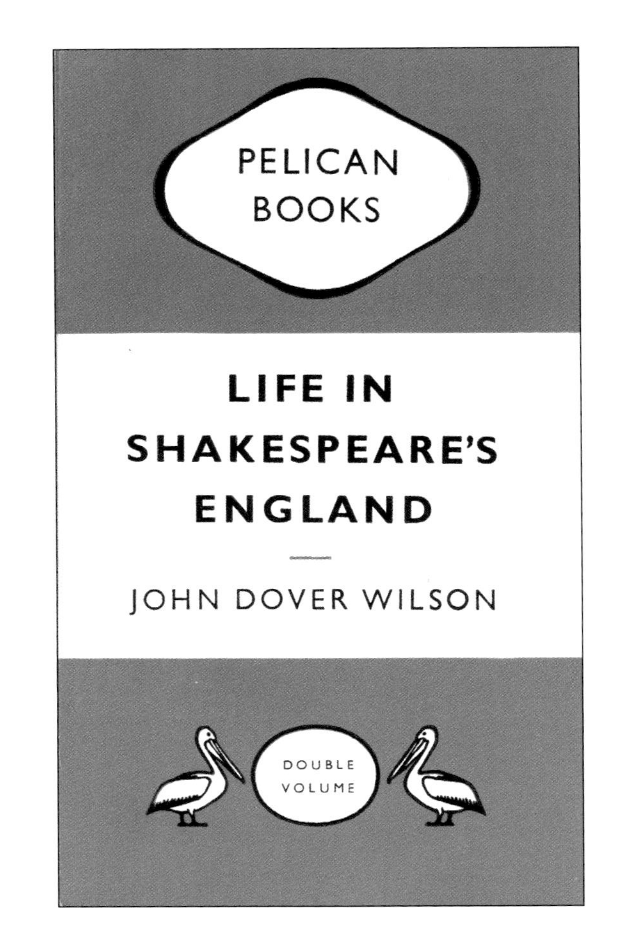

FIGURE 39

Life in Shakespeare's England: John Dover Wilson
Book Jacket Redesigned for Pelican Books by Tschichold
Pelican Number A 143, August 1944
4 3/8" x 7 1/8"

Some of the covers within the redesigned Pelican series maintained the original three horizontal bands (two pale aqua blue and one white). Eventually, the Penguin covers were replaced with the new Penguin jacket design with the introduction of a white rectangular window and surrounding pale aqua blue border and improved fonts and letter spacing.

Although he implemented a new identity for the Pelican book jackets and covers, the two design elements that were carried over from the original book covers were the pale aqua blue color coding and the sans serif font Gill Sans. (Figure 38) Some of the book covers within the redesigned series maintained the original three horizontal bands (two pale aqua blue and one white – Figure 39) as Tschichold introduced different weights of Gill Sans for hierarchy and emphasis and meticulous letter and word spacing for greater legibility for both the title and author's name. Further design modifications included a more accurate representation and visually pleasing redesign of the Pelican logo (standing version) placed at the bottom center of the cover. Two symmetrically placed Pelicans represented a double volume (double pelican). These updated Pelican covers were identical to the current revised Penguin fiction series. The only element that distinguished the revised Pelican and Penguin fiction titles was the different color coding, pale aqua blue for the Pelicans and orange for the Penguins.

Tschichold then began to focus his attention on the book jackets. The most distinguishing design feature was the introduction of a white rectangular window that allowed Tschichold greater flexibility with the typography and its placement within the white rectangular area. (Figure 40, 41) The surrounding pale aqua blue frame defines the four sides of the cover and adds an elegant and refined presentation that emulates similar classic treatments with its distinctive border. Within the pale aqua blue border, lettering appears in all upper case, with the title, A Pelican Book, carefully letter spaced and repeated on each of the four sides. For the typography, Tschichold used Gill Sans throughout, subtle variations on point size, with medium and bold styling for emphasis. The order of the typography on the white rectangle, from top to bottom, included the author's name in all uppercase followed by the title, appearing in upper and lowercase lettering often placed on one or two lines. Thin pale aqua blue hairline rules were placed between the author's name, title, and logo, generally two or three, depending on the length of the typography and if illustrations were included.

---

[19] Steve Hare. *Penguin Portrait, Allen Lane and the Penguin Editors* 1935-1970. (Harmondsworth, Middlesex, England: Penguin Books Ltd., 1995), p.53

FIGURE 40

Glass: E. Barrington Haynes
Pelican Number A166, November 1948
4 3/8" x 7 1/8"

Hand drawn mock-up by Jan Tschichold. The standard Penguin cover design was intended to be adaptable based on the book's content, for example, line illustrations, woodblocks, or simply typography with no images.

FIGURE 41

The Meaning of Art: Herbert Read
Pelican Number A213, September 1949
4 3/8" x 7 1/8"

Cover series redesigned for Pelican Books by Jan Tschichold.

Tschichold then centrally placed at the bottom of the book jacket the redesigned Pelican logo (flying version). The Pelican jackets and covers often appeared with delicately drawn black line illustrations, adding an elegant and refined feel, thus, giving each book jacket its own distinct personality. Aside from the pale aqua blue border Tschichold added a hairline rule just within the frame to compliment the horizontal pale aqua blue hairline rules. For the illustrated Pelican jackets Tschichold added four tiny fluerons on each of the four corners. This was a classical Renaissance decorative technique that adds beauty and character. The redesign of the book jackets would eventually replace the original three horizontal bands (two pale aqua blue and one white) on many of the new Pelican covers. The interior page spreads, reflect Tschichold's careful handling of the typography, particularly each Pelican title page. (Figure 42)

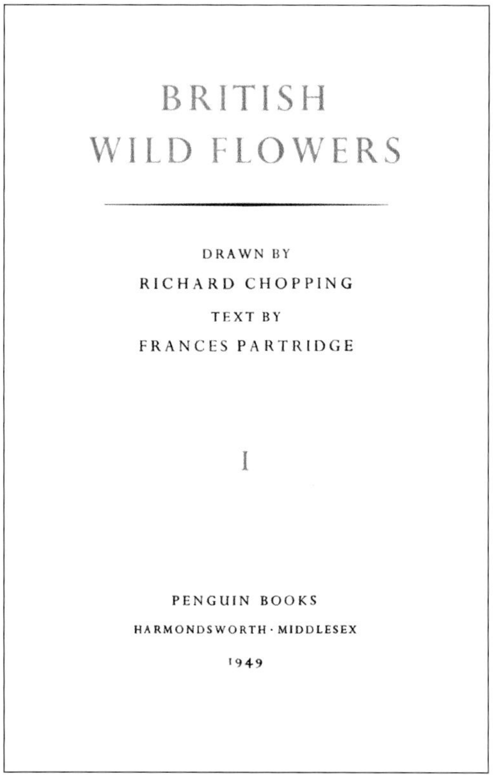

BRITISH
WILD FLOWERS

DRAWN BY
RICHARD CHOPPING
TEXT BY
FRANCES PARTRIDGE

I

PENGUIN BOOKS
HARMONDSWORTH · MIDDLESEX
1949

FIGURE 42

British Wild Flowers:
Text by Frances Partridge
drawn by Richard Chopping
Title-Page designed by Jan Tschichold
Pelican Books 1949
4 3/8" x 7 1/8"

The distinguishing typographic feature is the expressive uppercase monotype Perpetua throughout.

FIGURE 43

Cover design for *Das Kleine Pilzbuch*
The Little Fungi Book by Willi Harwerth
Insel-Verlag, Leipzig 1937
4 3/4" x 7 1/16"

The title in broken script (Fraktur), the German manuscript hand writing style invented by Leonard Wagner. The format of the Insel-Bücherei (Insel-Verlag picture books) was later used by Tschichold for The King Penguin Series, particularly the format, cover pattern technique, and the title plate with its dinstinctive ruled border and delicate fleurons.

The King Penguin Series

The King Penguin series, which covered art, science, leisure, and world history, was one of the first series to be printed in color and in hardcover by Penguin. This initiative was never really attainable in the company's past due to Penguin's lack of equity, and because of the low selling price of only sixpence per book. The books were underwritten by the financial success of the first batch of Penguin novels and subsequent landmark sales of Pelican Books and Penguin Specials. The former cover was indiscriminately designed with no original identity or corresponding style. Tschichold decided that the overall redesign of the King Penguins would emulate the prominent and much admired Insel-Verlag (Insel-Bücherei) picture books from Germany. (Figure 43) Each book numbered approximately 64 pages, with an equal distribution of text and images. The appearance was classic and elegant. (Figure 44, 45) They were smaller in bulk at a size of 4 3/4" x 7 1/16" (119mm x 179mm), and sold at twice the price of paperback Penguin Books. For King Penguins, Tschichold used unconventional classic typefaces; for example, Centaur, Pastonchi, Poliphilus, Scotch Roman, Lutetia and Walbaum.

Some of the titles released early on in the series established an unmistakable precedent for the breadth, essence, personality, and direction of King Penguins; *The Book of Ships* by Charles Mitchell, *Portraits of Christ* by Ernst Kitzinger (1912-2003) and Elizabeth Senior; and for successive volumes; *Seashore Life and Pattern* by T.A Stephenson, *A Book of Spiders* by A.T. Hollick and W.S. Bristowe, *Edward Gordon Craig* by Janet Leeper. (Figure 46, 47)

Tschichold had the daunting task of systematically organizing the efforts of manufacturers taking part in the evolution of each title. Often several different firms handled the various aspects of book production: binding, letterpress, photo-litho, and paper. Because of this, it was often difficult for Tschichold to impress upon each manufacturer its important role in the overall design of each title.

Often, the production process of each title in the King Penguin series was distributed to several factories throughout England. As the designer,

FIGURE 44

Elizabethan Miniatures: Carl Winter
King Penguin Series Cover Design by William Grimmond
Typography by Jan Tschichold
A King Penguin Book, Number K 8, First Published 1943
Revised, Reset and Reprinted 1948
4 3/4" x 7 1/16"

The typography appears to be hand drawn for this cover.

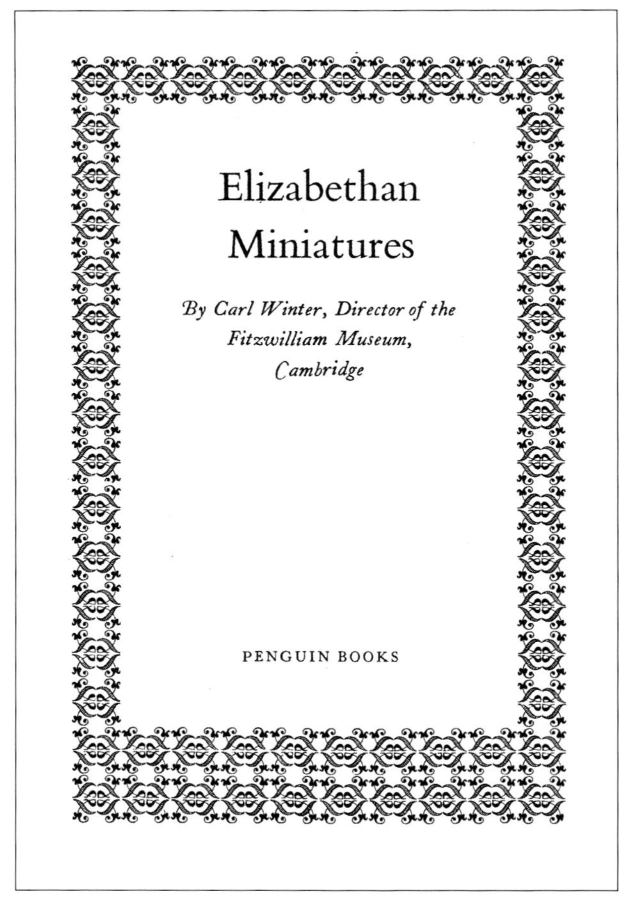

FIGURE 45

Elizabethan Miniatures: Carl Winter
King Penguin Series Title Page Design by Jan Tschichold
A King Penguin Book, Number K 8, First Published 1943
Revised, Reset and Reprinted 1948
4 3/4" x 7 1/16"

The elegant Roman serif lettering, centered placements, and meticulously composed illuminating decorative floral border technique is similar to Tschichold's styling of the 'Birkhauser-Klassiker' Series, Birkhauser Basel.

FIGURE 46

Edward Gordon Craig: Janet Leeper
King Penguin Series Cover Design by Jan Tschichold
A King Penguin Book, Number K 40, October 1948
4 3/4" x 7 1/16"

The typography appears to be hand drawn for this cover.

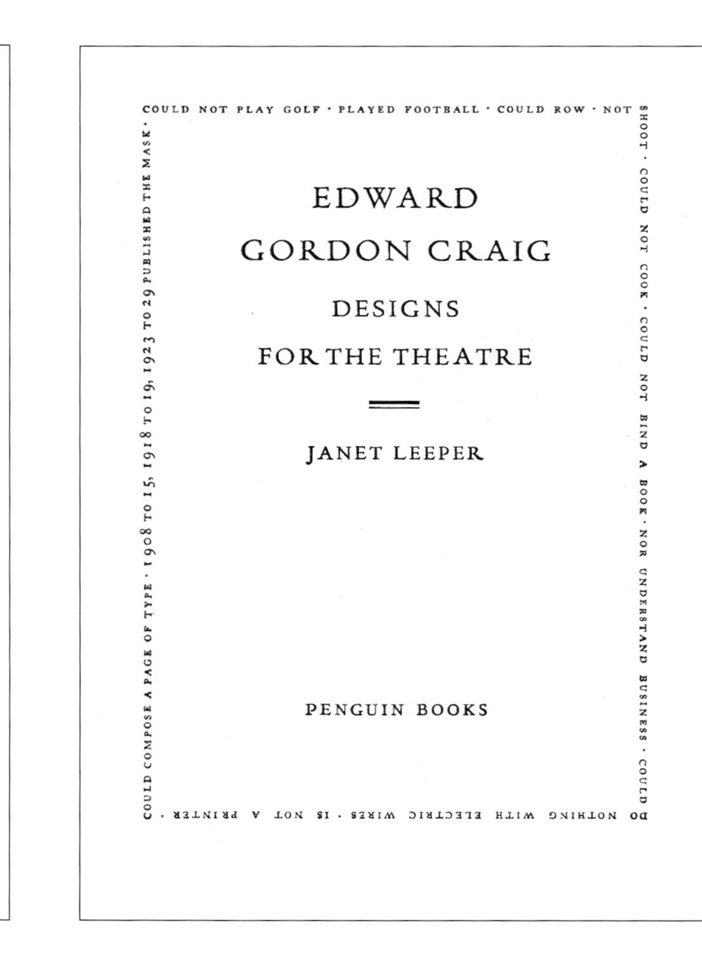

FIGURE 47

Edward Gordon Craig: Janet Leeper
Page Design by Jan Tschichold
A King Penguin Book, Number K40, October 1948
4 3/4" x 7 1/16"

The emblematic typographic component is the agreeable monotype Poliphilus.

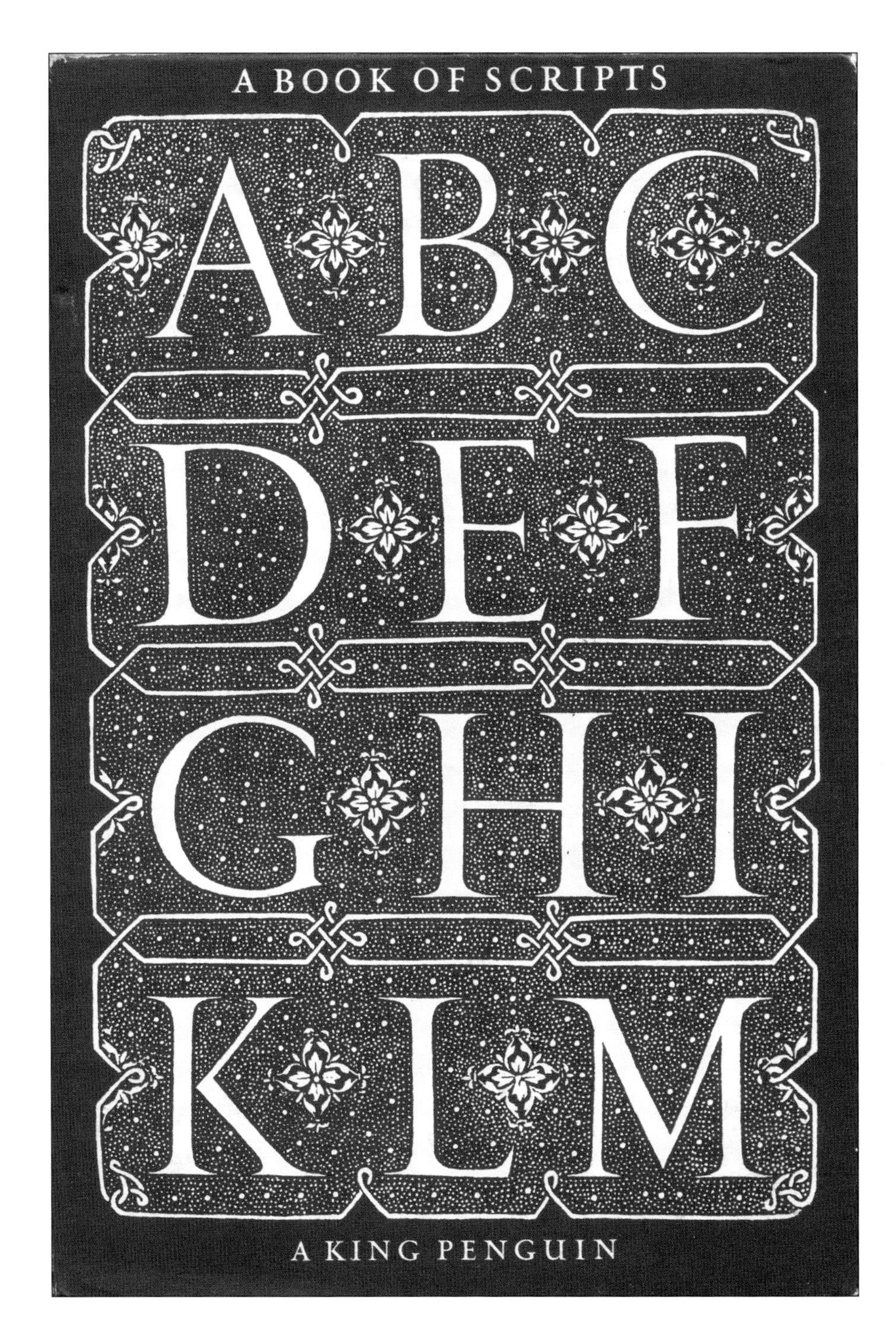

FIGURE 48

A Book of Scripts: Alfred Fairbank
King Penguin Series Cover Design by Jan Tschichold
A King Penguin Book, Number K48, November 1949
4 3/4" x 7 1/16"

Adapted from a page in Arte Subtilissima intitulada Orthographia Practica, A Classic work on Calligraphy and Engraving by the 16th Century Spanish Writing Master, Juan de Yçiar, Saragossa, 1547.

Tschichold had to systematically coordinate and educate each factory's efforts at producing a King Penguin book. Tschichold also began to apply the "Penguin Composition Rules" as well as the newly established "King Penguin Standard Grid." In addition to these design standards, Tschichold replaced the original dull grey paper to a warmer cream color for all of the Penguin series.

Of particular note in the King Penguin series is *A Book of Scripts* by Alfred Fairbank (1895-1982). (Figure 48) Tschichold adapted the cover design from a page in Arte Subtilissima intitulada Orthographia Practica, a classic work on calligraphy and engraving by the 16th century Spanish writing master, Juan de Yçiar (1515-90). Tschichold was concerned with the quality of reproductions, particularly when it involved calligraphy and exquisite lettering. For *A Book of Scripts,* Tschichold utilized his early training as a calligrapher by drawing the roman capitals by hand on the front and back cover, carefully restoring them to their original shapes. The National Book League recognized this title as one of the best designed books of 1949.

In addition, many volumes in the various series were recognized for design excellence and regularly competed with Cambridge and Oxford University Presses. (Figure 49, 50, 51, 52, 53, 54, 55, 56) The King Penguins were clearly the organization's most enthusiastic undertaking in book design. Many artists were commissioned to develop the illustration of both the covers and interior spreads including Lynton Lamb (1907-77), John Piper (1903-92), Edward Bawden (1903-89), Kenneth Rowntree, Peggy Jeremy, Ronald Searle (b. 1920), Paxton Chadwick, William Grimmond, Irene Hawkins, Mary Duncan, R.P. Howgrave-Graham, Rose Ellenby, and Thomas Bewick. (Figure 57, 58, 59, 60)

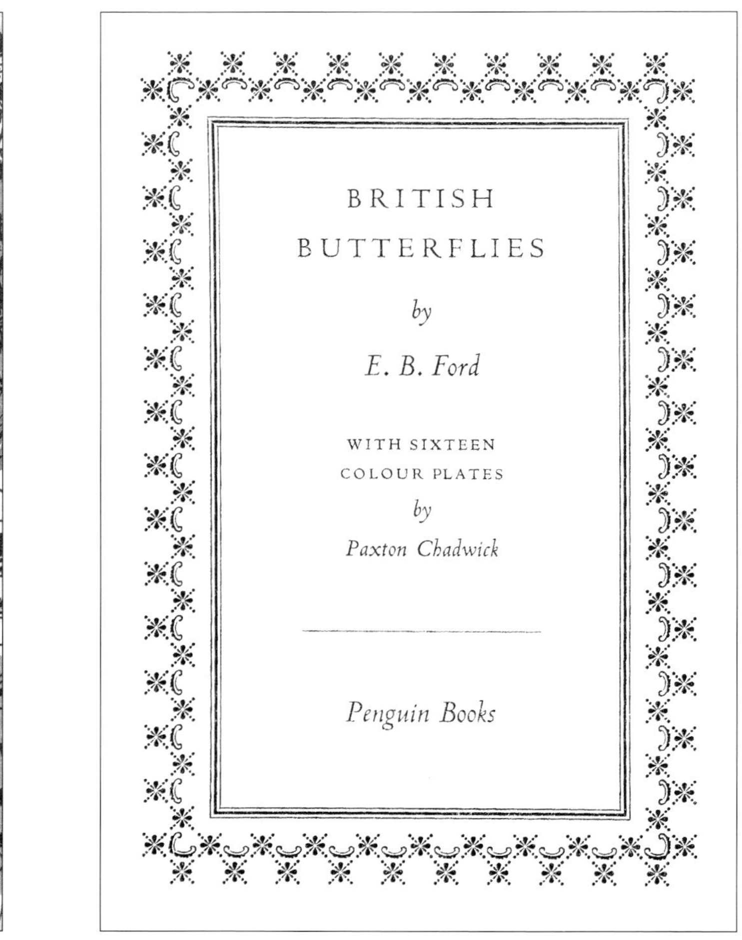

FIGURE 49, 50

British Butterflies: E.B. Ford
With Sixteen Colour Plates and Cover Illustration by Paxton Chadwick
King Penguin Series Design by Jan Tschichold
A King Penguin Book, Number K 41, October 1951
4 3/4" x 7 1/16"

The discerning typography is the graceful and clear-cut monotype Centaur.

POPULAR
ART
IN THE UNITED
STATES

BY ERWIN O. CHRISTENSEN
WITH ILLUSTRATIONS
FROM THE
INDEX OF AMERICAN DESIGN
NATIONAL GALLERY OF ART
WASHINGTON, D.C.

PENGUIN BOOKS
LONDON

FIGURE 51, 52

Popular Art in the United States: Erwin O. Christensen
King Penguin Series Cover Design by Jan Tschichold
A King Penguin Book, Number K 50, June 1949
4 3/4" x 7 1/16"

The typography is set in the classic vintage monotype Scotch Roman with a drop shadow added behind the title.

LIFE IN AN
ENGLISH VILLAGE

Sixteen Lithographs

by Edward Bawden

with an Introductory Essay

by Noel Carrington

FIGURE 53, 54

Life in an English Village: Edward Bawden and N. Carrington
King Penguin Series Cover Design by Jan Tschichold
A King Penguin Book, Number K 51, June 1949
4 3/4" x 7 1/16"

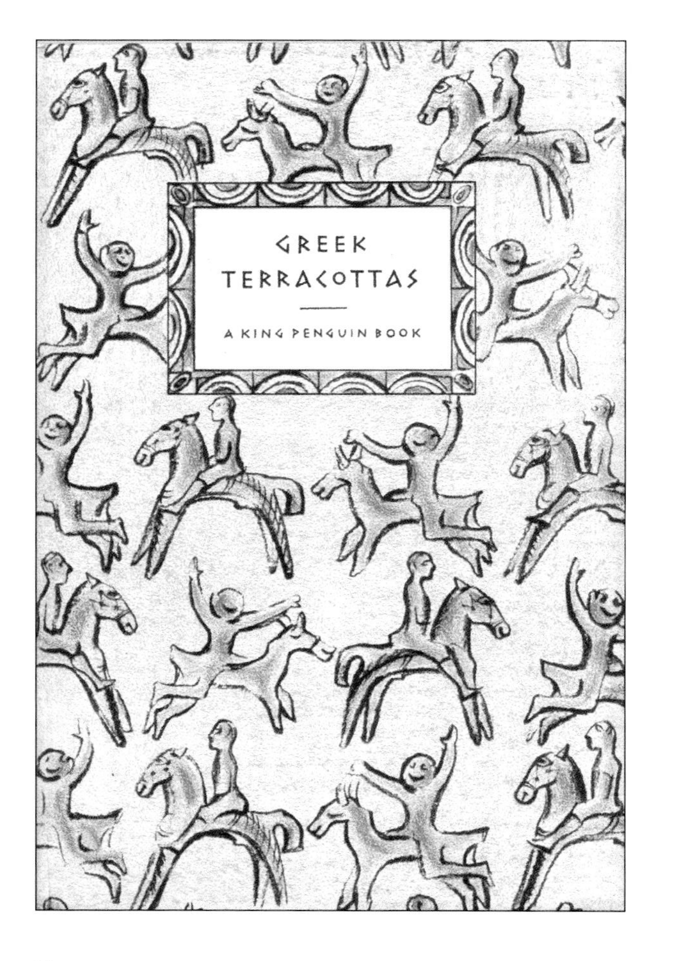

GREEK

TERRACOTTAS

T. B. L. WEBSTER

PENGUIN BOOKS

FIGURE 55, 56

Greek Terracottas: T.B.L. Webster
Cover Illustration by Enid Marx
King Penguin Series Cover Design by Jan Tschichold
A King Penguin Book, Number K 54
April 1951
4 3/4" x 7 1/16"

The typography appears to be hand drawn and is reminiscent of the Greek alphabet. On the title page, Tschichold introduces a monotype border with a geometric shapes similar to Greek sculpture and architectural detail.

FIGURE 57

Early British Railways: Christian Barman
King Penguin Series Cover Design by Jan Tschichold
A King Penguin Book, Number K 56
May 1950
4 3/4" x 7 1/16"

The typography on this cover is composed with the classic vintage monotype italic Scotch Roman which compliments the hand-lettered typography within the seal.

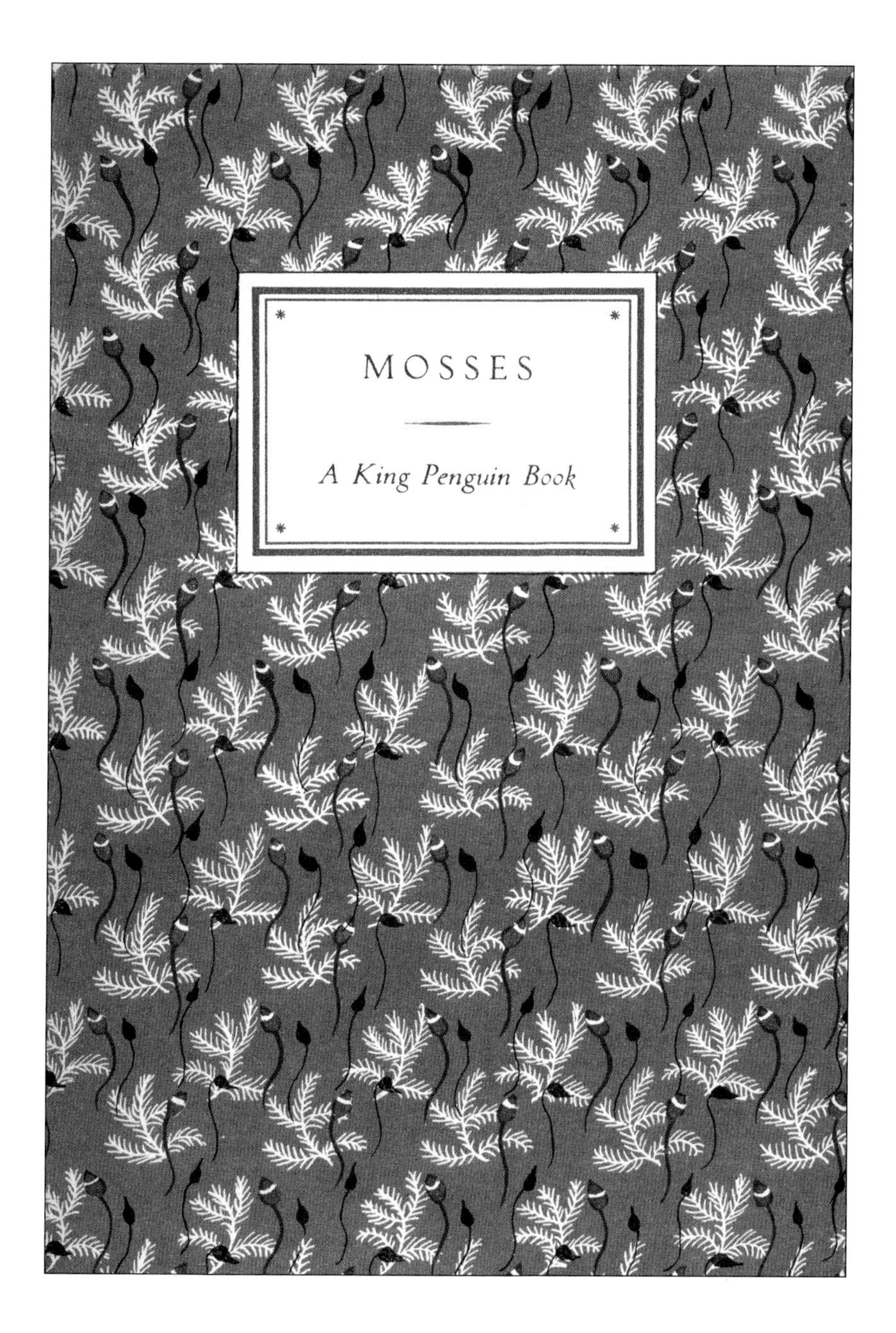

FIGURE 58

A Book of Mosses: Paul W. Richards
With 16 Plates from Johannes Hedwig's Descriptio Muscorum
King Penguin Series Cover Design by Jan Tschichold
A King Penguin Book, Number K 57, July 1950
4 3/4" x 7 1/16"

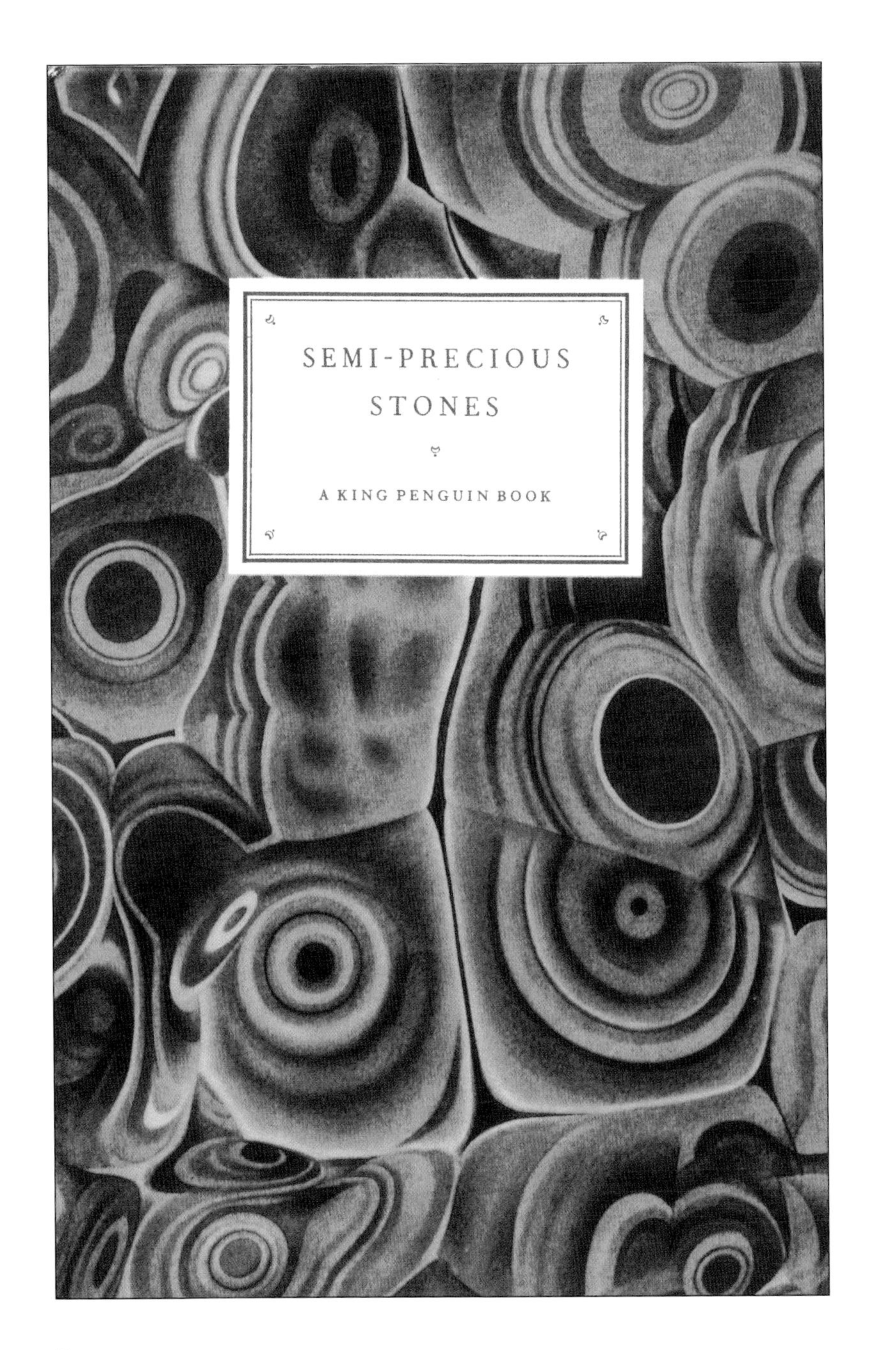

FIGURE 59

Semi-Precious Stones: N. Wooster
With Sixteen Colour Plates and Cover Illustration by Arthur Smith
King Penguin Series Cover Design by Jan Tschichold
A King Penguin Book, Number K 65, May 1953
4 3/4" x 7 1/16"

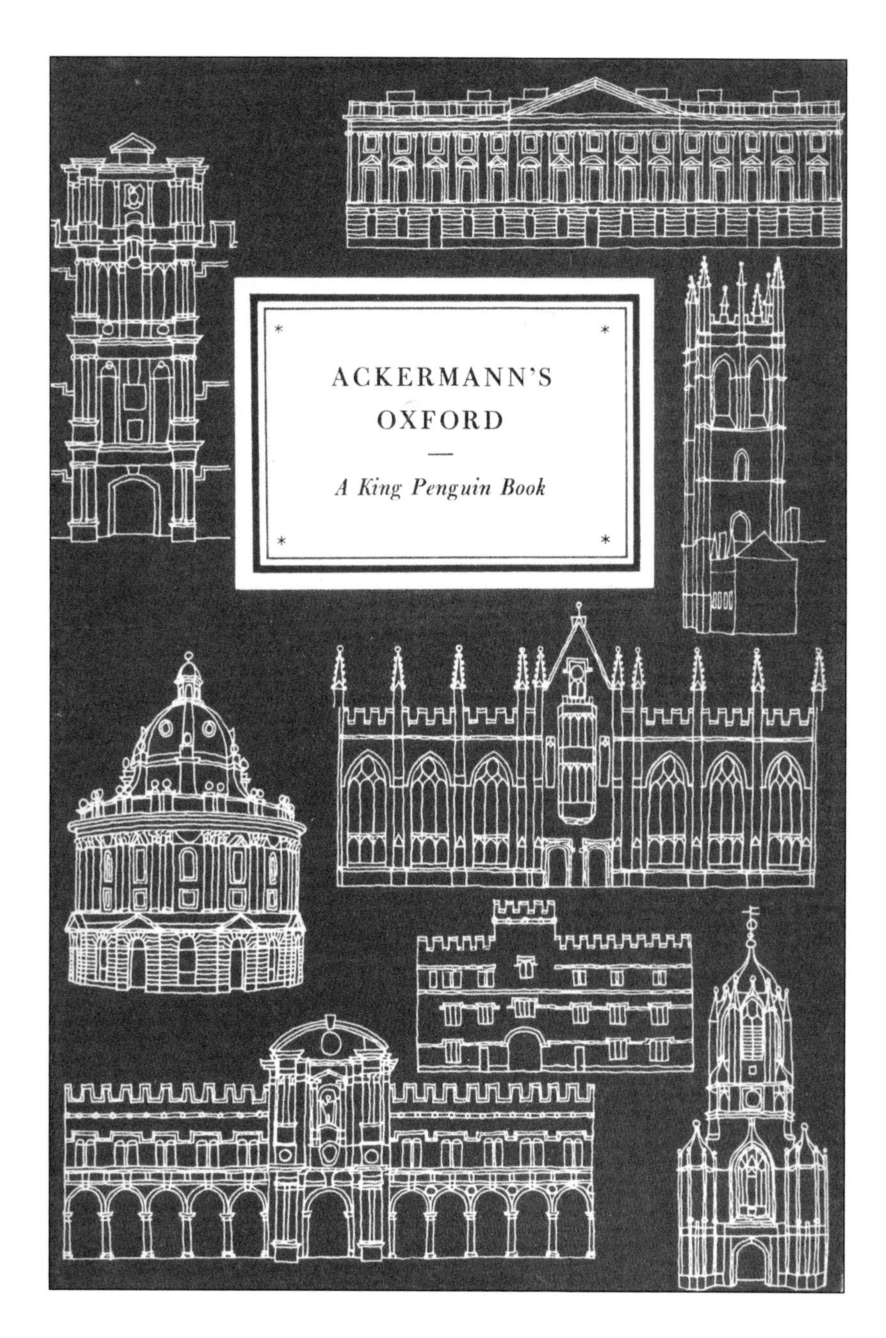

FIGURE 60

Ackermann's Oxford: H.M. Colvin
A Selection of Plates from Rudolph Ackermann's A History of the University of Oxford, its Colleges, Halls, and Public Buildings, 1814 and James Ingram's Memorials of Oxford, 1837
Cover Illustration by Gordon Cullen
King Penguin Series Cover Design by Jan Tschichold
A King Penguin Book, Number K 69, March 1954
4 3/4" x 7 1/16"

The Penguin Classics

In January 1946, Penguin Classics were launched as a new series of translations of Greek, French, and Latin classics, including such titles as *Ivan Turgenev: On the Eve* edited by G.C. Gardiner, *Honoré de Balzac: Old Goriot* translated by M.A. Crawford, and *Fydor Dostoyevsky: Crime and Punishment* translated by David Magarshack. Homer's *The Odyssey* translated by E.V. Rieu was the first volume of this new library of translations. These titles appealed to the many serious readers looking for foreign literature translated into English.

Within seven months of joining Penguin, Tschichold redesigned the following volumes within the Penguin Classics series: Sophocles: *The Theban Plays* edited by E.F. Watling, Voltaire: *Candide* edited by John Butt, Tacitus: *On Britain and Germany* edited by H. Mattingly, Dante: *The Divine Comedy I* edited by Dorothy L. Sayers, Xenophon: *The Persian Expedition* edited by Rex Warner, and Virgil: *The Pastoral Poems* edited by E.V. Rieu. The series appealed to the serious readers who had little to no knowledge of foreign literature.

Tschichold had aquired the former series cover design, whose elements, for example, title plate and roundel, were disordered and did not compliment one another. For the redesign of the Penguin Classics series, Tschichold reintroduces the common monochromatic frame appearing in rich purple or burnt sienna. Just within the frame, Tschichold adds a thick geometric line, a subtle detail that allows the cover to resonate and gives the series a classic and appealing personality. The illustrations, engravings, and roundels appearing on the covers and throughout the interior page spreads were commissioned by prominent English designers and artists. The roundels were created for many book covers within the series as iconic representations of the characters in the story, and to add character and finishing touch to the design. Tschichold employed the classic and assertive typographic features of Monotype Perpetua for many of the covers within the Penguin Classics. For the Chapter headings and body text, Tschichold would mix various weights of Monotype Bembo and Monotype Centaur Titling. The results were a stunning, classical, and unique quality that was heightened by the exquisite Perpetua setting and elegant roundel insignia. (Figure 61, 62, 63, 64, 65)

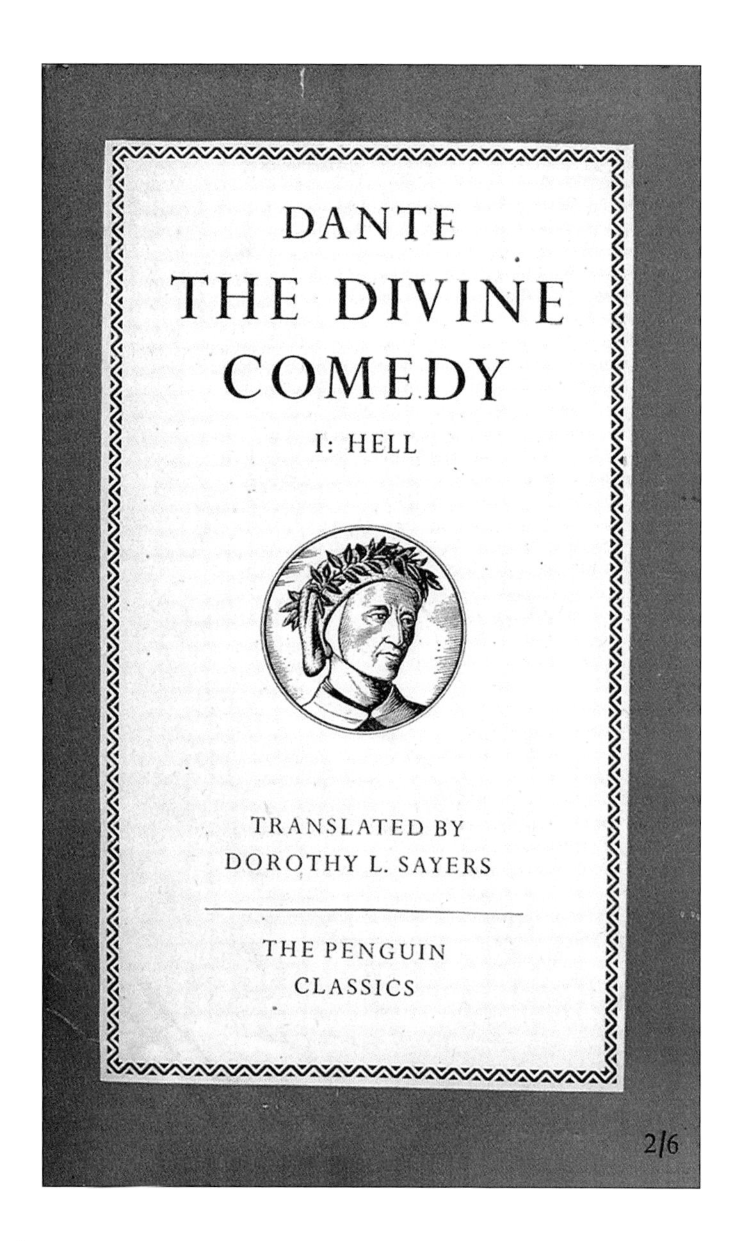

FIGURE 61

The Comedy of Dante Alighieri the Florentine, Cantica I Hell
translated by Dorothy L. Sayers
Cover Design by Jan Tschichold
The Penguin Classics, Number L 6, November 1949
4 3/8" x 7 1/8"

The singular characteristic of this cover design is the straightforward uppercase monotype Bembo throughout.

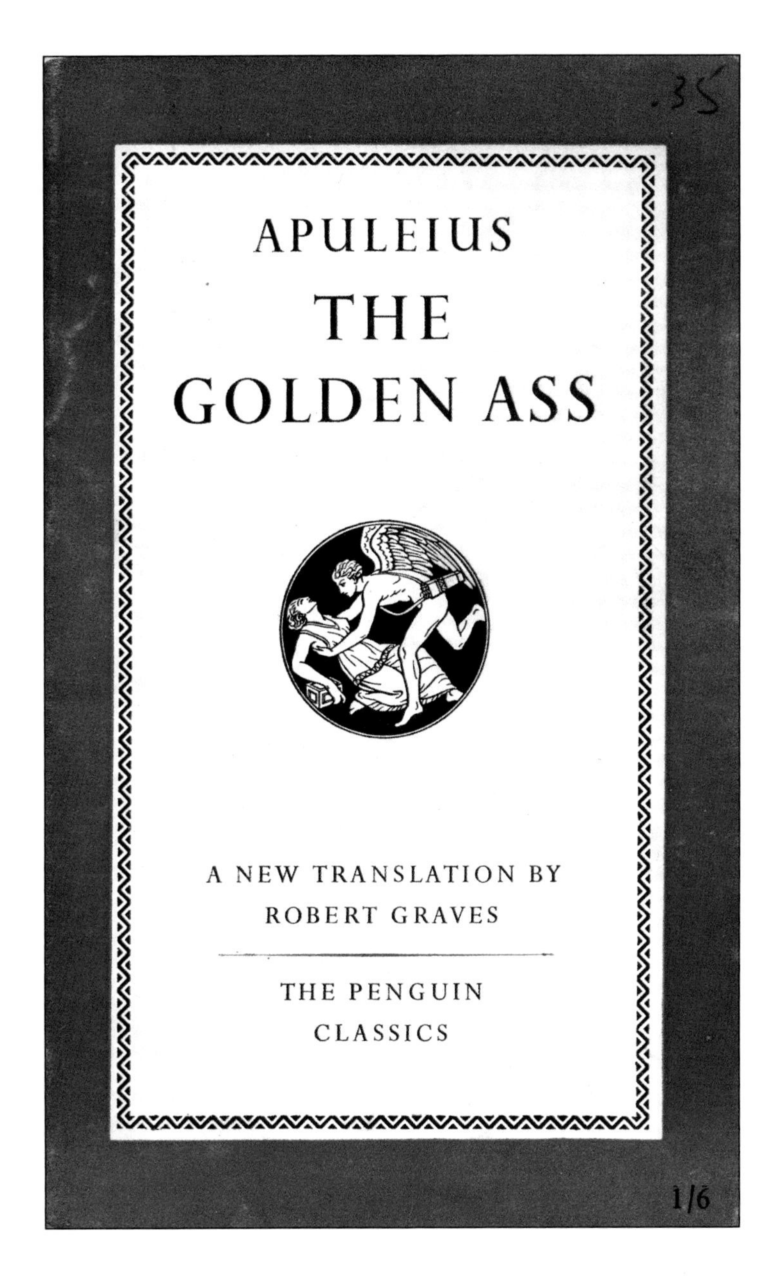

FIGURE 62

Apuleius: *The Golden Ass*, A New Translation by Robert Graves
Cover Series Design by Jan Tschichold
Penguin Classics, Number L 11, April 1950
4 3/8" x 7 1/8"

Tschichold's redesign of the Penguin Classics incorprates a unique frame-a common design element in many of the Penguin Cover series. The intricate difference with this particular border is the thick geometric line just within the frame. The distinguishing typographic feature is the expressive uppercase monotype Perpetua throughout. The roundels were commissioned by prominent English designers and add character and a finishing touch to the cover.

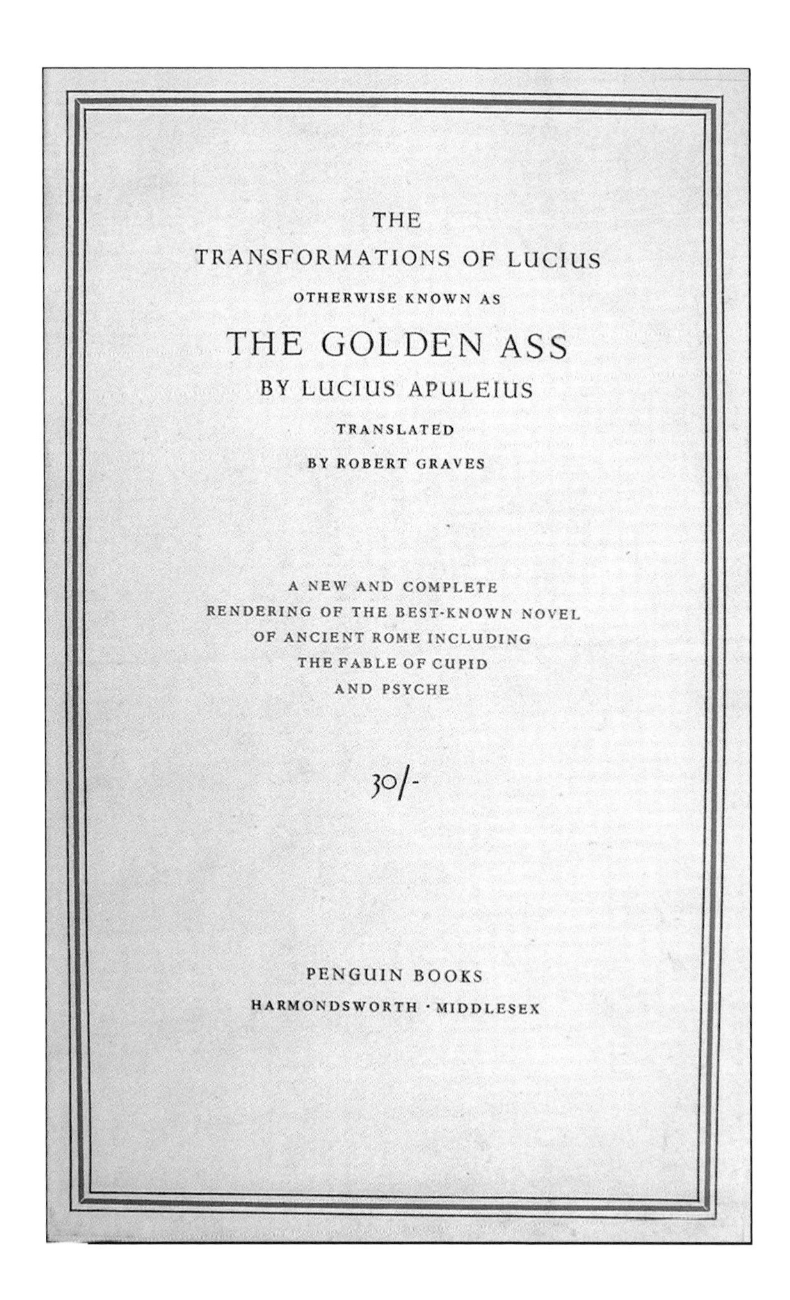
THE
TRANSFORMATIONS OF LUCIUS
OTHERWISE KNOWN AS
THE GOLDEN ASS
BY LUCIUS APULEIUS
TRANSLATED
BY ROBERT GRAVES

A NEW AND COMPLETE
RENDERING OF THE BEST-KNOWN NOVEL
OF ANCIENT ROME INCLUDING
THE FABLE OF CUPID
AND PSYCHE

30/-

PENGUIN BOOKS
HARMONDSWORTH · MIDDLESEX

FIGURE 63

The Transformations of Lucius otherwise known as The Golden Ass, by Lucius Apuleius (Edition de Luxe), translated by Robert Graves
Cover Design by Jan Tschichold
Penguin Classics, Number Q 13, December 1951
4 3/8" x 7 1/8"

The book's details included a beige cloth gilted stamped lettering on a vellum spine, Vellum tips, also referred to as French corners, and finished by hand to reinforce the spine and binding to avoid damage while handling. It was protected with a tan dustwrapper and fitted inside the original two-color card slipcase.

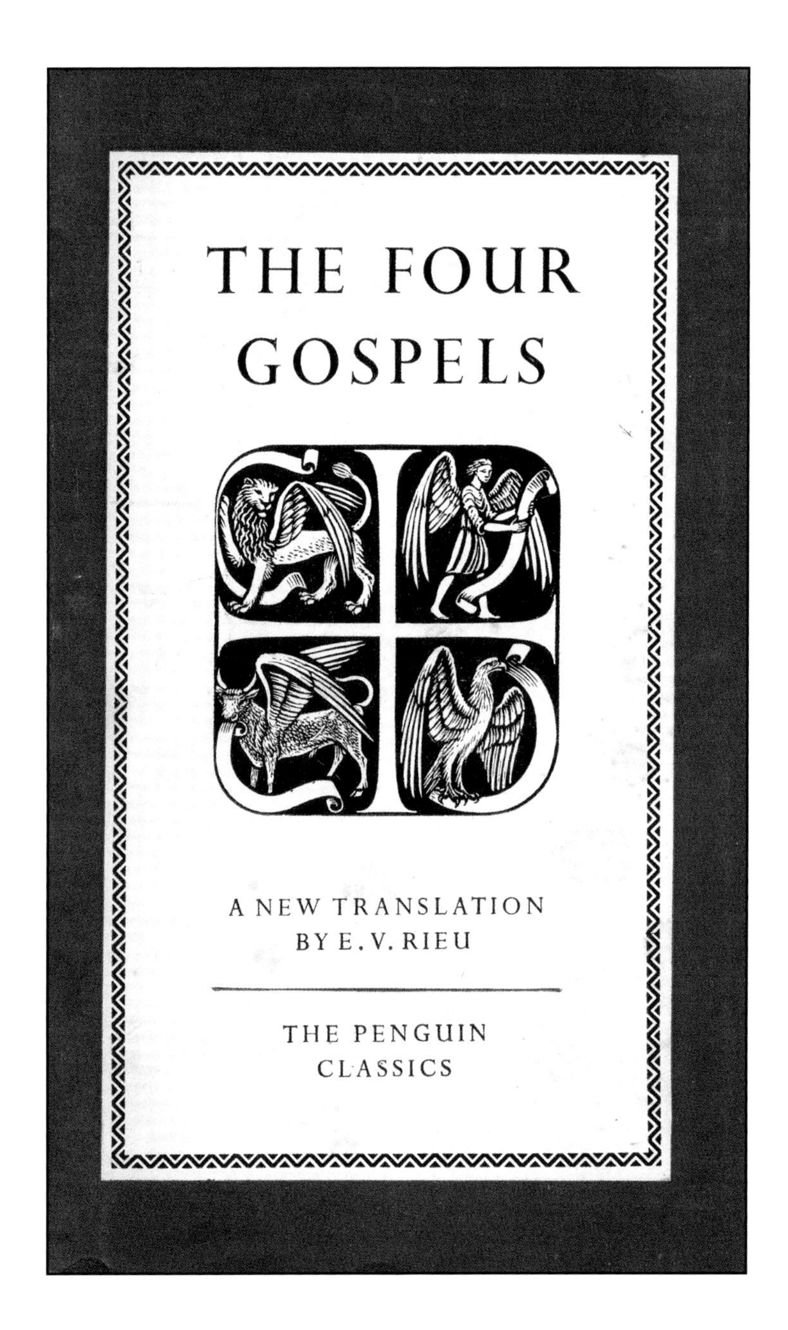

FIGURE 64

The Four Gospels: A New Translation by E.V. Rieu.
Cover Series Designed by Tschichold
Penguin Classics, Number L 32, November 1952
4 3/8" x 7 1/8"

The design on this cover was engraved in wood by Reynolds Stone. The discriminate typographic element is the expressive monotype Perpetua set in uppercase throughout.

THE GOSPEL AS RECORDED BY

MARK

THE FIRST WORD OF THE GOOD TIDINGS OF JESUS CHRIST SON OF GOD In accordance with the Scripture in the Prophet Isaiah, *Behold I send my Messenger ahead of thee to prepare thy way; the voice of one crying in the wilderness 'Prepare the way of the Lord: make his paths straight'*, John the Baptizer appeared in the wilderness proclaiming, for the forgiveness of sins, a baptism of repentance. All Judaea went out to him, and all the people of Jerusalem. They openly confessed their sins and were baptized by him in the River Jordan.

John wore clothing made of camel-hair, with a leather belt round his waist, and he ate locusts and wild honey. He preached in these words: 'He is on his way. One greater than I comes after me, whose sandal-straps I am not fit to stoop down and undo. I have baptized you in water; but he will baptize you in the Holy Spirit.'

And now Jesus appeared, coming from Nazareth in Galilee, and was baptized by immersion in the Jordan at the hands of John. He had no sooner come up out of the water than he saw

I

FIGURE 65

The Four Gospels: A New Translation by E.V. Rieu
Title Page Design by Jan Tschichold
Penguin Classics, Number L 32, November 1952
4 3/8" x 7 1/8"

The illustrations for each chapter were engraved in wood by Reynolds Stone. The discrete monotype Bembo is meticulously composed with Centaur Titling.

The Transformations of Lucius, otherwise known as The Golden Ass

One notable Masterpiece from the series of Penguin Classics is Tschichold's book design for *The Transformations of Lucius,* otherwise known as *The Golden Ass,* written by Lucius Apuleius, translated by the poet and novelist Robert Graves. First published as a softback in 1950, Penguin issued their own hardback version, a 298-page, 2,000 limited deluxe edition the following year. The books' detail included a beige cloth, gilted stamped lettering on a vellum spine, vellum tips, (also referred to as French corners), and finisheing by hand to reinforce the spine and binding in order to avoid damage while handling. For the lettering on the spine, *The Golden Ass,* Tschichold creates a hand drawn cursive lettering in a decorative and graceful script with vitality and harmony. Two rules of different weights had been added for visual support within the spine. The book was protected with a tan dustwrapper and fitted inside the original two-color card slipcase. Tschichold set the two-color card slipcase in all caps, monotype Perpetua in three distinctive groupings of typography. What made this design unique was the harmony and extreme clarity achieved by Tschichold's exquisitely centered arrangements, agreeable groupings, and elegant relationships of typography.

These three groupings were comprised of fourteen lines of type, centrally placed and similar point size throughout. However, the point size of the title, *The Golden Ass,* being the most important, was increased to a larger point and carefully letterspaced to draw attention. Also, the description of the books contents, comprised of five lines of type, was accentuated in an intense red and placed in the center of the cover. In addition, Tschichold included a three ruled frame device running around the edge of the slipcase to complement the typography in order to acheive balanced perfection. Tschichold set the book in monotype Lutetia, a typeface designed by Jan van Krimpen and printed by Silk & Terry on a specially made blue-white woven paper made by Wiggins, Teape & Co.

"James Laughlin, the distinguished publisher who founded *New Directions* in 1936, once wrote about *The Golden Ass* and called it *'a real corker.'* In an essay entitled 'The Pleasures of Reading the Classics in Translation' (Antaeus, 1987), he mentioned the fine translation by Robert Graves and said: *'Apuleius who lived in Carthage, was fascinated by magic. His tales are full of magical events. The original title of his book was Metamorphoses. The important transformation comes when a seductive sorceress applies an ointment which changes Lucius, the rather Candide-like young hero, into a donkey. This, for an author, yields the advantage of giving the narrator two points of view in satirizing human foibles. Toward the end the goddess Isis changes Lucius back to a man he is initiated into the old Egyptian Mysteries.'"* [20]

---

[20] Charles Antin. The Penguin Golden Ass, Jan Tschichold's Masterpiece. (AB Bookman's Weekly, June 1, 1998), pp.1465-1466.

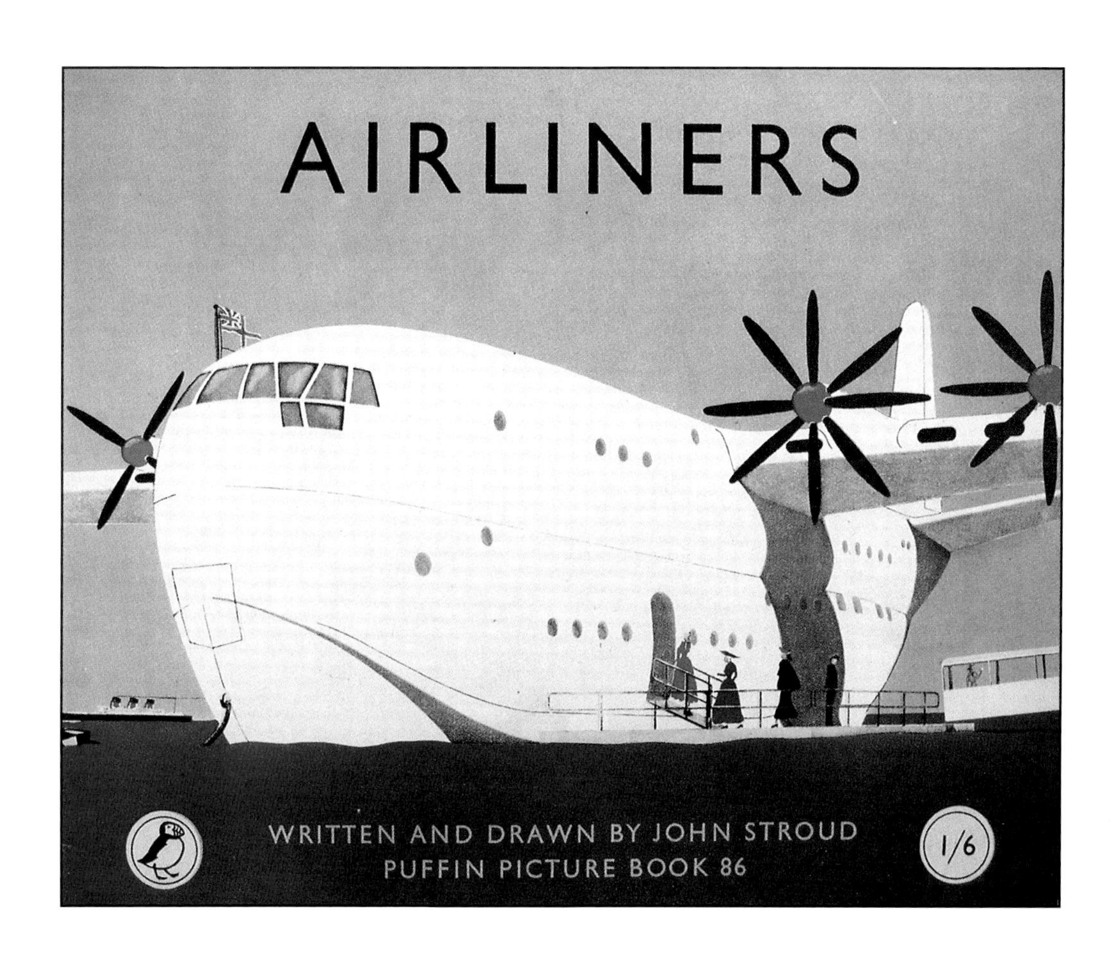

FIGURE 66

Airliners: John Stroud
Interior Page Design by Jan Tschichold
Puffin Picture Book, Number PP 86,
First Published October 1949
8 3/4" x 7 1/8"

Chapter 5
The Puffin Picture and Story Books

During World War II (1939-1945), Penguin began publishing books for children with the introduction of the popular Puffin Picture Books. This series was patterned on the eminent Russian children's books published after the 1917 Soviet Union Revolution. The Puffin Picture books included descriptive text with educational and recreational subject matter for the purpose of educating children and covered such topics as swimming, bird watching, spelling, nursery rhymes, and astronomy. (Figure 66) The books were oriented in a landscape format 83/4" x 71/8", consisting of thirty-two pages that included commissioned full colour illustrations on every page, drawn by prominent English artists such as Edward Bawden and C.F. Tunnicliffe. Many of the illustrations were reproduced by photolithography for the purpose of color and were an important component in the series success. The series editor Noel Carrington stressed the commissioned artists importance by saying:

"We owe much to the artists. Usually they have dedicated far more time and pains to the making of their books than seemed to be justified by the immediate reward. Some of the subjects meant months of preliminary field study or research.

I had a really stunning scheme for a book: 'Wild Flowers' by Paxton Chadwick, the whole job superbly finished in water-colours. When Allen and I looked through it he exclaimed: 'But this is absolutely tops! Who is this chap? Of course we must do it.' I said: 'But he makes conditions. It's to be in colour on every page.' (Puffins were usually black and white on every other opening). Here I brought out one of Chadwick's lithographic plates which he had done as a sample. It was really a masterpiece. (Figure 67, 68) *Allen compared it with the water colour and handed it around the table. Somebody said: 'Almost too good for a children's book.' 'Nonsense,' said Allen, 'nothing is too good for Penguins. We will double the print and bring the cost down. Bring this chap along to our next meeting. I want to see him."* [21]

In 1947, The Puffin Picture books presented Tschichold with the challenge of striking a delicate balance between text and illustrations, particularly, with the time consuming task of managing the page layout when the illustrations were often received in the incorrect sizes. Tschichold was able to carefully readjust and accommodate the different sized illustrations to create an appealing harmony and balance between text and illustrations. Before Tschichold's had arrived at Penguin, many of the books in this series relied on only one typeface, Times New Roman. In addition, the typography was poorly set in a disproportionately large setting, disagreeable leading, all uppercase chapter headings, and unbalanced column placements.

In contrast, one noteworthy example from the Puffin Picture Book series, designed by Tschichold is *Postage Stamps* (Figure 69, 70) by L.N. and M. Williams, Puffin Picture Book Number 69, first Published in 1950 and printed by W.R. Royle & Sons Ltd, London. The stamps were provided by Messrs Frank Godden Ltd, Bridger & Kay Ltd, and David Field Ltd, and the drawings are by Sydney R. Turner, Esq. For the cover design, Tschichold maintained the consistent border design, like many of the Penguin series, by skillfully integrating the colorful stamp montage inside the frame, thus, giving the book its unique character. In addition, Tschichold cleverly chose an appropriate image for the central typographic window frame, a Lundy Puffin stamp, a whimsical accent to the overall design. For the interior page spreads, Tschichold introduced a grid system to help with legibility, organization of the diverse stamp shapes, and an orderly arrangement of stamps and body text.

---

[21] Steve Hare. *Penguin Portrait, Allen Lane and the Penguin Editors 1935-1970.* (Harmondsworth, Middlesex, England: Penguin Books Ltd., 1995), pp.136-37

WILD FLOWERS

BRITAIN is rich in flowering plants. There are at least 1,200 different kinds, and some botanists say there are more like 1,600. Whatever the total number, it is only possible to deal with a few of them in this book. They grow in many different sorts of places; in the fields, woods, hedgerows and marshes, on heaths and hills and by the sea-shore.

Perhaps the most striking thing about them is the enormous variety of form and colour that is to be found not only in the flowers themselves but in the leaves, stems and roots. For example, leaves may be oval, long, lobed, divided, etc. They may grow with or without stalks, at different levels on the stem, in twos or more at thc same level, or radiate from the base, or in many other ways. Roots may take the form of tubers, bulbs, long tap-roots or they may be a compact mass of fibres. They may grow deep down or they may creep just below the surface of the soil.

Every part of a plant has some job to do in the life of the complete plant, but from the point of view of continuing a species, of maintaining the plant population, as it were, the flowers in particular play the key role. For it is in the flowers that the reproductive organs are to be found; and without these plant life would quickly die out.

2. HEARTSEASE, WILD PANSY (*Viola tricolor*) May to September. A perennial of fields and waste places. The flowers vary both in size and colour. Note the seed box with its three divisions.

FIGURE 67

Wild Flowers: Paxton Chadwick
Interior Page Design by Jan Tschichold
Puffin Picture Book, Number PP 81
First Published, April 1949
8 3/4" x 7 1/8"

Tschichold allows the illustration's exquisite shape to dictate the overall layout of the page as the justified body text serves to provide structure to the layout and compliment the flower illustration.

Composite flowers

Some flowers, like those of the dandelion, daisy and thistle types, present a new picture and are worth a special note. They are called composite flowers inasmuch as each flower-head consists really of a number of individual flowers or *florets*.

In the dandelion these are all strap-shaped (ligulate) and each is a perfect flower complete with anthers and stigma.

In the thistles the florets are all tube-shaped, while in the daisy there are two kinds, the central disc florets, which have a tube-shaped corolla, and the outer ray florets, which are flat.

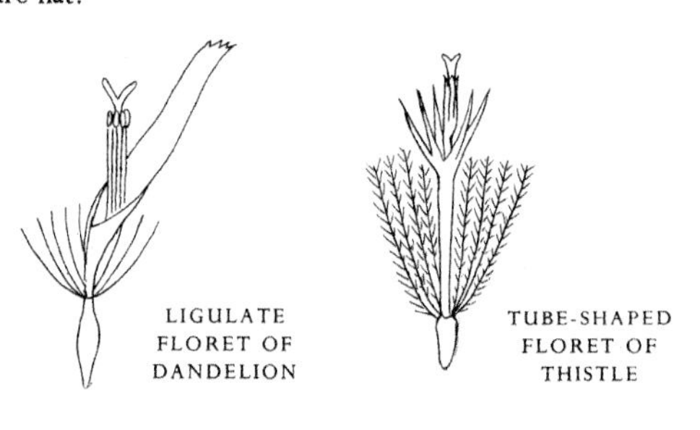

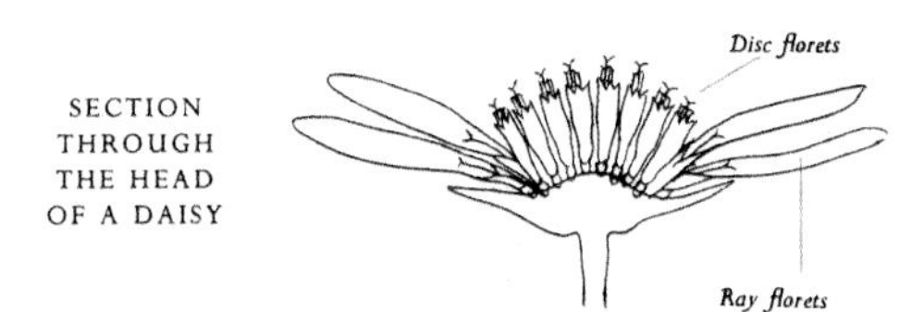

Examples of inflorescence, or the arrangement of flowers on the stems

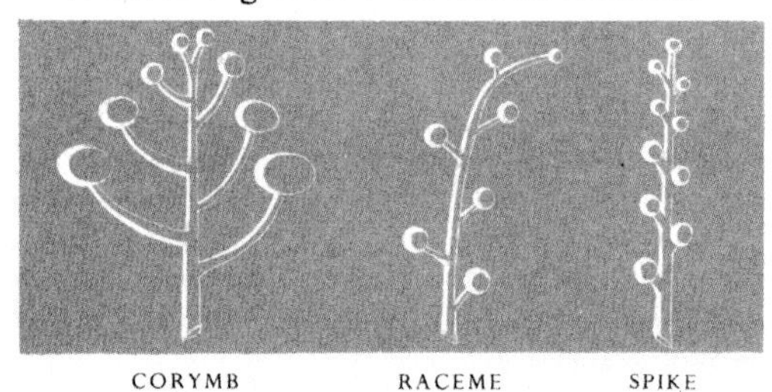

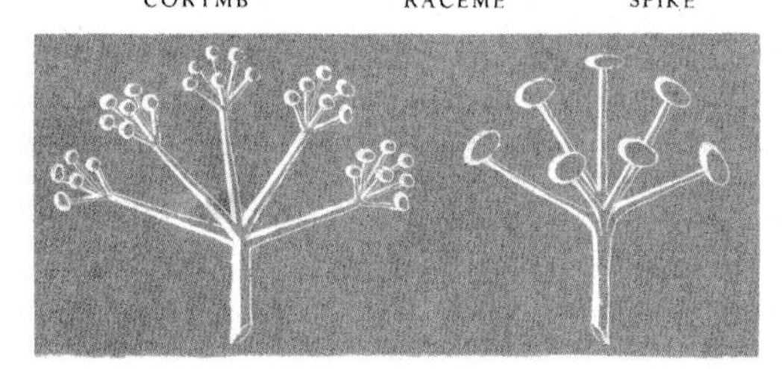

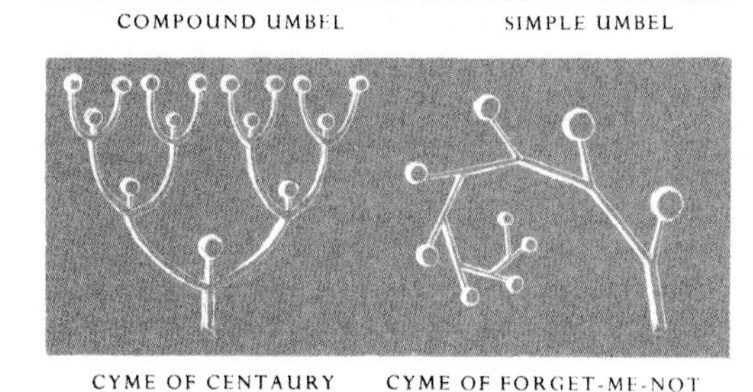

FIGURE 68

Wild Flowers: Paxton Chadwick
Interior Page Design by Jan Tschichold
Puffin Picture Book, Number PP 81
First Published April 1949
8 3/4" x 7 1/8"

Tschichold uses a grid to provide order and structure to the page layout. He also organizes the inflorescent examples of stems on flowers into boxed groupings for greater clarity and to compliment the justified body text and floating illustrations on the left hand side of the page layout.

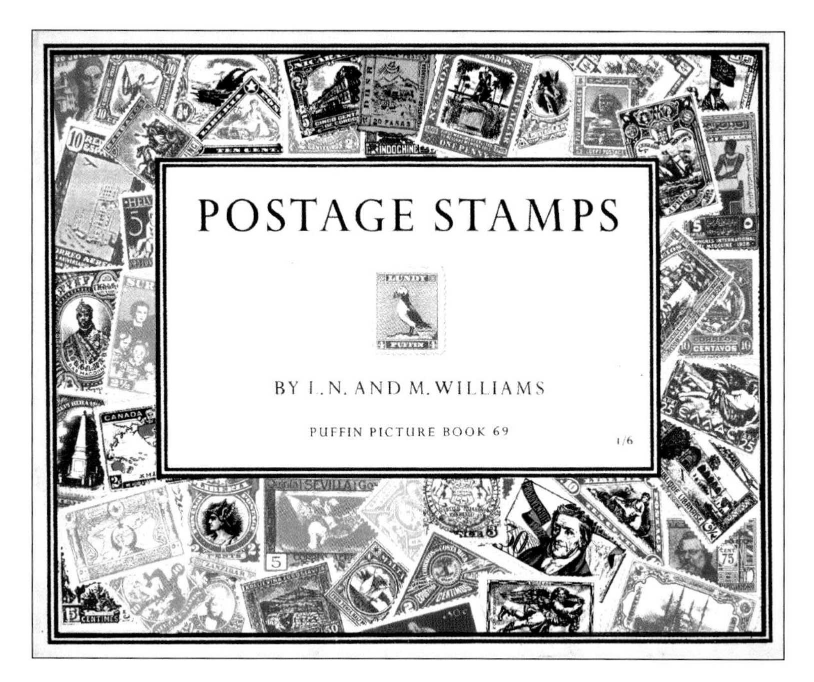

FIGURE 69

Postage Stamps: by L.N. & M. Williams, Cover Design by Jan Tschichold
Puffin Picture Book, Number PP 69, First Published April 1950, 8 3/4" x 7 1/8"

The upper case title, author's name, and book number are carefully positioned within the extraordinary illustrated collage of stamps. Tschichold cleverly chooses a Lundy Puffin Stamp for the very center, a whimsical accent to the overall design.

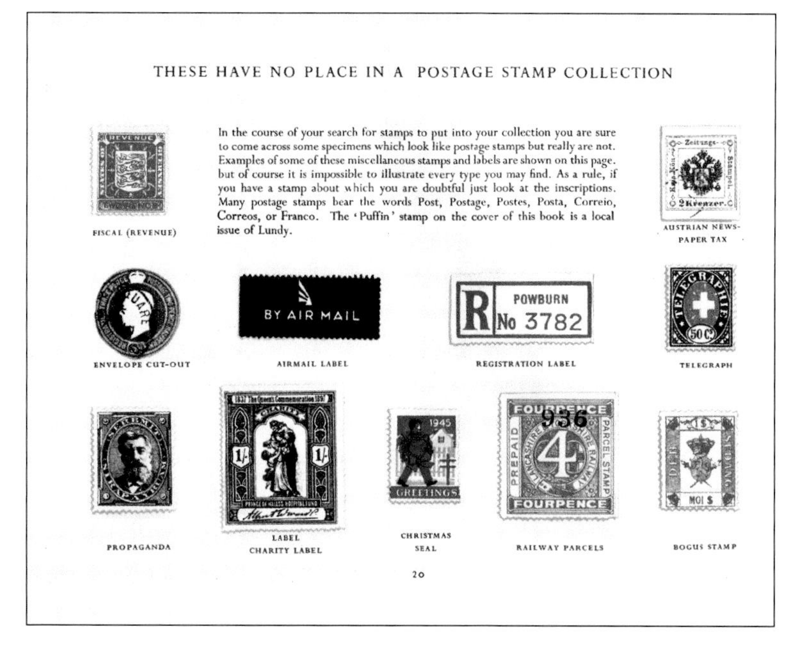

THESE HAVE NO PLACE IN A POSTAGE STAMP COLLECTION

In the course of your search for stamps to put into your collection you are sure to come across some specimens which look like postage stamps but really are not. Examples of some of these miscellaneous stamps and labels are shown on this page, but of course it is impossible to illustrate every type you may find. As a rule, if you have a stamp about which you are doubtful just look at the inscriptions. Many postage stamps bear the words Post, Postage, Postes, Posta, Correio, Correos, or Franco. The 'Puffin' stamp on the cover of this book is a local issue of Lundy.

FISCAL (REVENUE)

AUSTRIAN NEWS-PAPER TAX

ENVELOPE CUT-OUT

AIRMAIL LABEL

REGISTRATION LABEL

TELEGRAPH

PROPAGANDA

LABEL CHARITY LABEL

CHRISTMAS SEAL

RAILWAY PARCELS

BOGUS STAMP

20

FIGURE 70

Postage Stamps: by L.N. & M. Williams, Interior Page Design by Jan Tschichold
Puffin Picture Book Number PP 69, First Published April 1950, 8 3/4" x 7 1/8"

Tschichold's use of a grid becomes almost visible with the placement and structure of the postage stamps. The body text has been set with left and right justification to simulate a rectangular or square shape-a subtle way of integrating the body text and stamps.

Puffin Story Books soon followed in 1941. Some included reprints of famous children's classics such as *Coconut Island* by Robert Gibbins, *Worzel Gummidge* by Barbara Euphan Todd (1890-1976), and *Treasure Island* by Robert Louis Stevenson (1850-94). Other titles written specifically for the series included *Enjoying Painting* by A.C. Ward, *The Puffin Puzzle Book* by W.E. Gladstone, and *Going to the Ballet* by Arnold Haskell.

The Puffin Story Books were first published in December 1941 and were geared specifically for children ages six to fifteen. Many books were written and commissioned for the series covering a wide range of topics such as adventures, games, discoveries, fairy tales, selected stories and verses, song books, and enjoying painting.

Aside from enchanting illustrated covers, Tschichold inherited a series that used unpleasing typography with no visual connection to the illustrations and lacked unique characteristics corresponding to the books story. One particular book within the series that Tschichold focused his attention on was *Through the Looking Glass and What Alice Found There.* (Figure 71, 72) The story was first published in 1872, and republished in Puffin Story Books and edited by Eleanor Graham in October 1948. Tschichold cleverly adorns the front cover with an illustration drawn by John Tenniel of a young girl stepping through the looking glass and a similar illustration of the young girl stepping out the other side onto the back cover. The illustrations served as a visual metaphor for reading and experiencing the story from beginning to end. The typography treatment for the back cover was placed backwards and read from right to left, an occurrence that happens when reflected into a mirror. The illustration on the front cover was sized proportionately to be the same width as the line length of the typography for a seemless integration of text and image.

The typography was set in monotype Scotch Roman to reflect the period of when the story was first published in the late 1800's. The title, author's name, and illustrator's name are all set in uppercase and simply placed on a central axis. The words, *A Puffin Story Book*, was set in monotype italic Scotch Roman at a smaller point size for less emphasis. The title page spread includes a beautiful illustration on the left page and carefully positioned all

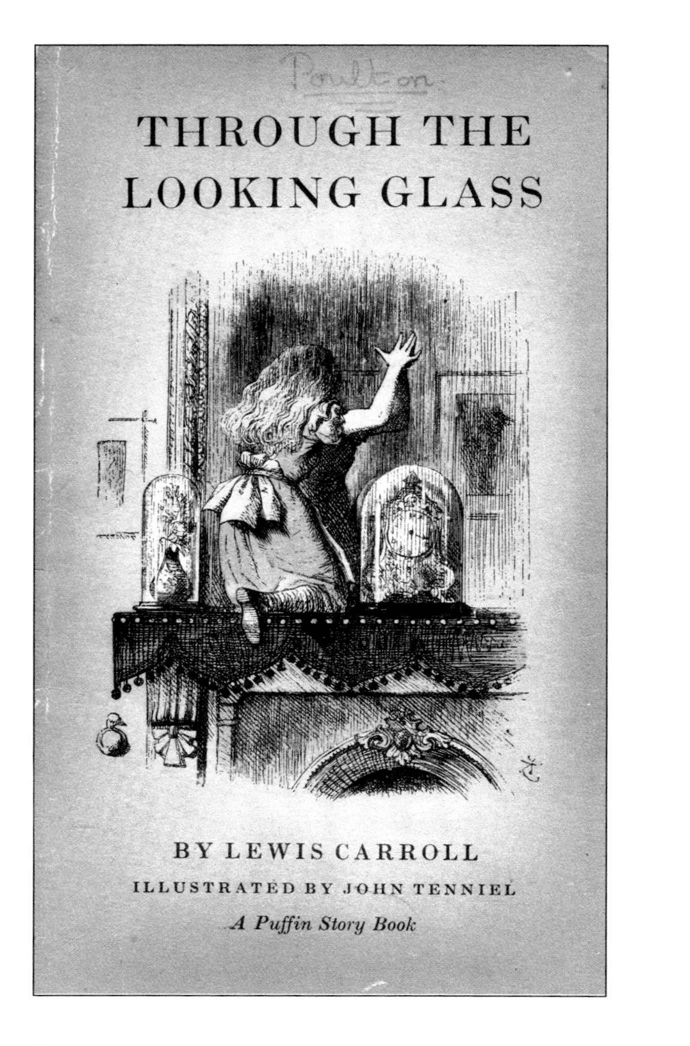

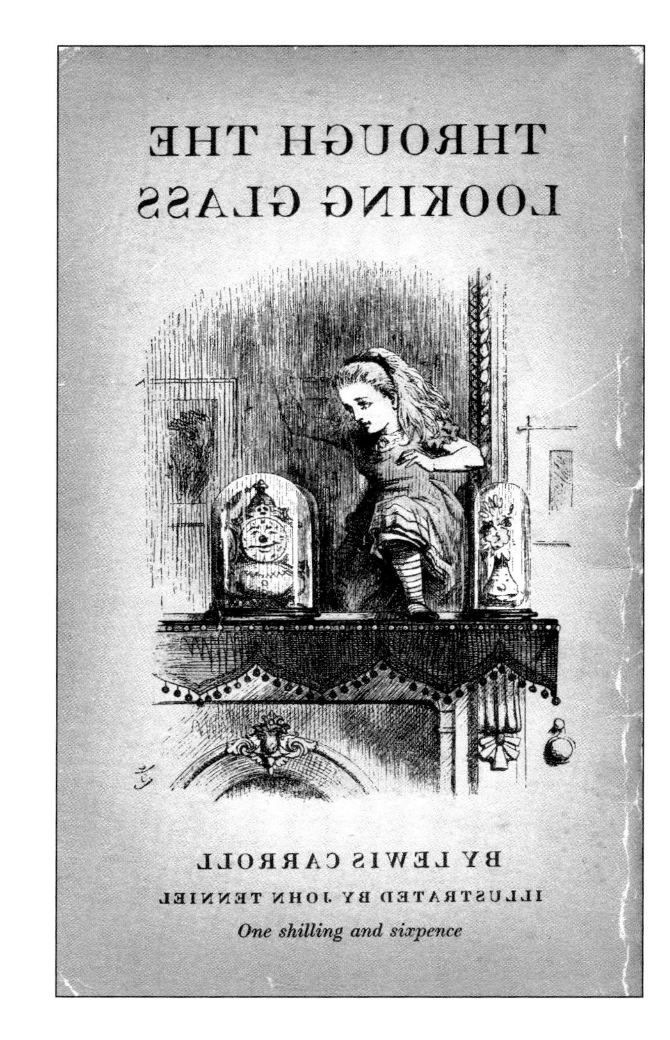

FIGURE 71 & 72

Through the Looking Glass: by Lewis Carroll
Front & Back Cover of Puffin Story Book Cover Design by Tschichold
A Puffin Story Book, Number PS 44, October 1948
4 3/8" x 7 1/8"

The distinguishing typographic feature is the classic vintage monotype Scotch Roman. Each of the five lines of typography is carefully letter spaced to align the width of the illustration. In addition, the subtle styling of the lettering is unobtrusive and compliments the delicate qualities of the illustration. The typography and illustration on the back cover are cleverly inverted to represent the story Through the Looking Glass.

uppercase monotype Scotch Roman in three distinct groups of type on the right page. The interior spreads included fifty extraordinary illustrations by Tenniel and justified monotype Scotch Roman for the body text. The monotype Scotch Roman's generous x-height allows for highly legible type set at a small point size. One noteworthy quality was the physical character and smooth paper, which is only appreciated when one holds it in their hands. The book was printed by Richard Clay and Company, Limited Bungay, Suffolk. For further examples of book covers designed by Tschichold within the Puffin Picture and Story Books series, see Figure 73, 74, 75.

FIGURE 73

A Puffin Book of Verse: Edited by Eleanor Graham
Illustrated by Claudia Freedman
Front Cover of Puffin Story Book Cover Design by Tschichold
A Puffin Story Book, Number PS 72, May 1953
4 3/8" x 7 1/8"

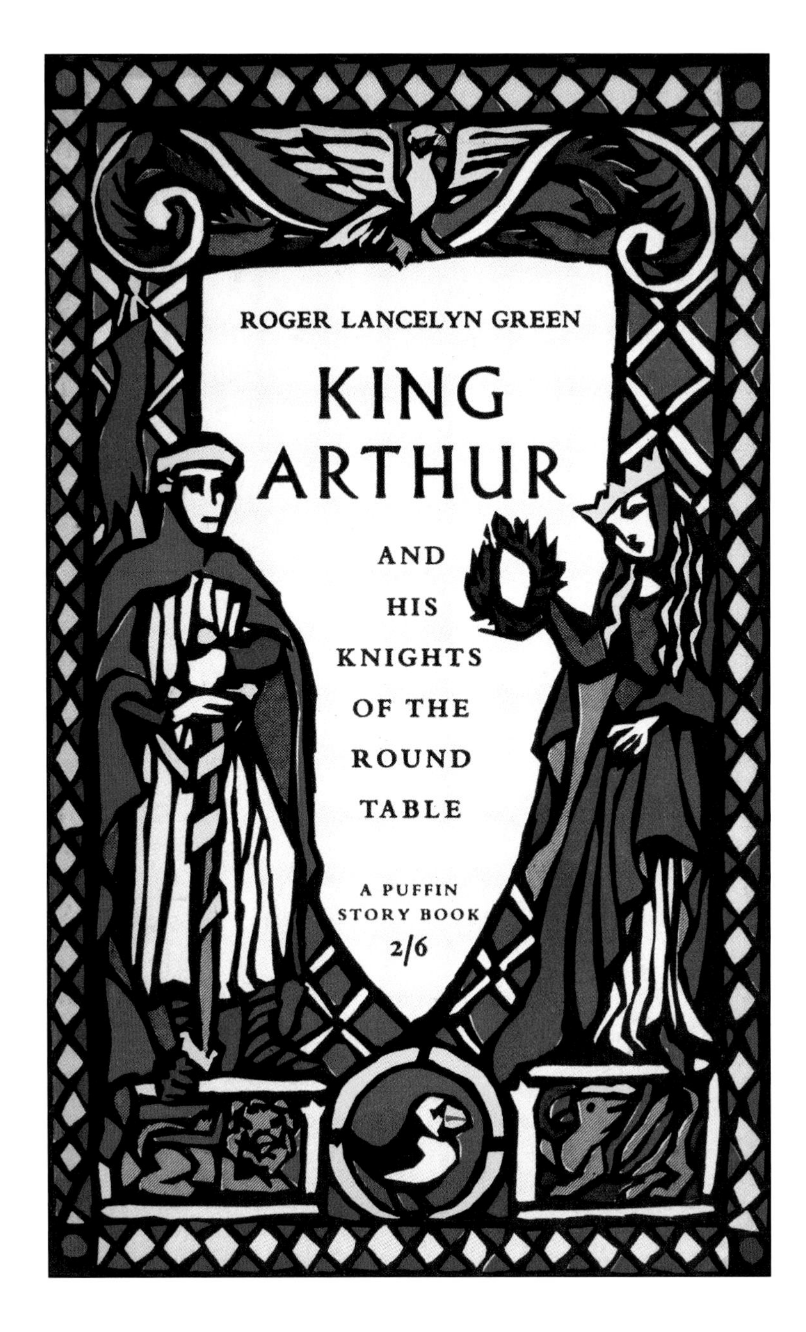

FIGURE 74

King Arthur and his Knights of the Round Table: Roger Lancelyn Green
Illustrations by Lotte Reiniger
Cover and Series, Redesign by Tschichold
A Puffin Story Book, Number PS 73, May 1953
4 3/8" x 7 1/8"

A wood block effect has been applied to the illustration to give this cover a distinct personality. The artist, Lotte Reiniger, uses a new method by cutting the illustrations out of thin black paper with a pair of special scissors. The subtle scissor cuts are mounted on transparent paper as a set of much smaller pictures were made for the book. The weight of the upper case typography and its crude character compliments the illustration.

The High Toby
A play for the Toy Theatre by J. B. PRIESTLEY
with scenery and characters by DORIS ZINKEISEN
A PUFFIN CUT-OUT BOOK
Two shillings and sixpence

FIGURE 75

The High Toby: J.B. Priestley
Scenery and Characters by Doris Zinkeisen
Cover Design by Jan Tschichold
Puffin Cut-Out Books, Number PC 5, First Published
November 1948
8 3/4" x 7 1/8"

The typography is composed with the dainty characteristics of monotype Bell.

Chapter 6
Penguin Expanded Series

Among those titles mentioned, new projects and development occurred in early 1947 to expand Penguin's readership, such as Penguin Music Scores, Penguin Poets, Penguin Guides, and The Building of England to raise readers' awareness of England's environs and beautiful surroundings. Penguin continued to experiment with further innovations and launched Penguin Parade, edited by Denys Kilham Roberts, a quarterly publication devoted to essays, poems, and woodcuts by contemporary writers and artists. Penguin Parade was revived in 1948, after production had stopped during the war, and its editor, J.E. Morpurgo, assembled international critical writings on artistic and social development.

Penguin Music Scores

The Penguin Music Scores series was developed to help guide the knowledgeable and passionate listener towards a greater understanding of the musical compositions. These compact musical guides were edited by Gordon Jacob and included biographical notes of such masters as Sergei Rachmaninov, Peter Ilich Tchaikovsky, Johannes Brahms, Franz Liszt, and Joseph Haydn.

No previous design had existed for the Music Scores series, and Tschichold was able to tackle the new design assignment with a fresh and inventive approach; he began by introducing a white title plate positioned just slightly above center on the cover. Figure (76, 77) The white window shade included the featured musicians last name, for example, Beethoven, set in all uppercase monotype Caslon Old Face, followed by the title of the musical composition,

FIGURE 76, 77

Beethoven: Coriolan and Egmont Overtures
Penguin Music Scores Series Cover Design by Jan Tschichold
Penguin Music Scores, Number SC 3, June 1949
5 1/8" x 7 3/4"

The decorative repeated Curwen Press patterned paper was designed by the german designer Elizabeth Friedlander (1903-84). Both the cover and title page are set in the beautiful monotype Caslon Old Face.

BEETHOVEN

Overtures Coriolan Op. 62 and Egmont Op. 84

WITH A BIOGRAPHICAL NOTE AND AN INTRODUCTION
BY W. MCNAUGHT

PENGUIN BOOKS
HARMONDSWORTH · MIDDLESEX

offset in an enchanting monotype italic Caslon Old Face. Only three lines of text are used within the white title plate for each Music Score cover. Tschichold then added one thick and one thin hairline rule just within the white panel. The decorative and exquisite repeated Curwen Press patterned paper in a sophisticated monochromatic earthtone color palette was designed by the German designer Elizabeth Friedlander (1903-84). A new patterned paper and monochromatice earthtone color was introduced for each book to invoke the spirit and energy of the music composition.

Tschichold carefully carried over similar typographic styling from the cover to the title page. The typography was centrally placed in a symmetrical format and an elegant swelled rule was inserted to divide the composer and musical composition from the biographer's name in a simple, restrained, elegant manner. The interior spreads are composed on a grid as the body text was set in left and right paragraph justification for clarity and legibility. The musical note page spreads are organized in a manner to help the reader with ease of reading.

Penguin Poets

The Penguin Poets may arguably be the most beautiful and elegant of all the Penguin series designed or redesigned by Tschichold. The series included an extensive catalogue of old and new poetry such as works by T.S. Eliot, Scotland's national poet Robert Burns, John Donne, Alexander Pope, and a selection of great English poems from Chaucer to Rossetti.

The early Poet designs were not suitable for the subject of poetry or styling characteristic of poetic works. For the Penguin Poets cover, Tschichold incorporated an exquisite floral monotype border, befitting romantic and poetic imagery, similar to the covers he designed in the mid 1940's for Swiss publishers, within a frame composed of various weighted hairline rules. For the typography, Tschichold has meticulously placed the type into distinct groupings, placed centrally within a long rectangular window. The type treatments include mixings of all uppercase and upper and lower case groups all set in the graceful, hand written features of monotype Bell. All the groupings are consistent in point size, excluding the title of the work,

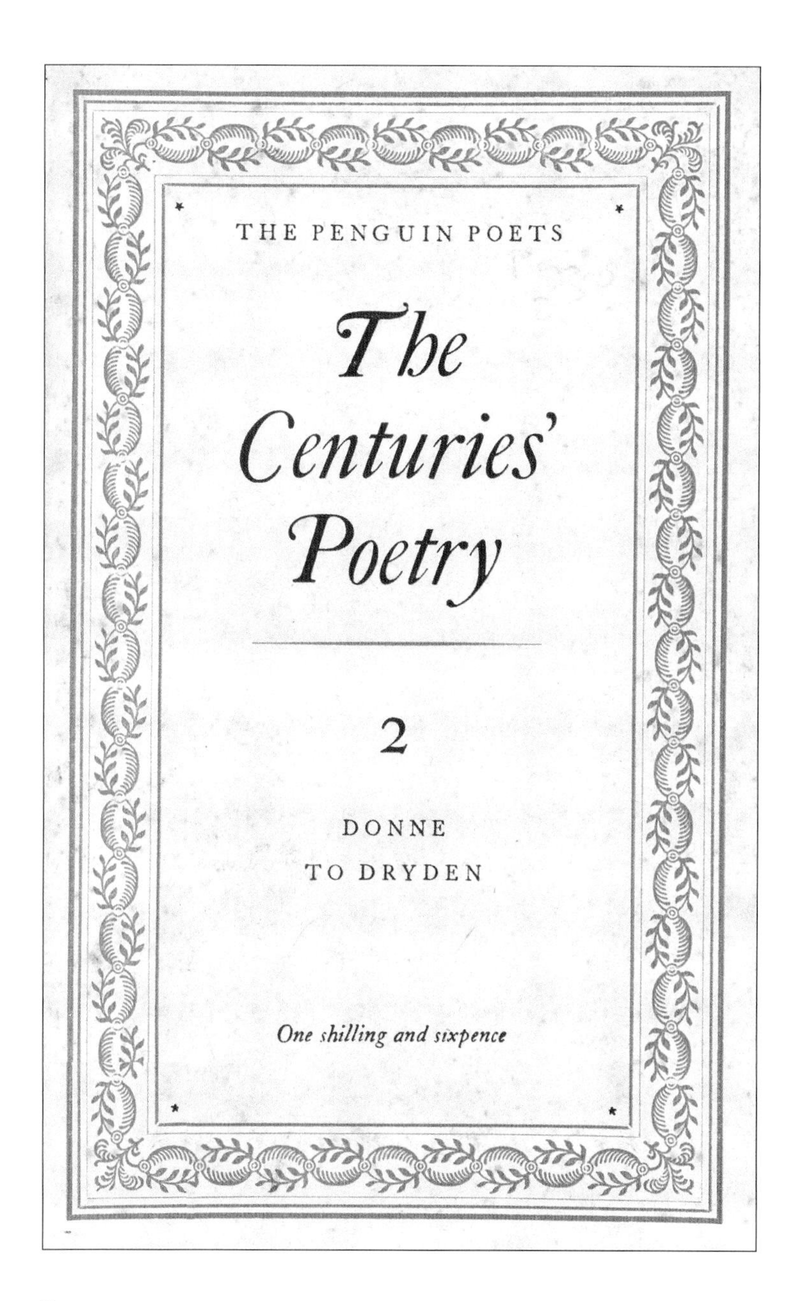

FIGURE 78

The Centuries' Poetry (2): Donne to Dryden
Edited by D. Kilham Roberts
Penguin Poets Cover Series Design by Jan Tschichold
The Penguin Poets, Number D 7, September 1949
4 3/8" x 7 1/8"

The typography on this cover is composed with the stunning monotype Caslon Old Face and compliments the elegant border design.

set in a much larger point size, for emphasis and hierarchy. Of particular note in the Penguin Poets cover is the beautiful yellow, cream colored paper stock, accented with a faint pale green color for the monotype border and swelled rule. These delicate features give this series a retrained yet equisite and stunning look and feel. (Figure 78)

Penguin Handbooks

The Penguin Handbooks series were published in December 1942, as useful manuals written by recognized experts for readers unfamiliar with a new activity or professional interest or whose hobbies include vegetable gardening, parenting, breeding farm animals, cooking, chess, and painting. Each book provides an introduction to the leisure activity, historical highlights from the 19th century to present day, bibliography and index. (Figure 79, 80, 81)

The former design was comparable to the earliest Penguin series with a superfluous floral motif pattern within the white horizontal panel. For the redesign of each book cover in the series, Tschichold created a rectangular frame composed of individual panels with thumbnail-sized illustrations and symbols representing the books subject matter, for example, a variety of vegetables and chess pieces. The illustrations are generally in one color or reversed out to white and set on a neutral or dark background such as black or one color. A long white rectangle includes all of the typography, author's name, title of the book, and a brief commentary highlighting the subject matter. Tschichold meticulously places the typography on a centered axis and precisely spaces out the type and leading, thus, creating clear-cut groups to help with readability and a succinct and consice relationship between the typography and the long rectangular shape.

The title and author's name is set in monotype Gill Sans and the commentary, organized on six to nine lines of type, is set off in oblique styling. The interior spreads include a simple composed title page, justified body text, and illustrations sprinkled throughout the handbook. The interior pages are well-organized and restrained and reflect Tschichold's composition rules. The series was composed and printed by the Camelot Press Ltd.,

London and Southhampton. In contrast to the former design, Tschichold has introduced unequivaocal individuality, functional appearance, and refined characteristics.

Additional periodicals coincided with Penguin's diversifications with the launch of the Penguin Musical Magazine, Russian Review, Penguin Film Review, as well as two journals, New Biology and Science News. Penguin launched the Film Review in August 1946 and the Music Magazine in February 1947, just as Tschichold was coming on board as leading typographer of design.

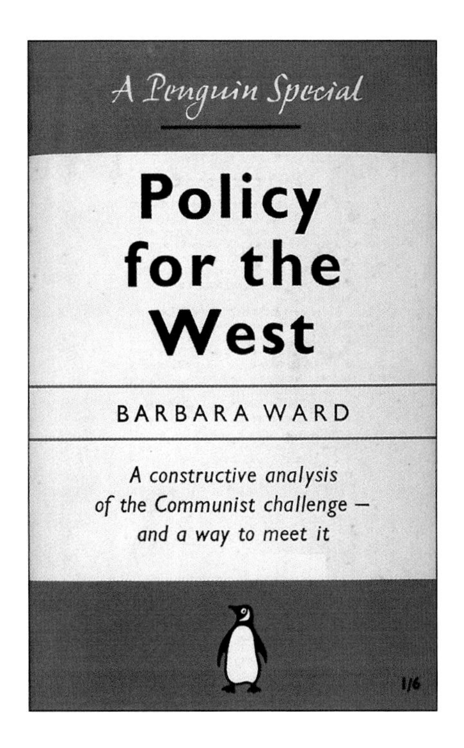

FIGURE 79

Policy for the West: Barbara Ward
Series Cover design for A Penguin Special by Jan Tschichold
Number S 158, January 1951
4 3/8" x 7 1/8"

The quirky and eccentric monotype Gill Sans mixed with the hand drawn calligraphy for 'A Penguin Special' gives this cover a unique personality. Tschichold's study of natural and pure of cancellaresca cursive script such as works by the Spanish writing master Francisco Lucas, Englishmen Jean de Beauchesne and John Baildon as well as the calligraphic engravings of the Frenchmen Benignus Morellus informed his use and styling of calligraphy at Penguin. Penguin Specials was one of the few Penguin covers where Tschichold applied his calligraphic skill.

THE PENGUIN
New Writing
Paul Bowles: By the Water
William Sansom: A Wedding
Vitaliano Brancati: Sebastiana
Donald Ford: The Green Door
Tom Hopkinson: The Matelot and the Piece of Cake
Kathleen Raine: Michael Roberts
Robert Liddell: Angelos Sikelianos
J. P. Hodin: Cornish Renaissance
John Lehmann: The Life of the Prodigal Son
Poems by C. Day Lewis, Anne Ridler, J. C. Hall,
Hal Summers, Saba, Lynette Roberts and Denton Welch
Illustrations by Figari, Cavalcanti
Sven Berlin and others
EDITED BY JOHN LEHMANN
One shilling and sixpence
39

FIGURE 80

New Writing: Edited by John Lehmann
Series Cover design for Periodical Publications by Jan Tschichold
Number NW 39, 1950
4 3/8" x 7 1/8"

The featured typeface is the quirky and essentric monotype Gill Sans mixed with the hand drawn calligraphy for *New Writing*. Tschichold's study of natural and pure forms of cancellaresca cursive script such as works by the Spanish writing master Francisco Lucas, the Englishmen Jean de Beauchesne and John Baildon, as well as the calligraphic engravings of the Frenchmen Benignus Morellus informed his use and styling of calligraphy at Penguin. *New Writing* was one of the few Penguin covers where Tschichold applied his calligraphic skill.

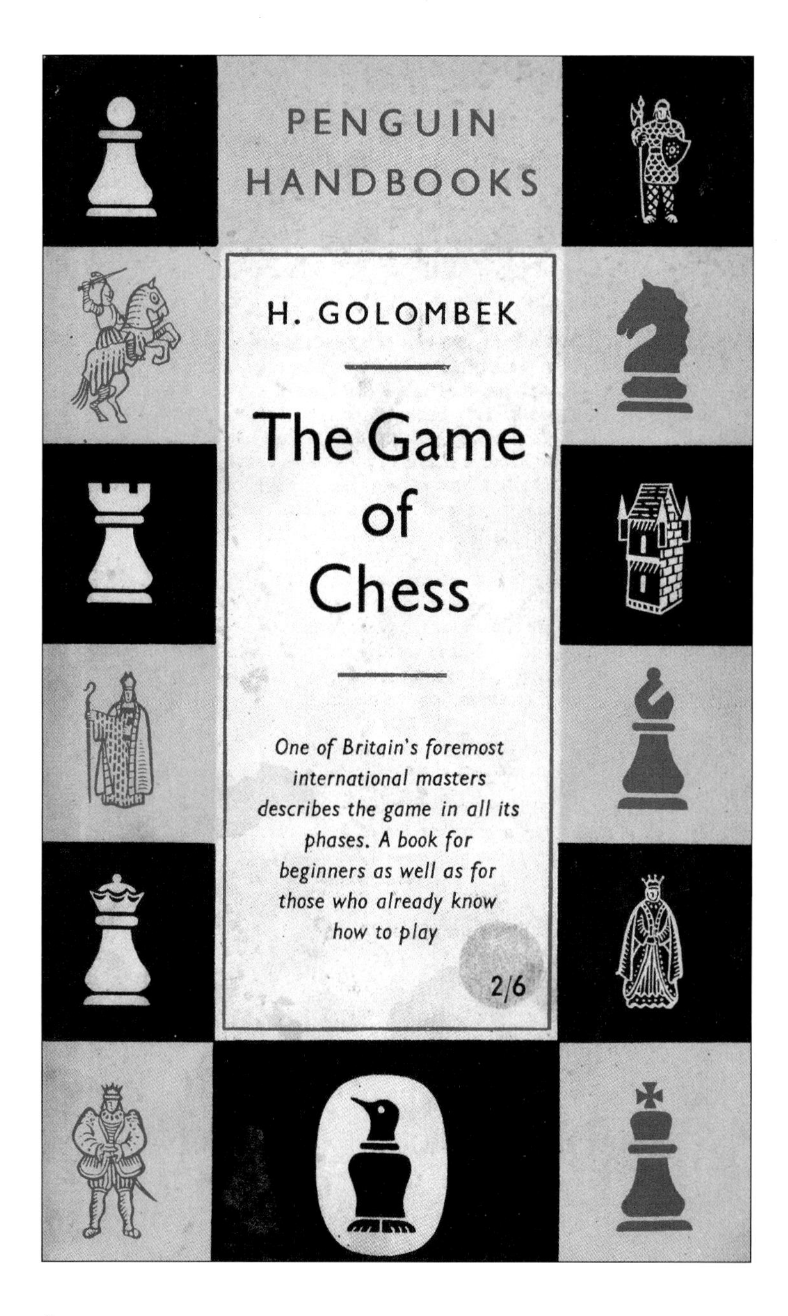

FIGURE 81

The Game of Chess: Harry Golombek
Penguin Handbook Series Cover Design by Jan Tschichold
Penguin Handbooks, Number PH 24, October 1954
4 3/8" x 7 1/8"

The typography is set in monotype Gill Sans, a popular typeface in England, inspired by Edward Johnston's Railway type. Tschichold cleverly incorporates the Penguin logo, located at the bottom of the cover, as one of the chess pieces.

Science News

The Science News, a periodical publication, was first published in June 1946, for serious readers interested in general science. The topics included ground already covered in science research, old discoveries, new research, as well as the way science evolves. It was written and explained in detail the way things work by scientists who study various subjects such as Physics, Molecular structure in Plants, Bacteriology, Veterinary Surgery, X-ray crystallography, Biochemistry and Medicine. Each volume contains an editorial, recent progress, correspondence, books received, photographs, glossary, and Index.

Tschichold implemented a simple yet elegant cover design for Science News. The design had a very "workman-like" presence with all of the typography delicately placed on the center axis. It is interesting to note that for this periodical, Tschichold decided not to use the common border theme; instead, he simply positioned the type in a rectangular, tapered effect running down the cover. The beautiful and elegant swelled rules, not only divide the three distinct groups (for example, science news 14, subject matter, and penguin logo), but also reinforce the shape of the centered type within the book's format. Tschichold has also reversed the type, Science News and Penguin books, to white, in order to create balance from the top to the bottom of the typography. The background is furnished in a deep and rich red crimson and evokes a sophistication reflected also in the subject matter. In addition, the typography has been set in all upper case, monotype Perpetua and upper and lower case monotype Times New Roman to convey a simple yet classical presence.

Penguin Reference Books

The Penguin Reference Books were first published in April 1943, for readers interested in the world through definitions and explanations of terms on subjects such as Geography, Science, Music, Psychology, Biology, and the Penguin English-German and German-English Dictionary. Each volume is written by prominent scholars and important contributors to their respective

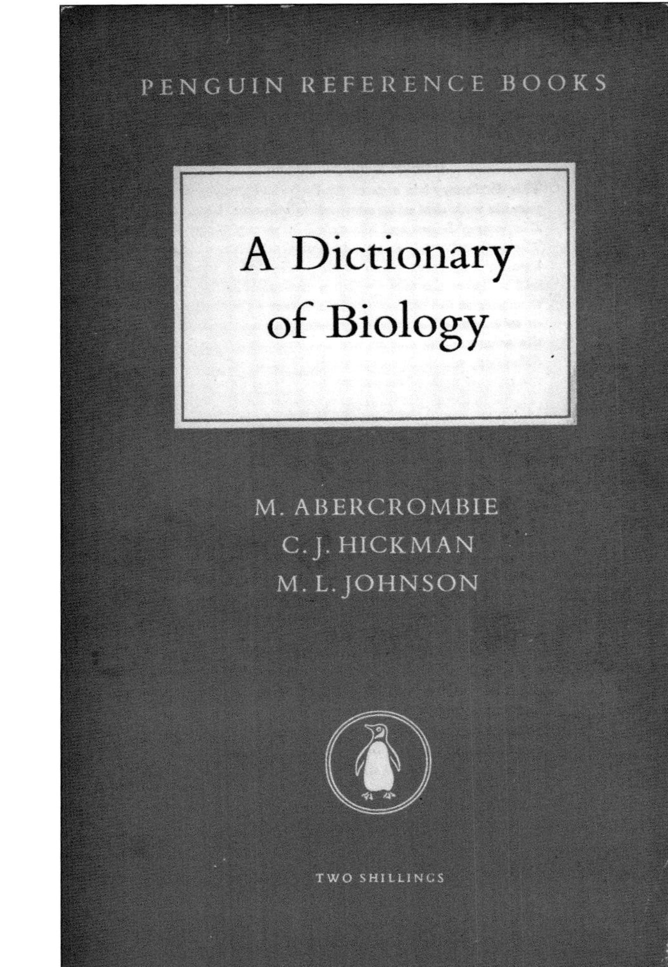

FIGURE 82 & 83

A Dictionary of Biology: M. Abercrombie, C.J. Hickman, and L.M. Johnson
Series Cover design for the Penguin Reference Books
Penguin Reference Books, Number R 3
February 1949
4 3/8" x 7 1/8"

Original hand drawn comp by Jan Tschichold. The adaptable monotype Poliphilus is the emphasis for the title named after Aldus Manutius' 1499 edition of Fra Francesco Colonna's Hypnerotomachia Poliphili (The Strife of [illegible]). The smaller all uppercase typography is set in monotype Bembo.

fields of study. Readers are able to cross-reference items of interest regarding relevant information and encourage them to probe further and discover new information. In addition, diagrams and map projections accompany the alphabetical terms.

Tschichold designed the reference books with basic design elements to create a look that is simple and functional, much like the books contents. (Figure 82, 83) The white title plate in the shape of a rectangle is positioned in the top half of the composition. A thin white rule runs around the perimeter of the title plate to add emphasis to the typography within the shape. The background is a deep burgundy tone in stark contrast to the white elements on the cover. The distinguishing typographic feature for the upper and lowercase title is the adaptable monotype Poliphilus, named after Aldus Manutius' 1499 edition of Fra Francesco Colonna's *Hypnerotomachia Poliphili* (The Strife of Love in a Dream or The Dream of Poliphilus). The smaller, all uppercase, reversed typography is set in monotype Bembo. It is interesting to note the subtle detailing surrounding the Penguin logo in the form of two circles which appear to be in unison with the surrounding white rule encompassing the title plate. The series was composed and printed by Hunt, Barnard and Company, Ltd., Great Britain.

The Artist at Work

In 1949, Tschichold designed one noteworthy book, first published in 1951, which stands out from all the other Penguin series, *The Artist at Work,* which represents, in book form, the exhibition of the same title, suggested and planned in 1944 for the British Institute of Adult Education (Arts Council of Great Britain) by Ellen M. Kemp and designed by H. Ruhemann. The layout Tschichold formulated was asymmetric and outside the classical symmetrical formula and styling for all of the other Penguin series. Tschichold's decision to apply an assymetrical styling makes it clear that he did not completely abandon "The New Typography" and the "functional" principles of the Bauhaus.

H. Ruhemann and E. M. Kemp

The artist at work

PENGUIN BOOKS

FIGURE 84

The Artist at Work: H. Ruhemann and E.M. Kemp
Series Cover Redesign for the Planning, Design, and Art Books by Jan Tschichold
Planning, Design, and Art Books, Number E 37, December 1951
9" x 7 1/2"

The quirky and playful monotype Gill Sans is featured throughout. This series and cover design was the only asymmetrical layout by Jan Tschichold during his tenure at Penguin Books.

The styling of *The Artist at Work* utilizes a grid, providing Tschichold with a system to work within, and was a logical reaction to what the book's contents dictated in his application of asymmetric layout. (Figure 84, 85) This partly had to do with the function of the asymmetrical layout, similar to an art exhibition catalogue and the variety of works of art at different sizes, silhouettes, and sections of painting in detail. The list and variety of works Tschichold had to arrange included inspiration, planning style, optical principles, watercolour, pastel, texture, the French impressionists, and contemporary British painters. Since there was no previous series or redesign for this title, Tschichold was able to take a more liberal and fresh approach to the assignment. Often, Tschichold's assignments included redesigns within the existing series, but this particular title offered him a new design challenge for the book's layout.

Tschichold decided to create a landscape format at 9 1/4" x 7 3/8" (235mm x 187mm) to provide him with the flexibility to place images side by side, in order to show developmental stages of a painting and to compare styles of various periods. Tschichold developed a grid and separated the page spreads into two and three columns, however, some of the pages included one column of text and as many as six images comprising the entire width of the page. The justified columns of body text are generally equal widths throughout except for the appendix and list of illustrations, which were increased twice the width. For the placement of the text and images, Tschichold creates unconventional spatial arrangements, bold rectangles of text, and juxtoposition of san serif typography that creates a uniformity of proportion and impeccable balance. Tschichold developed a masterful grid system and utilized each page's "white space" by prudently placing the columns of typography and images within that space for balance and clear and precise communication. In addition, Tschichold styled each page differently to avoid repetition, and similitude in order to enable all the parts to be dissimilar to each other and to render contrast as well as a dynamic and coherent whole.

Tschichold's aim was simplicity and clarity when choosing an all-purpose, upper and lower case, san serif typeface throughout. The medium, bold,

Picasso (1881–). The traditional means of expression proved too narrow for his imagination, and he widened the limits of the different *media*: graphic arts, painting, relief, sculpture, ceramics, crossing from one field into another. He explored the potentialities of visual art, in numerous revolutionary styles and techniques, often arriving at absurd extremes. When we do not understand Picasso we often suspect irony and blasphemy, but his delivery has always the mark of conviction and authority. Eventually he created a few pictures of a peculiarly powerful rhythm by swinging electric torches in the darkness. The lines drawn in the air were photographed. He has thus for the first time realized 'photography' in its most literal meaning: 'writing or drawing with light.'

46. *Pablo Picasso*. The Blue Ship, 1912.

47. *Pablo Picasso*. Portrait of Mme Picasso, 1917–18.

The plate on the right is characteristic of Picasso's inventiveness. The impasto (thick texture), the deep impressions, probably made with the finger, together with delicate scumbles (translucent application), have probably never before been done in ceramics.

48. *Pablo Picasso*. Horse's Head, 1937.

49. *Pablo Picasso*. Head, Majolica plate, 1949.

FIGURE 85

The Artist at Work: H. Ruhemann and E.M. Kemp
Style and Nature Page Design by Jan Tschichold
Planning, Design, and Art Books
Number E 37, December 1951
9" x 7 1/2"

and oblique range of weights provided not only contrast, but expressiveness while enhancing the effect of the typeface on the page. For the cover, the grid becomes invisible as the author, title, and publisher are placed in a simple arrangement composed of only three lines. The title and logo are reversed out in white on a slate-gray paper cover. The contrast in layout and the difference in feeling of this title to the rest of the Penguin series is remarkable.

The Pelican History of Art

The publishing of the *Pelican History of Art,* like many other Penguin series, grew from earlier publications and definitive books on a broad spectrum of academic interests, to accommodate serious readers, including students of higher learning. More specifically, the series focused on the history of art and subjects such as Painting in Britain; The Art and Architecture of India: Hindu, Buddhist, Jain; Architecture in Britain; and Art and Architecture in France. The series' editor, whose specialty was the study of art, was Nikolaus Pevsner.

Tschichold's primary responsibility was implementing the plate grid with standard instructions and a prospectus cover in 1948. However, the first book in the series, Z1, *Painting in Britain:*1530-1790 by Ellis K. Waterhouse, was not published until May 1953. The prospectus cover, certainly one of the most exquisite and impressive designs by Tschichold, was composed with seven lines of typography, centrally placed, with two contrasting point sizes. The smaller of the two sizes is set in all uppercase monotype Bembo and delicate letterspacing. The larger typography, *The Pelican History of Art,* again, with delicate letterspacing and all uppercase type, is set in the impeccable monotype Felix Titling. The beautiful Pelican symbol, designed specifically for the series, was drawn by Berthold Wolpe (1905-89), the German-born typographer, and adds beautiful detailing and a finished look to the design. The series was cloth bound, accompanied with illustrations, and in a larger format than the typical Penguin size. The original design appeared in Black and amber on a soft-hued paper.
(Figure 86, 87, 88)

THE

TO BE PUBLISHED BY

PELICAN

PENGUIN BOOKS LIMITED

HISTORY

HARMONDSWORTH · MIDDLESEX

OF ART

FIGURE 86

Prospectus Cover design for *The Pelican History of Art* by Jan Tschichold
Edited by Nikolaus Pevsner
The engraved pelican symbol is by Berthold Wolpe, 1947
First Published 1953
9 3/4" x 12"

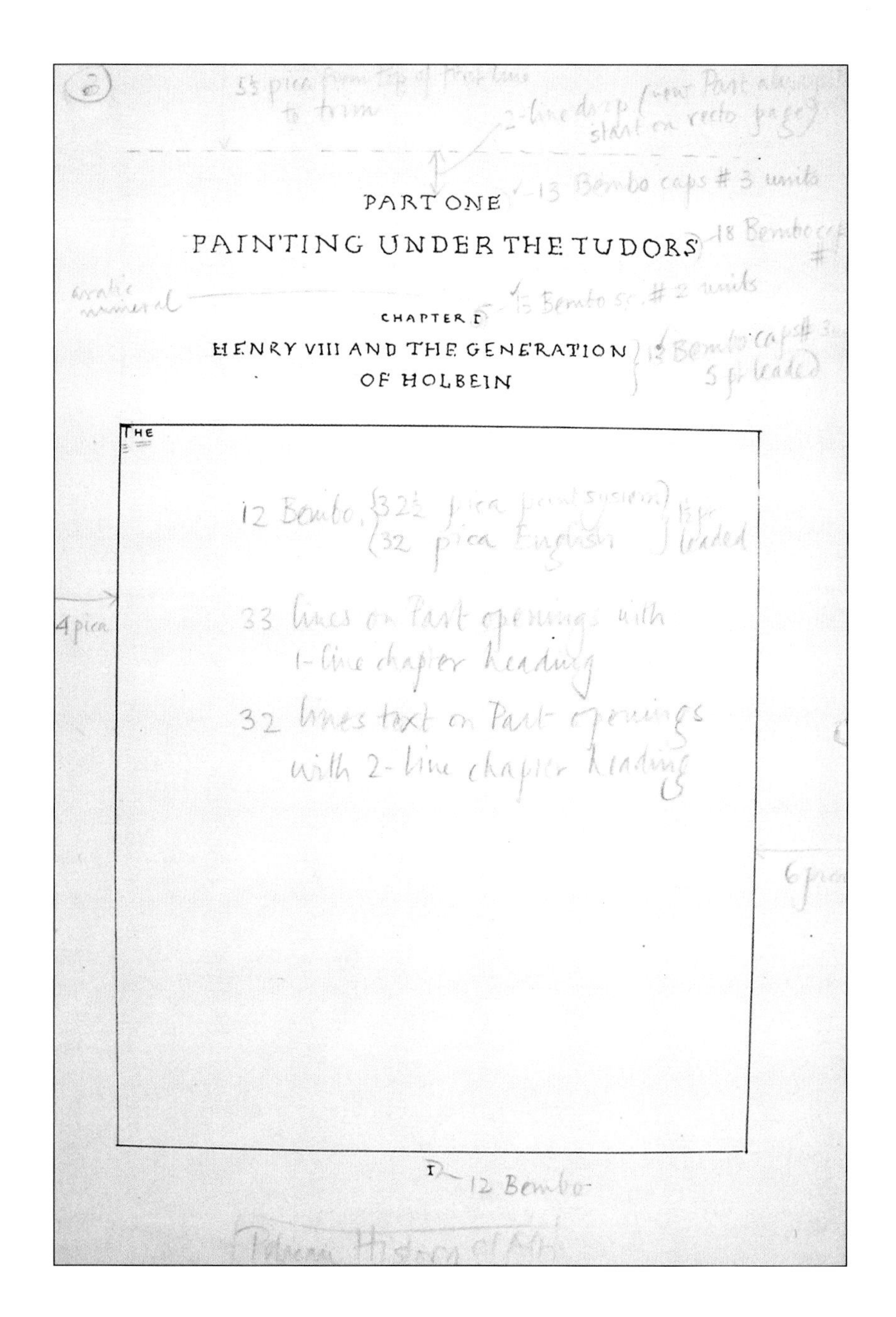

FIGURE 87

Preliminary Page for *The Pelican History of Art,* Painting in Britain: 1530-1790, Ellis K. Waterhouse, Edited by Nikolaus Pevsner, May 1953
9 3/4" x 12"

Preliminary Pencil Sketch by Jan Tschichold.

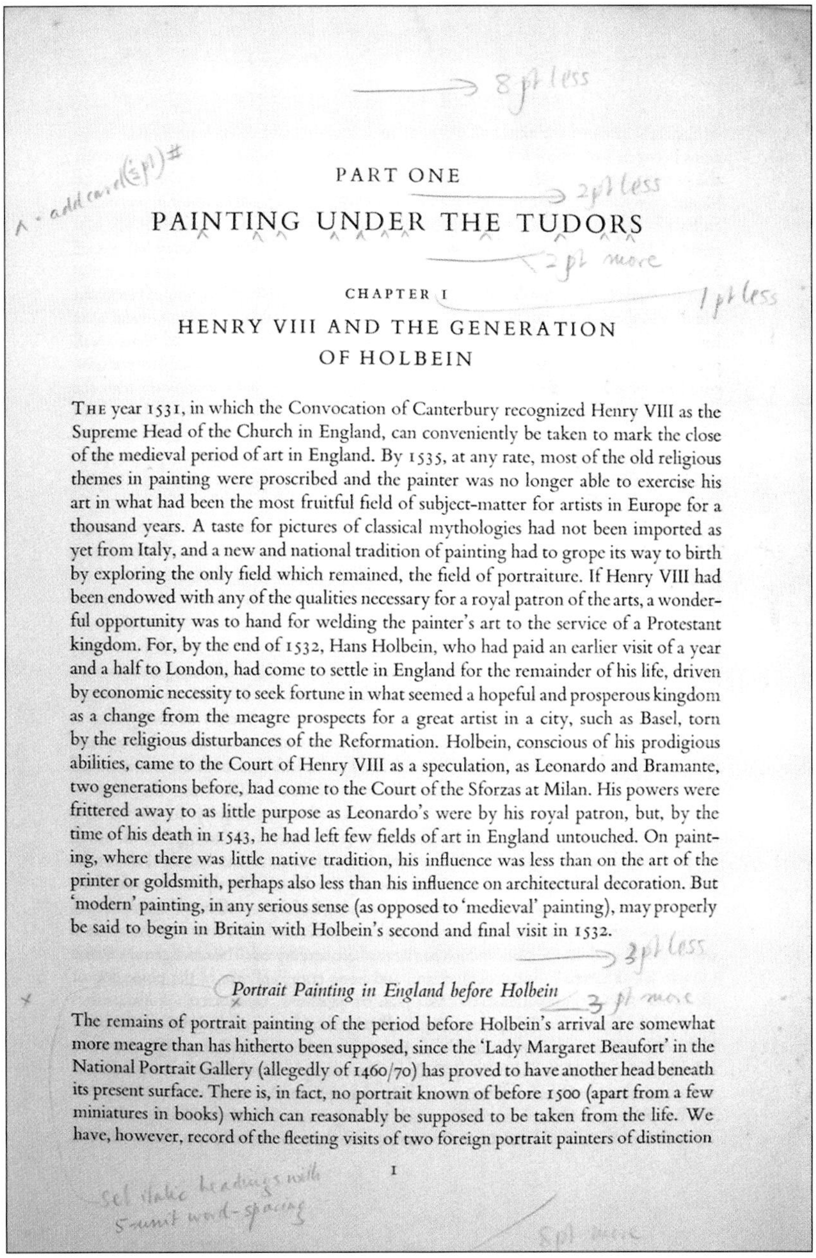

PART ONE

PAINTING UNDER THE TUDORS

CHAPTER I

HENRY VIII AND THE GENERATION OF HOLBEIN

THE year 1531, in which the Convocation of Canterbury recognized Henry VIII as the Supreme Head of the Church in England, can conveniently be taken to mark the close of the medieval period of art in England. By 1535, at any rate, most of the old religious themes in painting were proscribed and the painter was no longer able to exercise his art in what had been the most fruitful field of subject-matter for artists in Europe for a thousand years. A taste for pictures of classical mythologies had not been imported as yet from Italy, and a new and national tradition of painting had to grope its way to birth by exploring the only field which remained, the field of portraiture. If Henry VIII had been endowed with any of the qualities necessary for a royal patron of the arts, a wonderful opportunity was to hand for welding the painter's art to the service of a Protestant kingdom. For, by the end of 1532, Hans Holbein, who had paid an earlier visit of a year and a half to London, had come to settle in England for the remainder of his life, driven by economic necessity to seek fortune in what seemed a hopeful and prosperous kingdom as a change from the meagre prospects for a great artist in a city, such as Basel, torn by the religious disturbances of the Reformation. Holbein, conscious of his prodigious abilities, came to the Court of Henry VIII as a speculation, as Leonardo and Bramante, two generations before, had come to the Court of the Sforzas at Milan. His powers were frittered away to as little purpose as Leonardo's were by his royal patron, but, by the time of his death in 1543, he had left few fields of art in England untouched. On painting, where there was little native tradition, his influence was less than on the art of the printer or goldsmith, perhaps also less than his influence on architectural decoration. But 'modern' painting, in any serious sense (as opposed to 'medieval' painting), may properly be said to begin in Britain with Holbein's second and final visit in 1532.

Portrait Painting in England before Holbein

The remains of portrait painting of the period before Holbein's arrival are somewhat more meagre than has hitherto been supposed, since the 'Lady Margaret Beaufort' in the National Portrait Gallery (allegedly of 1460/70) has proved to have another head beneath its present surface. There is, in fact, no portrait known of before 1500 (apart from a few miniatures in books) which can reasonably be supposed to be taken from the life. We have, however, record of the fleeting visits of two foreign portrait painters of distinction

1

FIGURE 88

Preliminary Page for *The Pelican History of Art*, Painting in Britain: 1530-1790, Ellis K. Waterhouse, Edited by Nikolaus Pevsner, May 1953
9 3/4" x 12"

Preliminary Pencil Marks by Jan Tschichold.

Penguin Progress, the free booklet edited by J.E. Morpurgo, was a condensed, fully and clearly expressed review of the fields of Penguin publications and was mailed specifically to all Penguin readers. Tschichold utilized his calligraphy and drawing skills on the titles of fourteen issues of Penguin Progress. Figure (89, 90)

The Penguin Modern Painters

The Penguin editor's most ambitious development was the unveiling of the new Penguin Modern Painters series. Each book provided reproductions of an artist's work and familiarized readers with the painting of contemporary artists. Some of the titles in the series from 1947-1949 included *Edward Bawden* by J.M. Richards, *Ben Nicholson* by John Summerson, and *Paul Klee* by Douglas Cooper, all of which were recognized by the National Book League as some of the best designed books of their respective years, due, no doubt, to the graphic design efforts of Tschichold. However, the former series design that Tschichold adopted contained a disfigured version of the penguin logo and poorly composed typography (Figure 91, 92)

Tschichold retained the size 8 5/8" x 6 7/8" (220mm x 175mm) landscape format and applied a classical serif typeface throughout each Modern Painters series. The Cover, title, and copyright pages were methodically designed as the typography was placed in the center of each page and carried an elegant feel as emphasis was placed on the editor and artist's name to establish hierarchy. The cover in thin, green-blue paper boards was simply designed and included The Penguin Modern Painters, inverted in white, the title, *Paul Klee,* in black all upper-case lettering, and the carefully redrawn Penguin symbol, inverted in white and placed within two circles. The interior spreads were designed with two columns of serif type justified body text, centrally placed on each page. The Paintings included 16 Colour and 16 Black and White Plates made by The Sun Engraving Co. Ltd., and printed by John Swain & Sons Ltd. (Figure 93, 94)

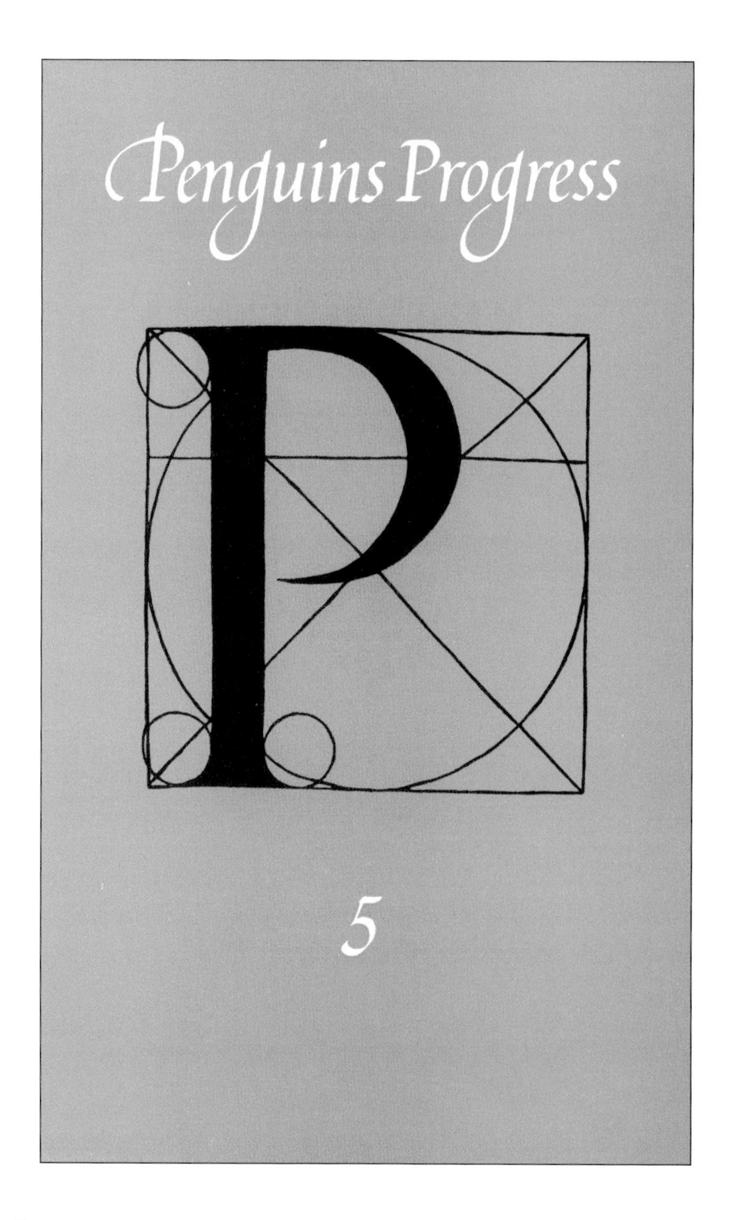

FIGURE 89

Cover design for the house-magazine '*Penguin Progress*' by Jan Tschichold
Penguin Progress, Number 5, 1948
4 3/8" x 7 1/8"

Tschichold chooses a beautiful arrangement of calligraphy and subtle decorative linear element integrated with the letter P. The letter P is set in monotype Felix Titling, originally designed by the fifteenth century Veronese calligrapher Felice Feliciano. Penguins Progress was one of the few Penguin covers where Tschichold applied his calligraphic skill.

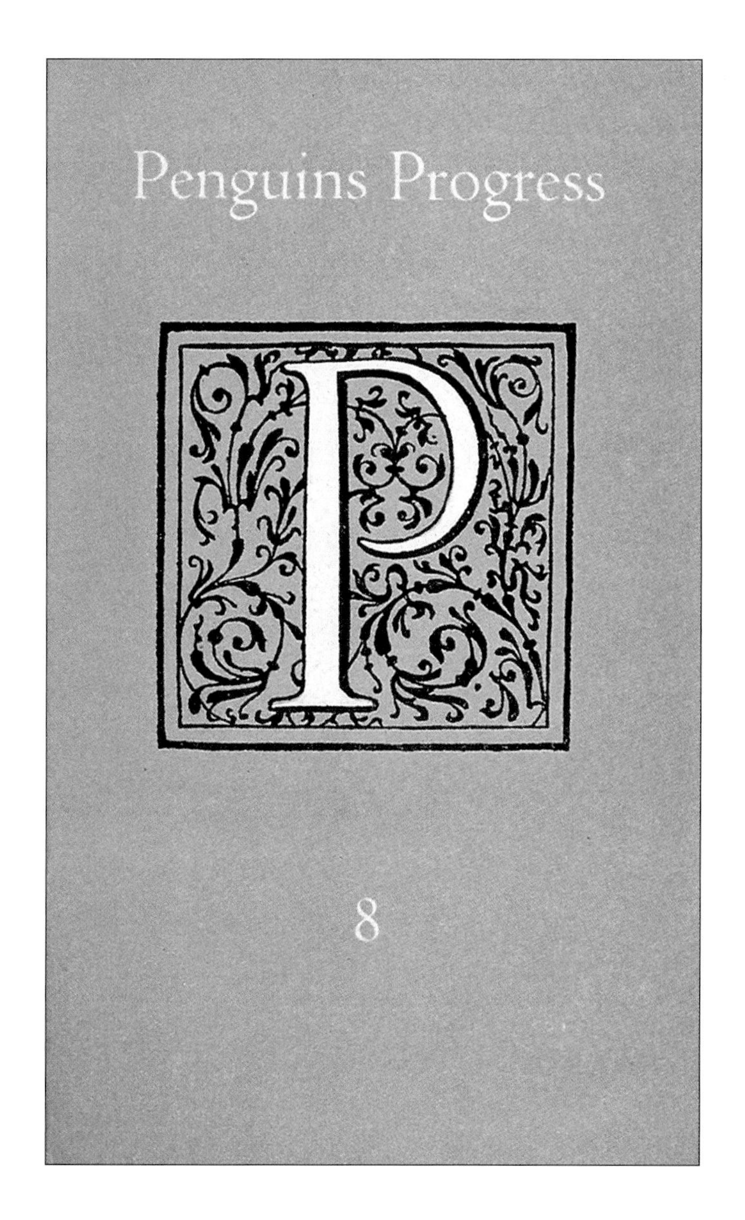

FIGURE 90

Cover design for the house-magazine '*Penguin Progress*' by Jan Tschichold
Penguin Progress, Number 8, 1949
4 3/8" x 7 1/8"

Tschichold chooses a beautiful hand drawn decorative letter P set in monotype Felix Titling with a drop shadow combined with stunning intricate coiling spiral motifs imitating the initials of the manuscript book. The distinguishing title is composed with the slender and well-defined features of monotype Centaur.

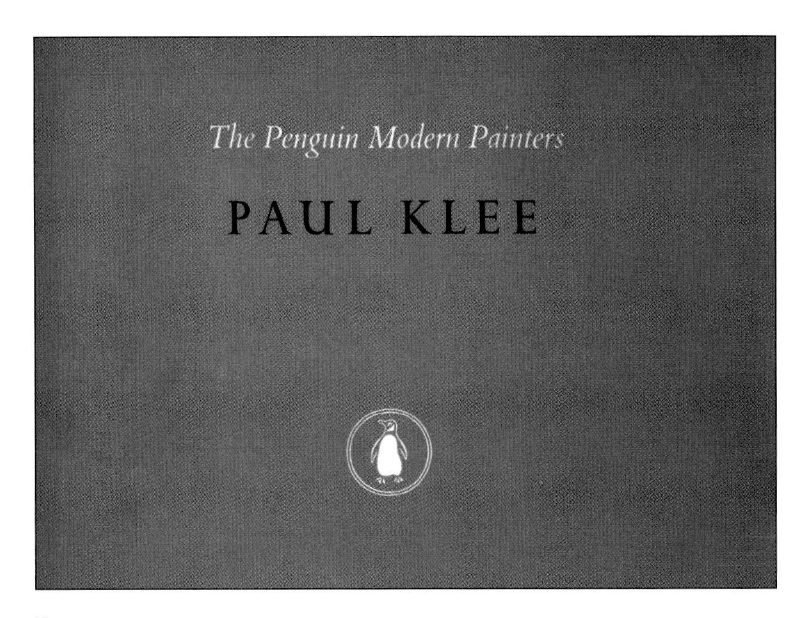

FIGURE 91

Paul Klee: Douglas Cooper
Penguin Modern Painters Series Cover Design by Jan Tschichold
Penguin Modern Painters, Number MP 16, July 1949
8 3/4" x 7"

Monotype Perpetua and italic monotype Bembo are the featured typefaces.

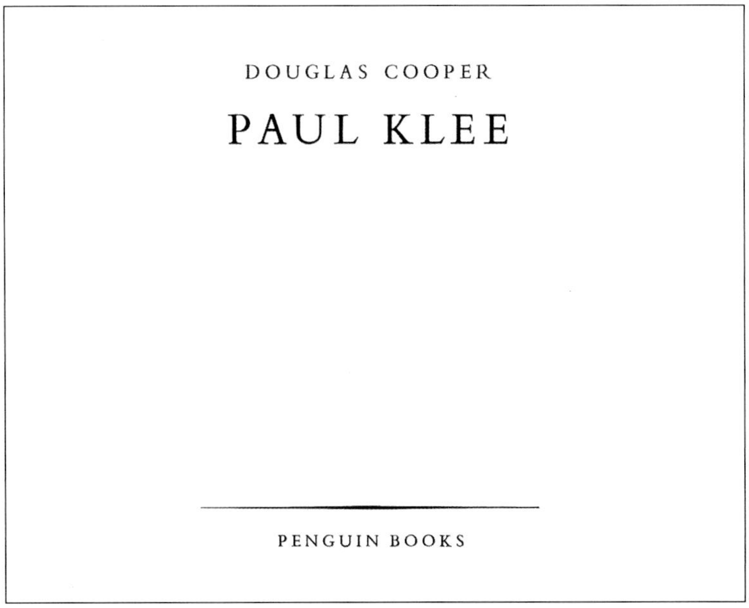

DOUGLAS COOPER

PAUL KLEE

PENGUIN BOOKS

FIGURE 92

Paul Klee: Douglas Cooper
Penguin Modern Painters Title Page Design by Jan Tschichold
Penguin Modern Painters, Number MP 16, July 1949
8 3/4" x 7"

For the title page Tschichold uses monotype Bembo with a beautiful swelled rule.

BLACK-AND-WHITE PLATES

2. *Portrait of a Doll.* 1915. 10½×7½ inches. Wash drawing. Owned by Atelier Paul Klee, Bern.
4. *Bull's Head.* 1931. 13¼×19 inches. Water-colour. Owned by Herr Rolf Bürgi, Bern.
6. *The Meadow.* 1935. 7½×11¼ inches. Water-colour. Owned by Galerie Louise Leiris, Paris.
8. *The Large Dome.* 1927. 11⅞×10⅝ inches. Pen-and-ink drawing. Owned by the Paul-Klee-Stiftung, Bern Museum.
10. *Acrobats.* 1935. 12×18½ inches. Gouache. Owned by Galerie Louise Leiris, Paris.
12. *Battle-scene from the Tragi-Comic Opera 'Sinbad the Sailor.'* 1923. 12⅝×19⅛ inches. Water-colour. Private Collection, Basle.
14. *The Little Man is Off on His Own.* 1937. 18½×13 inches. Gouache. Owned by Galerie Louise Leiris, Paris.
16. *Young Man at Rest.* (Self-portrait.) 1911. 5⅛×8 inches. Wash drawing. Owned by Herr Rolf Bürgi, Bern.
18. *Migrant Fish.* 1926. 10×13 inches. Pen and ink. Owned by Herr Rolf Bürgi, Bern.
20. *In the Spell of the Stars.* 1921. 9⅞×12⅝ inches. Water-colour. Owned by Miss Jane Greenough, Idaho.
22. *Exotic Garden.* 1926. 20½×16¼ inches. Oil. Owned by Buchholz Gallery, New York City.
24. *Park Beside a Lake.* 1920. 6×8⅞ inches. Wash drawing. Owned by Atelier Paul Klee, Bern.
26. *The Vigilant Angel.* 1939. 19¼×13 inches. Gouache. Owned by Douglas Cooper.
28. *Head Hewn with an Axe.* 1935. 12½×9¼ inches. Water-colour. Owned by Galerie Louise Leiris, Paris.
30. *Comedian.* 1904. 5×5½ inches. Etching.
32. *St Beatenberg.* 1909. 7⅞×6⅞ inches. Ink drawing. Owned by Herr Rolf Bürgi, Bern.

16

FIGURE 93

Paul Klee: Douglas Cooper
Penguin Modern Painters Typographic Layout by Jan Tschichold
Penguin Modern Painters, Number MP 16, July 1949
8 3/4" x 7"

Tschichold carries the monotype Bembo typeface for all of the spreads with a delicate arrangement of typography

FIGURE 94

Paul Klee: by Douglas Cooper
Penguin Modern Painters Page Design by Jan Tschichold
Penguin Modern Painters, Number MP 16, July 1949
8 3/4" x 7"

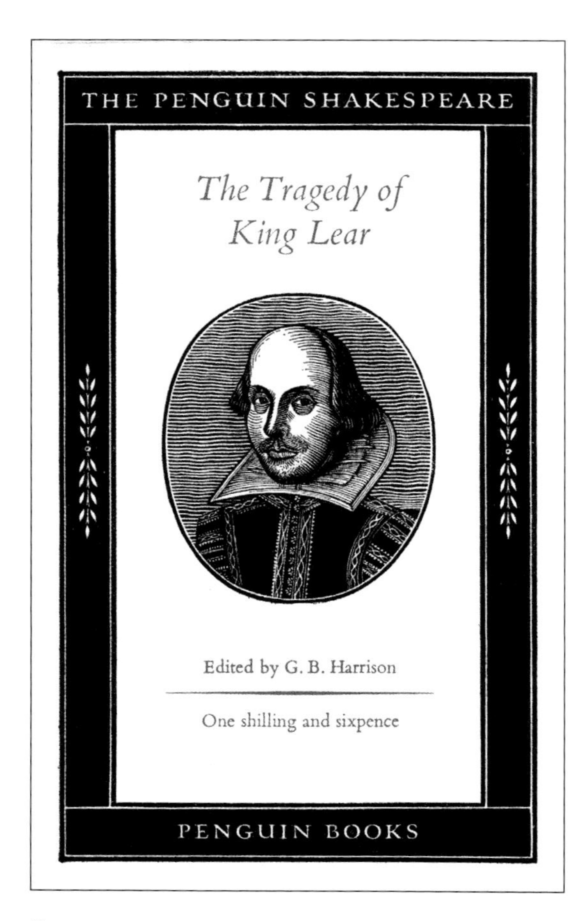

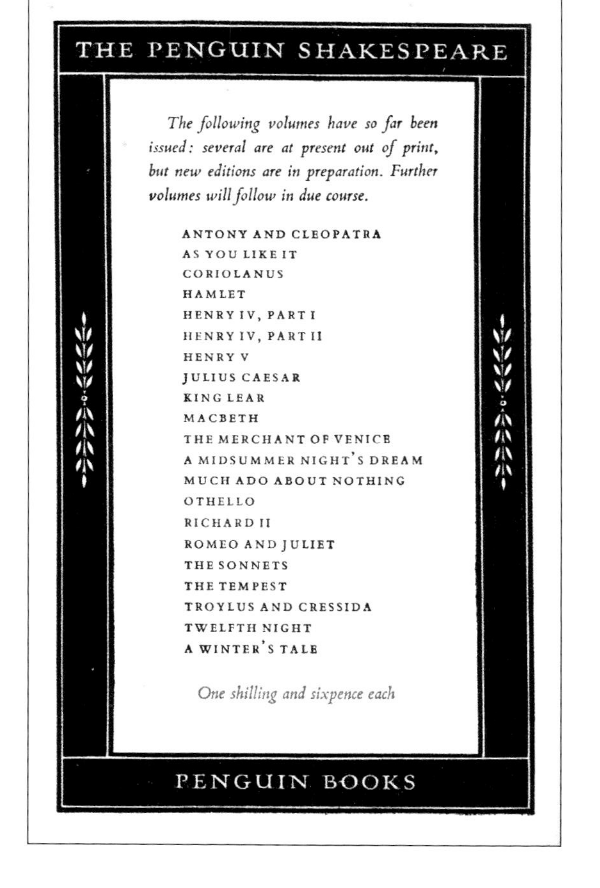

FIGURE 95 & 96

William Shakespeare: *The Tradegy of King Lear*, Edited by G.B. Harrison
Series Jacket design for the Penguin Shakespeare by Jan Tschichold
The engraved portrait is by Reynolds Stone, Penguin Shakespeare Number B 4,
This edition first published 1937, Reprinted 1940, Revised and Enlarged 1949
4 3/8" x 7 1/8"

The cover typography is composed with monotype Bembo. This type face became an "everyday" for Tschichold and became a favorite for classic works. Tschichold created the frame and lettering within the frame at original size using scraper board which was carefully made with a pin held in a pen-holder fastened with string. On his first attempt, the letter-spacing, serifs and decorative leaf motif were to proportion without any alterations or revisions.

The Penguin Shakespeare Series

The Penguin Shakespeare series, edited by G.B. Harrison, made its first appearance in 1937. Some of the Shakespearian titles included *Twelfth Night; Hamlet, Prince of Denmark; Henry V; King Lear; As You Like It; A Midsummer Night's Dream; The Tempest; The Merchant of Venice; Richard II; Romeo and Juliet; Julius Caesar; and Macbeth.* This collection was produced principally for the general reader and included extensive notes, a biography, and glossary. The series was discontinued during the war years and republished with the introduction of *The Winter's Tale* in September of 1947. As for the typography of the Penguin Shakespeare series, Lane noted:

"It was during our search for the right typeface for the Shakespeare that we hit on the Monotype Times Roman, in which all Penguin Books are now being set. Having been designed specially for printing long runs on cheap paper, it should have occurred to us earlier as being the ideal typeface for our purposes; but it was actually only when we came up against the innumerable difficulties in producing a typographically satisfactory Shakespeare page that we definitely decided to use it regularly. Its really fine range of small caps., titling, and italic made it ideal for separating speakers' names, headlines, and stage directions from speeches. And for some reason or other we felt that Shakespeare needed a strong, black typeface, and certainly Times New Roman gives a fine "colour" to a page." [22]

Eventually, Tschichold would replace the Times Roman typography with Monotype Bembo for the body text and settle upon a less flimsy pale yellow paper. The preceding cover design included unsightly typography, a variation of the deformed logo and a carelessly drawn Shakespeare portrait. Each New Shakespeare cover included a superior and improved engraved portrait of Shakespeare by Reynolds Stone. The distinguishing typographic feature is the exquisite monotype Bembo. This typeface became an "everyday" for Tschichold and became a favorite for classic works. (Figure 95, 96)

[22] Allen Lane, *Penrose Annual, A Review of the Graphic Arts.* Volume 40, Penguins and Pelicans, 1938 (Lund Humphries & Co. Ltd., London, UK) pp. 43-44.

I. 1

Thunder and lightning. Enter three Witches.
FIRST WITCH: When shall we three meet again?
In thunder, lightning, or in rain?
SECOND WITCH: When the hurly-burly's done,
When the battle's lost, and won.
THIRD WITCH: That will be ere the set of sun.
FIRST WITCH: Where the place?
SECOND WITCH: Upon the Heath.
THIRD WITCH: There to meet with Macbeth.
FIRST WITCH: I come, Graymalkin.
ALL: Paddock calls anon:
Fair is foul, and foul is fair,
Hover through the fog and filthy air.
Exeunt.

I. 2

Alarum within. Enter King Duncan, Malcolm, Donalbain, Lennox, with Attendants, meeting a bleeding Captain.
DUNCAN: What bloody man is that? He can report,
As seemeth by his plight, of the revolt
The newest state.
MALCOLM: This is the Sergeant,
Who like a good and hardy soldier fought
'Gainst my captivity: hail brave friend;
Say to the King, the knowledge of the broil,
As thou didst leave it.
CAPTAIN: Doubtful it stood,

FIGURE 97

William Shakespeare: *The Tragedy of Macbeth*
Page design for the Penguin Shakespeare by Jan Tschichold
Penguin Shakespeare, Number B 12
This edition first published 1937, Reprinted 1940, 1941
Revised and Enlarged, 1950
4 3/8" x 7 1/8"

WILLIAM SHAKESPEARE

THE SONNETS

AND

A LOVER'S COMPLAINT

PENGUIN BOOKS
HARMONDSWORTH · MIDDLESEX
ENGLAND

FIGURE 98

William Shakespeare: *The Sonnets and A Lover's Complaint*
Series Jacket design for the Penguin Shakespeare by Jan Tschichold
The engraved portrait is by Reynolds Stone
Penguin Shakespeare, Number B 18
This edition first published 1938, Reprinted 1940, 1941,
Revised and Enlarged 1948
4 3/8" x 7 1/8"

Tschichold continued a graceful and elegant styling and consistency, like many of his other series redesigns, from front to back cover. Tschichold created the frame and lettering within the frame at original size using scraper board which was carefully made with a pin held in a pen-holder fastened with string. On his first attempt, the letter-spacing, serifs, and decorative leaf motif were to proportion without any alterations or revisions. The title, editor, and price was centered above and below the engraved portrait of Shakespeare and styled in monotype italic and regular Bembo with red ink. (Figure 97, 98)

Monotype typefaces

During the 1920s and 1930s The Monotype Corporation, under the direction of "typographic consultant" Stanley Morison (1889-1967), raised the standard of British publishing and printing by reviving a series of classical typefaces; Baskerville, Bell, Bembo, Caslon Old Face, Centaur, Ehrhardt, Fournier, Garamond, Goudy Modern, Imprint, Perpetua, Plantin Light, Poliphilus, Romulus, Scotch Roman, Spectrum, Times New Roman, and Walbaum, for machine composition. By the time Tschichold arrived at Penguin Books, the setting of type by machine had become an accepted practice by printers and publishers, as composition machines had become more proficient, and books composed and printed by mechanical means were considered as superb as those created by hand. The revolution of mechanical production moved quickly through the printing trade as composition machines became more proficient.

Morison's greatest contributions were his design supervision of a major newspaper, *The Times of London,* and subsequent design of the typeface Times New Roman, which became one of the most widely used typefaces throughout England in the twentieth century. In addition, Morison played an important role as typographic advisor to both the Cambridge University Press and The British Monotype Corporation, where he was responsible for the imaginative growth of its type library from 1920 until after the Second World War.

In 1935, Penguin Books' first typographer, Edward Young, emulated Albatross Books' style, format, and color, when he set out to design Penguin Books' various series. Old Style No. 2, Gill Sans, and Times New Roman were the only representative fonts used during the first ten years of production. Tschichold adopted The Monotype Corporation's most distinguished typefaces for Penguin Books, skillfully identifying the right face for every variety of book and choosing the font that would most appropriately suit the personality of the given text, for example, Caslon Old Face with its distinctive and charming oblique styling for the Penguin Musical Scores, the often relied on Bembo with its discrete qualities for the Penguin Shakespeare series, and the elegant and slender features of Bell for many of the Penguin Poets. Tschichold stated,

"That faces of both kinds are available today is the special achievement of Stanley Morison (1889-1967) during twenty-five years' activity with a leading English firm. The rebirth of the classic types brought with it a typographic revival the world over that is at least as important as the cleaning-up process of the New Typography was for Germany." [23]

In addition to the Monotype family of fonts, Tschichold adopted a series of classical typefaces from the Intertype and Linotype Corporations.

Erik Ellegaard Frederiksen

To help with the challenging task of designing and coordinating the sheer volume of Penguin titles, Tschichold hired only one assistant, Erik Ellegaard Frederiksen (1924-1997), who, when he joined Penguin in 1948, had just completed his student training in Denmark.

Frederiksen wrote of the experience and training he received from Tschichold during this period:

"This period was the typographic foundation of the rest of my life. Our desks were at right-angles, so he could see what I was doing. More important for me, I could watch the way he worked. When I asked him about uncertain

[23] Ruari McLean, *Jan Tschichold: Typographer,* Glaube und Wirklichkeit, *Schweizer Graphische Mitteilungen,* June, 1946, Appendix 3: Belief and Reality, (Boston: David R. Godine, Publisher, Inc., 1975), p. 137.

points, he was always willing not only to answer the specific question, but to teach me the reasons, the background. He lent me books, Updike and others . . . Only later did I realize the reason for his solutions, always based on a historical background. He was totally uncompromising in maintaining design standards. . . . His craftsmanship was great. I remember that Reynolds Stone had engraved the Shakespeare portrait, in a medallion for the Penguin Shakespeare covers. But Tschichold wanted to make the surrounding border himself. He used scraper-board in actual size, and drew the lettering with a pin held in a pen-holder. He did not need to correct anything: letterspacing, serifs, everything was correct at the first attempt!

All our work was done with the utmost care . . . all our layouts were minutely accurate. We knew that we could never meet the printers, who were scattered all over England. All our communication was by writing. A very few questions were answered by telephone. It forced us to take the utmost trouble with our layouts. . . . distance does not matter if your specifications are complete." [24]

The Penguin Logo

Around 1935, long before Tschichold's arrival at Penguin Books, Lane was trying to come up with a name for his new publishing company. He was fixed on the idea of an animal logo and was inspired by a stylized picture of an Albatross for a colophon designed by Mardersteig at Albatross Books. Aside from being an important element on each cover design, the trademark had to be simple to pronounce, and simple to remember. During a final meeting, the prospective pool of animals and birds were wittled down to a half dozen or so candidates when suddenly the secretary Joan Coles uttered:

"*What about Penguins?*" [25] Lane then replied: "*It was the obvious answer, a stroke of genius*" [26]

---

[24] Ruari McLean, *Jan Tschichold: Typographer* (Boston: David R. Godine, Publisher, Inc., 1975), pp. 98-99.

[25] Steve Hare. *Penguin Portrait, Allen Lane and the Penguin Editors 1935-1970.* (Harmondsworth, Middlesex, England: Penguin Books Ltd., 1995), p.5

[26] Steve Hare. *Penguin Portrait, Allen Lane and the Penguin Editors 1935-1970.* (Harmondsworth, Middlesex, England: Penguin Books Ltd., 1995), p.5

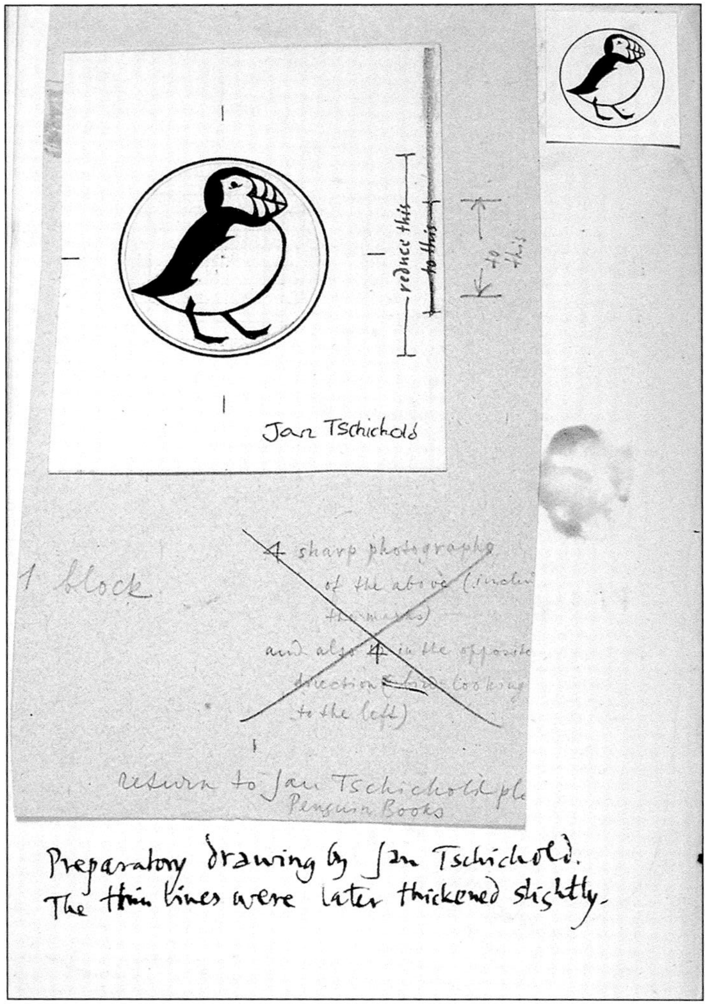

FIGURE 99

Some of the Puffin Symbols Original Preparatory Work by Jan Tschichold, 1947

FIGURE 100

Some of the Penguin Symbols Original Preparatory Work by Jan Tschichold, 1947

"The name Penguin was the secretary's inspiration, 'I wanted a name that could be fixed in the mind and eye, pictorially,' he says. the moment my secretary said, 'Why not a Penguin?' we knew it wouldn't be anything else. From a trade point of view it was easy to draw in many different ways in black and white without losing his dignity. Everyone loves a penguin. It has brought us a fantastic amount of goodwill. Besides it has an endearing dignified flippancy, and it seemed to us to symbolise exactly the light-hearted way we went into the whole thing." [27]

Edward Young, a young Penguin worker with some amateur talent, began developing sketches of penguins, immediately after the meeting was concluded. The idea was to reflect a light-hearted dancing variation of the bird:

"I went straight off to the Zoo to spend the rest of the day drawing Penguins in every pose from the dignified to the ridiculous, and the following morning produced, at first shot, the absurdly simple cover design which was soon to become such a familiar sight on bookstalls." [28]

At the time of his arrival at Penguin in 1947, Tschichold also focused on the Penguin logo. The logo was badly drawn, pudgy and did not accurately represent a Penguin. In addition, the rendering lacked the characteristics that Lane initially suggested when the firm first began searching for a mascot, distinguished yet playful. Several variations existed, and all were being used indiscriminately. Tschichold redrew the symbol by attempting to match up the original design as best he could as well as the Pelican and Puffin, then in use. Each of the series was embroidered with complimentary bird symbols; Penguins, Pelicans, Puffins, and Ptarmigans. These redesigned animal logos were cast from a monotype matrix and were more precise depictions, and often were reflected, inverted, or surrounded by circular or oval frames. These variations with frames allowed Tschichold to be more flexible as various versions of the logos could be easily adapted to the spines, front and back covers, title pages, etc. In addition, Tschichold paid careful attention to the logo sizes so that they would make for a more well-balanced layout and harmonious design. (Figure 99, 100, 101, 102, 103, 104, 105, 106)

---

[27] Sir Allen Lane. *Scope*, 'Man of the Month', (August 1954), p.56

[28] Steve Hare. *Penguin Portrait, Allen Lane and the Penguin Editors 1935-1970.* (Harmondsworth, Middlesex, England: Penguin Books Ltd., 1995), p.5

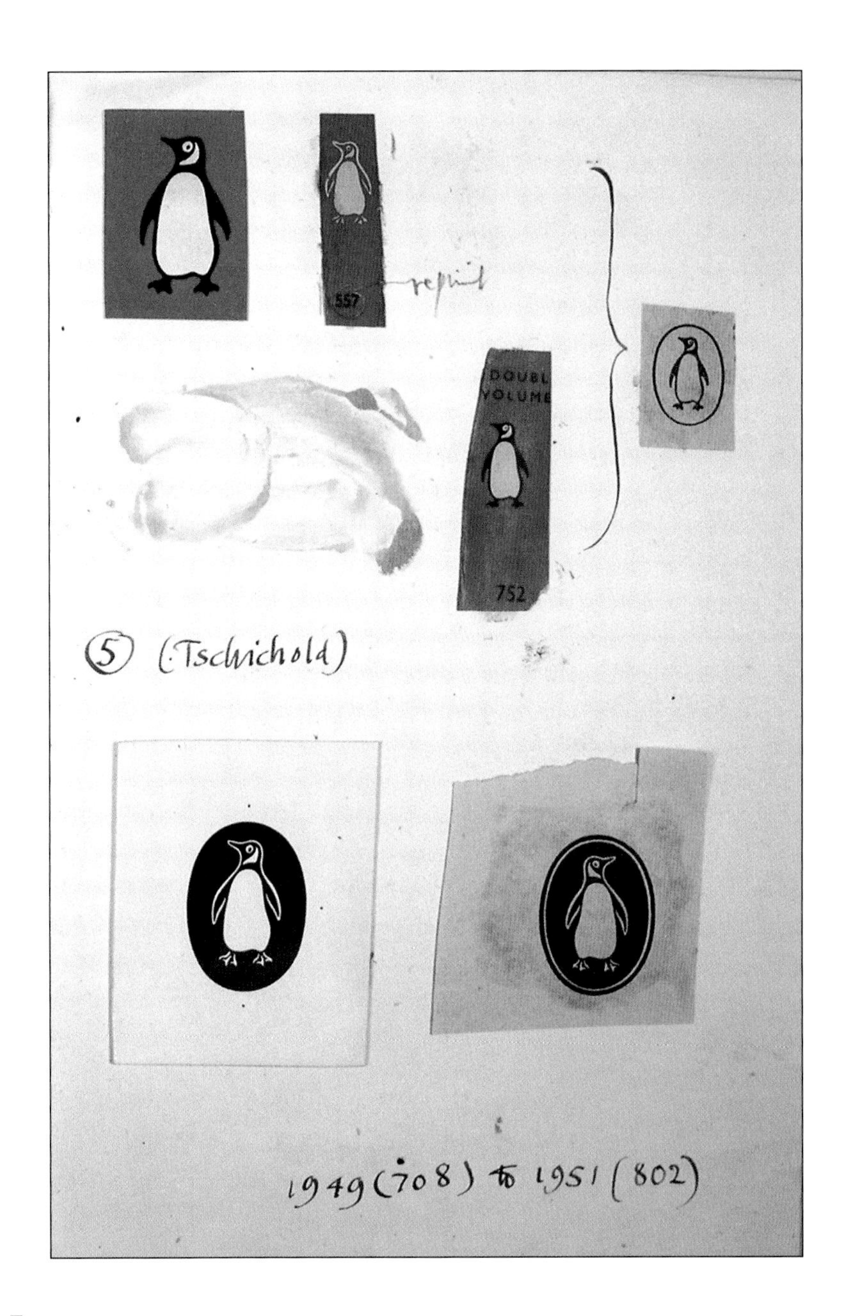

FIGURE 101

Some of the Penguin Symbols Original Preparatory Work by Jan Tschichold, 1947

Figure 102

Some of the Penguin Symbols Redrawn by Jan Tschichold, 1947

Several different variations of the Penguin logo closely modelled on the original logo. Tschichold inverted the Penguin logo and added shapes such as a circle and oval for multiple uses such as spines, front and back covers, title pages, double volumes, etc. Each Penguin series has a slight variation on the Penguin logo.

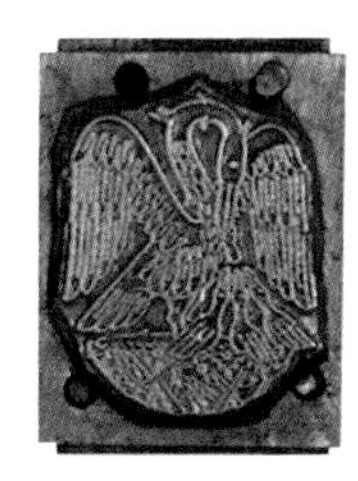

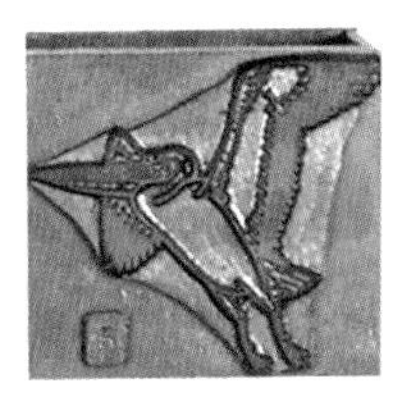

FIGURE 103

Monotype Metal Blocks
Symbols designed by Jan Tschichold
The engraved pelican symbol is by Berthold Wolpe, 1947

Several different variations of the Penguin logo closely modelled on the original logo as Metal Blocks.

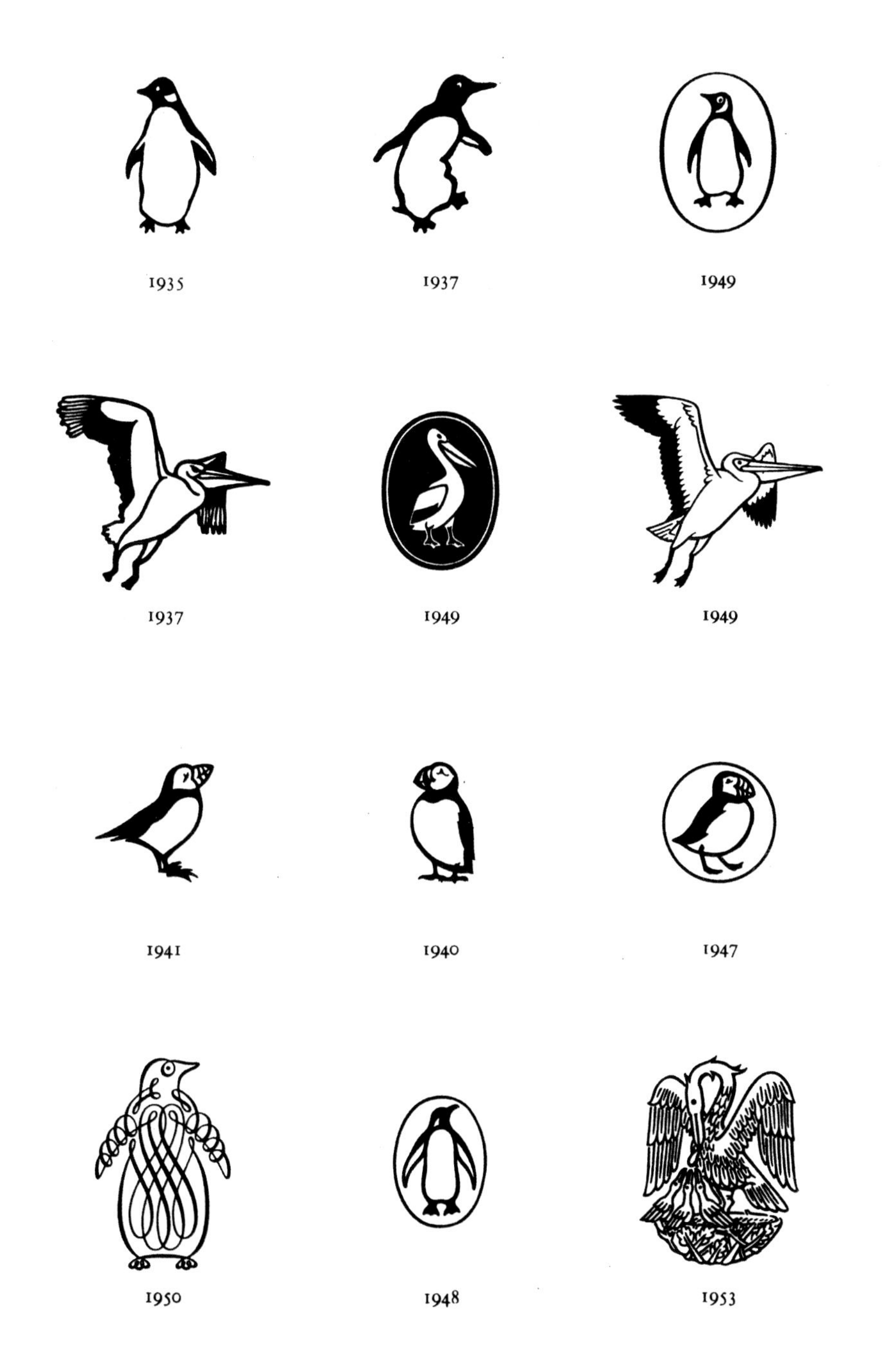

FIGURE 104

Chronology of some early devices 1935-1953

Beginning in 1935-37 are the original Penguin and Pelican logos designed by Edward Young. From 1947-49 Tschichold updated the Penguin and Pelican logos with delicate refinements and added exquisite lines and black ovals around the Penguin, Pelican, and Puffin logos. The calligraphic Penguin logo from 1950 was designed by Hans Schmoller. The logo from 1953 was designed for *The Pelican History of Art* by Berthold Wolpe.

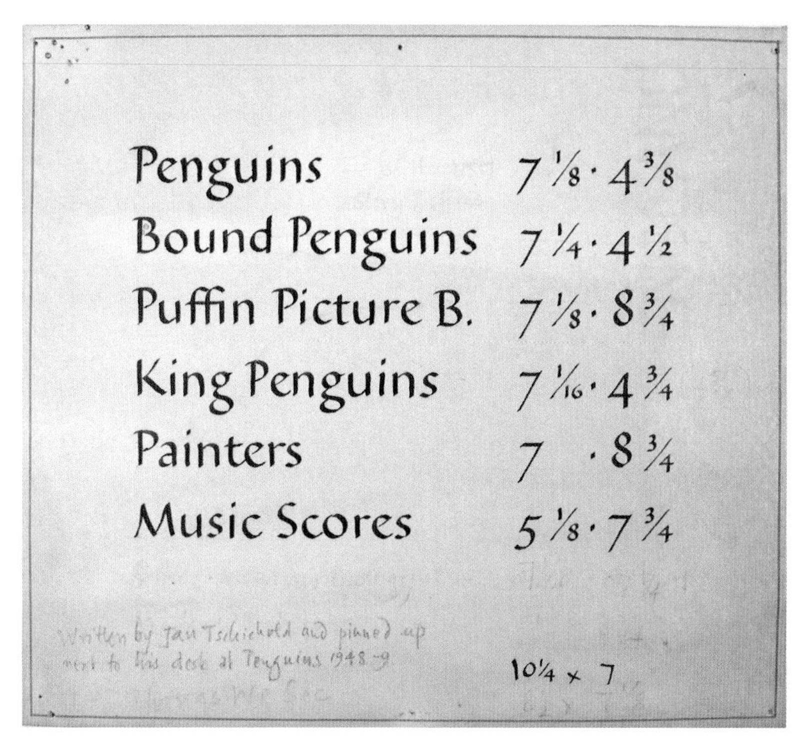

FIGURE 105

Some of the Penguin Book Series sizes written by Jan Tschichold and pinned up next to his desk at Penguin 1948-49

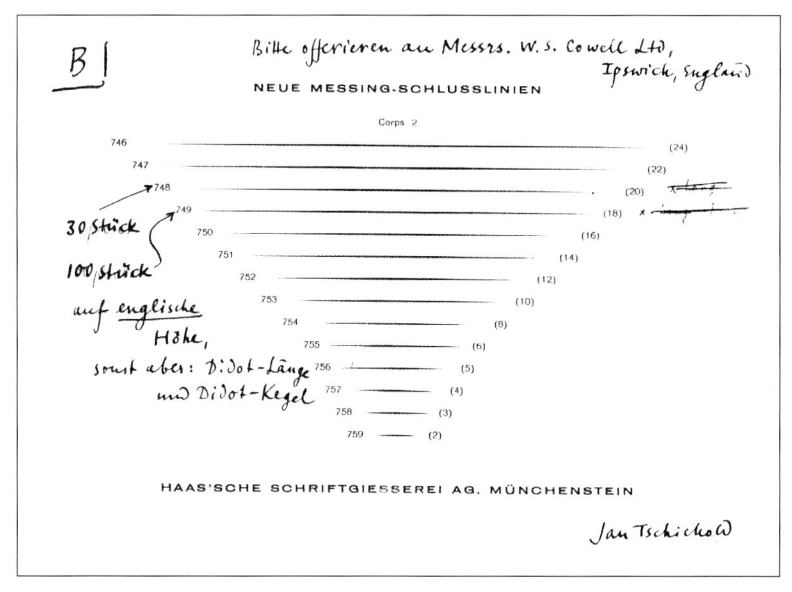

FIGURE 106

Some of the Penguin Book Series Rules written by Jan Tschichold and pinned up next to his desk at Penguin 1947-49. These swelled rules were used by Tschichold on many title pages to set off the title from the author's name. Tschichold ocassionally used these rules as a design element for some of the Penguin covers, for example, the Penguin Classics, the Penguin Poets, Science News, Penguin Shakespeare, and Penguin Reference Books.

The Penguin Roundels

In addition to hiring the engraver, Reynolds Stone, to provide the Shakespeare portrait medallion for each book comprising the Penguin Shakepeare Series, Tschichold recruited and commissioned artists for all the series who drew their illustrations directly onto transparent film, litho plates, and for photographic reproduction by either photo-litho, photogravure, and letterpress. For the Penguin Classics, each book was individually distinguished by the roundel medallion design on each cover. (Figure 107) These round decorative elements originated from coins in Roman times. Artists who have designed these roundels for the Penguin Classics include John Diebel, Cecil Keeling, Andrea Lee, William Grimmond, Elizabeth Friedlander, and Berthold Wolpe (1905-89). In the 19th Century, wood-engraving was practiced primarily for illustration, as British artists began to

Figure 107

Left to Right: Classic Roundels: Mediaeval Latin Lyrics, Herodotus, Tacitus, Camoens, Tolstoy, Ovid

These vignettes were commissioned by prominent English designers. An appropriate iconic symbol was produced to represent a classic from the Library of New Translations.

experiment, creating an individualistic medium in the early 20th Century. This provoked an extreme division between those who desired that the craft be identical with etching and those artists evolving their own craft. In the 1930s, it gained momentum as a popular art form, particularly in commercially produced books.

Back to Switzerland

Tschichold resolved to return to Switzerland in December 1949, having felt that his work at Penguin was complete, coupled with the substantial drop in the value of the English pound. His last task was recommending Hans Schmoller (1916-85) from the Curwen Press as his successor.

Tschichold's design assistant, Erik Ellegaard Frederiksen (1924-97), left Penguin on the same day as his mentor, but returned to Penguin in February 1950 to help Schmoller transition into his new job. The tradition of typographic excellence in book design continued at Penguin Books. As Penguin's production director, Schmoller maintained and built upon the design standards and composition rules implemented by Tschichold. During his 25-year tenure, Schmoller carefully modified and adapted the composition rules to reflect the continuous technological developments in the publishing and printing industry. Tschichold commented on his successor by saying: "I am also glad that my work is being well taken care of by H.P. Schmoller, a first-class book designer, and its fundamental lines can hardly be altered." [29]

---

[29] Ruari McLean, *Jan Tschichold: Typographer,* Mein Reform der Penguin Books, *Schweizer Graphische Mitteilungen,* No. 6, 1950 (Boston: David R. Godine, Publisher, Inc., 1975), p. 147.

Chapter 7
Tschichold's Legacy

Tschichold's three-year reorganization at Penguin Books, individual attention to the design of each book, and distribution of the Penguin composition rules had an enormous influence on the entire British printing industry. Of all the early specialists of "contemporary typography," Tschichold stood apart from his contemporaries due to his early training in written letters, calligraphic writing, knowledge of roman alphabets, old type specimens, and study of Italian Renaissance writing masters.

The tradition of typographic excellence in book design continued at Penguin Books Ltd, with the succession of compatriot, Hans Schmoller (1916-85) in December, 1949. Schmoller was born in Berlin in 1916 and recieved his early training working in metal, designing and arranging type as an apprentice compositor. He later became Penguin's production director, and it was in this position that he made his contribution as a typographic designer by maintaining for twenty-five years the "Penguin style": design standards and composition rules that Tschichold implemented during his three year tenure at Penguin. Schmoller carefully modified and adapted the composition rules to reflect the continuous technological developments in the publishing and printing industry. Schmoller's perfectionism, eye for detail, and crafting of each book helped to maintain Penguin's reputation for printing superior quality paperback books. The nickname, 'Half-Point Scmoller' was given to him by his production staff, as he was the only person who "could distinguish between a Garamond full point and a Bembo at two hundred paces." [30]

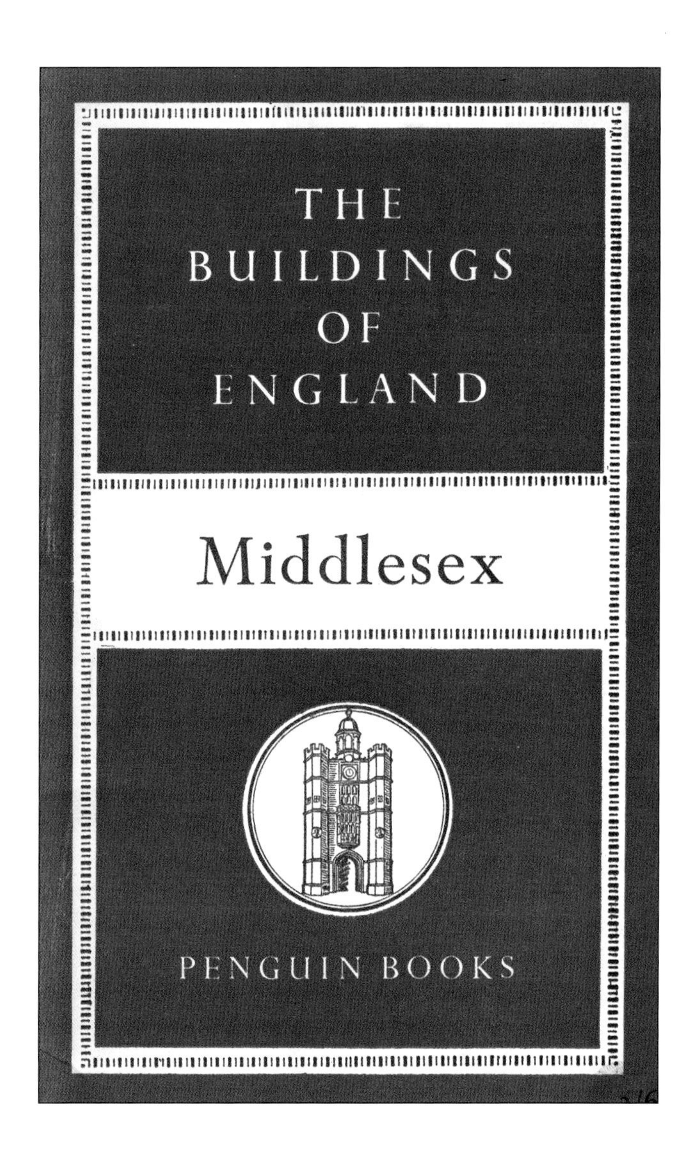

FIGURE 108

Middlesex: The Buildings of England by Nikolaus Pevsner. Cover Series Designed by Hans Schmoller, Buildings of England, Number BE 3, October 1951
4 3/8" x 7 1/8"

Tschichold's design influence is evidenced with Schmoller's choice of typography and centered styling. The white horizontal band technique can be traced back through several of the Penguin covers to the very beginning with the introduction of the Penguin fiction titles. The significant design modification on this cover is the slender band of white, which includes the county name, Middlesex, for emphasis. A thick white border encompasses the shape of the book to create a highly structured architectural window. The subtle detailing is in the form of a rhythmical monotype border to replicate the delicate edging of a building detail. The typography is carefully positioned and set in the lyrical uppercase monotype Perpetua. The word Middlesex is set in monotype Bell. Schmoller adorns the cover with a circular illustrated architectural roundel to promote individual character.

Following in the footsteps and the design tradition implemented by Tschichold at Penguin, is Schmoller's cover design for *The Buildings of England* series, first published in 1951. (Figure 108) They were planned to examine architectural features of all ecclesiastical, public and municipal buildings in each town and village of all the counties in England. Each book provides facts and lists buildings of architectural or historical interest within a specific county, such as churches, glass, historical monuments, houses, church furnishings, church painting, village buildings, country houses, schools, London transport tube stations, garden suburbs and cottages. Each volume covers the counties from prehistoric to the present. A general architectural introduction provides information regarding historical developments, geology in the region, prehistoric remains, the Middle Ages, and up to the middle twentieth century. In addition, each book includes a map referencing entries in the text, numerous photographs, glossary, and an index of plates, artists, and places.

For the cover design, Schmoller incorporates a thin white horizontal band across the center of the cover. The foundation for the basic horizontal banding technique can be traced back through several of Tschichold's Penguin covers, particularly, the Penguin Series. However, for this series, the white band has been reduced to a thin stripe that incorporates just one word, the county name, set in upper and lowercase monotype Bell. Schmoller designed the cover deliberately in this way to add emphasis to the county name. Aside from the white band is a thick white frame that encompasses the format of the book to create a structured architectural window. Schmoller then adds a rhythmical monotype border to the white areas to replicate the delicate edging or cornice of a building. For the remaining typography, Schmoller sets the words, *The Buildings of England* and Penguin books in the delicate all uppercase monotype Perpetua, inverted on the rich terra cotta background. To give each book its own distinct personality, Schmoller graces the cover with a circular illustrated architectural medallion composed of a finely

---

[30] Alan Bartram, *Making Books: Design in British publishing since 1945*. (The British Library & Oak Knoll Press, 1999), p. 53.

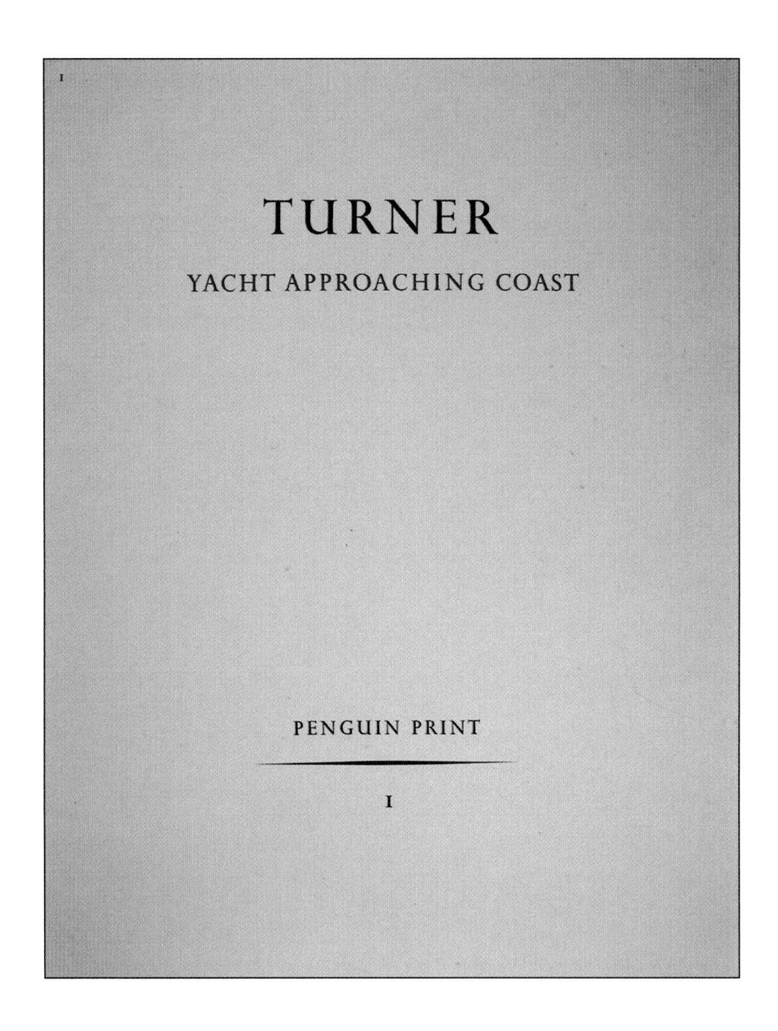

FIGURE 109

J.M.W. Turner: *Yacht Approaching Coast*
Title Page design by Jan Tschichold
Penguin Prints, Number PR 1, 1948
6" x 8 1/4"

This title page is noteworthy for its pure and simple elegance, composed in all upper case type and exquisite swelled rule. The featured typeface is the expressive uppercase monotype Perpetua throughout.

detailed rendering. Of particular note is the detailing of the spine, set in italic monotype Bell and placed within a white band with styling similar to the cover design.

Tschichold was the first designer at Penguin to separate the profession of graphic designer from production editor. Tschichold's careful planning, precise control, and demanding instructions to the machine compositors and printers enabled suberb craftsmanship and the highest quality of book production. Tschichold tried to strike a balance between exceptional handicraft and the restrictions, requirements, and demands of mass-produced books. Tschichold developed a design philosophy based on craftsmanship of the past and attempted to apply his design attitudes to the mass-production of books. Parallels can be drawn between Tschichold and the Kelmscott Press. Both were dedicated to reclaiming the charm and exquisiteness of incunabula books a variety of typeface designs based on earlier classical models, attention to the smallest details, faithful adherence to design specifications for printers and compositors, quality paper, decorative borders, and hand drawn lettering.

Tschichold's unrelenting design approach and individual attention to the design of each book was often overlooked and under appreciated by other designers and British publishers in the 1950s. (Figure 109) However, the distribution of the Penguin composition rules has had an enormous influence on the entire British printing industry.

In 1946, Rurai McLean (b. 1917) was hired by Lane to manage the production of the Puffin Picture Books children's series as well as Penguins Progress, a handbook introducing new Penguin publications. By March of 1947, Tschichold had arrived at Penguin and was assigned an office close to McLean's office. McLean would often consult with Tschichold regarding the artwork and page layout for the Puffin Picture Books and witnessed firsthand Tschichold's extraordinary skill at resolving scrupulous typographic problems, such as incorrectly sized illustrations within the page layout. McLean left Penguin and soon joined George Rainbird's (d. 1986) studio. Rainbird and McLean went into partnership as Rainbird, McLean Ltd.

in February 1951. McLean's continued correspondence with Tschichold, design experiences and aquired skills as a result of working with Tschichold at Penguin, influenced his design approach at Rainbird, McLean Ltd. In the early to mid 1950s, Rainbird, McLean Ltd. established a reputation and became preminent publishers of well designed books whose clients included William Collins, Festival of Britain, Lincoln Cathedral, National Magazine Company, and Geoffrey Grigson.

Tschichold exhibited that the function of typography is not so much the stylish results, but the less apparent, consistent adherence to a standardized format, grids, composition rules, and managing the details. He emphasized to his design colleagues and those who followed and admired his design aesthetic that accuracy and attention to detail are as important to book production as editing. Early in his career, Tschichold understood the importance of the "New Typography" and its attempt at purification and clarity in modern typographic design. At Penguin, however, Tschichold used a classical design approach, which was based on a realistic assessment of the requirements and restrictions imposed on book design.

The enforcement of composition rules and introduction of grids, the utilization of appropriate classic fonts to a specific title, the elegant human touch of calligraphy, and the precise stroke of a pen or brush all contributed to the beautiful body of books designed by Tschichold at Penguin. Penguin books' impeccable design standard established a precedence of uniformity and improved the overall aesthetic of books throughout Britain. Tschichold emphasized the importance of enforcing composition rules and a grid on the consistency of the entire series. Adherence to his design principles gave Tschichold the time to concentrate on the character of each book and add his personal esthetic touch. His conviction and adherence to these principles, reflected in the sheer volume of elegant books he designed, contribute to the quality of his work and his legacy as a designer. Tschichold's tenure at Penguin, during which he designed or prepped for press 500 elegant books—sometimes one per day—was a significant chapter in his career. He could claim to be the first typographer to successfully design and manage, on such a wide-ranging scale—book series, editors, compositors, binders, and printers—the mass production of books for a publishing firm. (Figure 110)

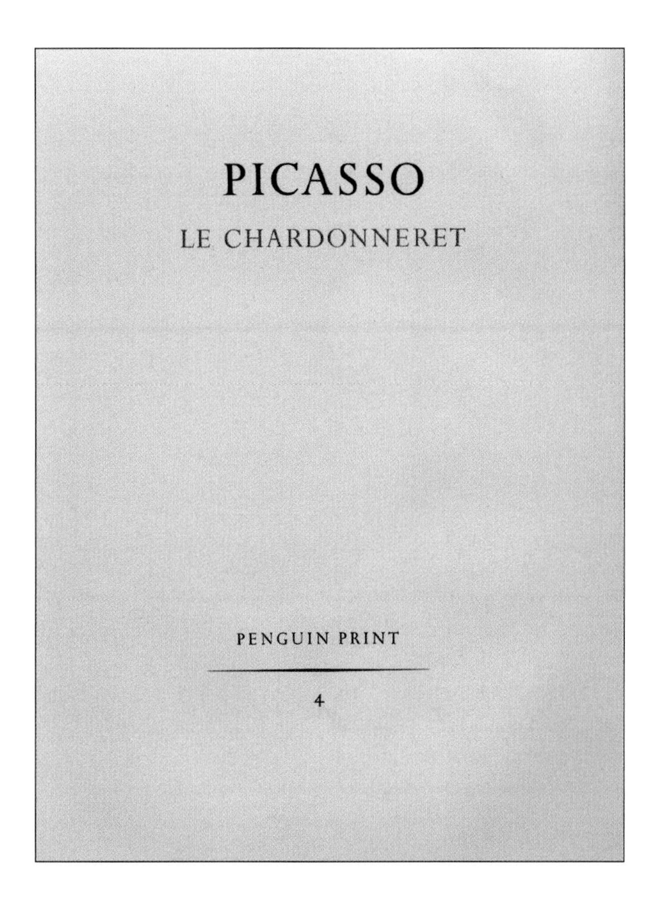

FIGURE 110

Title Page design for Picasso: *Le Chardonneret* by Jan Tschichold
Penguin Prints, Number PR 4, 1948
6" x 8 1/4"

This work's distinguishing typographic feature is the expressive uppercase monotype Perpetua throughout. This title page is noteworthy for its pure and simple elegance, composed in all upper case type and exquisite swelled rule.

Late in his career he reflected on his experience and efforts at Penguin Books by saying "*I could be proud of the million Penguin books for whose typography I was responsible. Beside them, the two or three luxurious books I have designed are of no importance. We do not need pretentious books for the wealthy, we need more really well-made ordinary books.*"

Appendix 1: My Reform of Penguin Books
Mein Reform der Penguin Books
Schweizer Graphische Mitteilungen, No.6, 1950

Penguin Books are probably, after Hutchinson, the biggest English publisher. they produce about 15 million books a year (at the lowest possible prices); there are about sixteen titles every month, in editions of from 50,000 to 100,000. They do not own either a printing works or a bindery. Furthermore, present circumstances compel them to hold their complete stock in their own warehouse, an average of 8 to 10 million books at any given time.

The man who controls typographical design in an English publishing house is called the typographer. The typographer's communication with printers and binders is by letter. Penguin Books uses a large number of printing and binding firms all over the British Isles. Distances are so great that visits even to a firm in London are only occasionally possible: any visit takes nearly a whole day, most of which is spent in travelling. Corrections can hardly ever be made quickly. In exceptional circumstances, they may be made within a week, but more often it takes weeks or even months before one can see a revise. These delays do not make a typographer's life any easier. But now, along came a man who not only wanted nearly everything changed, but also, in this most conservative of countries, produced an entirely new set of typographical rules!

After only a few days in my new job, I saw how urgent it was to establish strict rules for composition. The printers who set the type either had no composition rules at all, or worked to nineteenth-century conventions, or followed one set or another of house rules. Luckily, even in England, the machine compositors can be directed and are ready to follow good composition rules: I had hardly any problems with them, and after about a year (the production of a single book often takes as long, or longer) I could see the improvement in straightforward composition as a result of my Penguin Composition Rules, which ran to four printed pages. Although the general practice in both England and Scotland, was, as it had been in the nineteenth century, wide spacing between words and preferably no leading at all between the lines, I insisted on close spacing and leading. I also insisted on the use of the en-dash, with the word space of the line on each side, instead of the em-dash set solid, which greatly improved the appearance of the page. Finally, the practice of putting extra space after full points had to be abolished. These were only the most obvious rules: my list of rules covered a mass of other details.

If it was comparatively easy to persuade the machine compositors to accept these (for Britain) apparently revolutionary rules, with the hand compositors I came up against a stone wall. They simply could not understand what I meant by 'capitals must be letter-spaced'. Because every day I had to wade through miles of corrections (often ten books daily) I had a rubber stamp made:''Equalize letterspaces according to their visual value'. It was totally ignored; the hand compositors continued to space out the capitals on title-pages (where optical spacing is essential) with spaces of equal thickness. Because in England there is no commonly accepted correction mark for 'space in' or 'space out', I was forced literally thousands of times to mark between every individual capital, for example, '1/2 pt in' or '2 pts out'. That a good hand compositor should always look carefully at capitals and space them by eye is in Britain (as opposed to the USA) entirely unheard of or at least never done. Compositors do not seem to be interested in their work. Printers have told me that compositors who try to produce better results get into severe trouble with their colleagues. So, with everything set by hand – titles, decorations, capital letters and advertisements – I had terrible difficulties, that would never have occurred in Switzerland.

Things began to improve towards the end of my time there, in the summer of 1949. Probably my layouts were generally given to the same compositors, and they eventually began to understand what I wanted. For this reason my layouts had to be far more exact than would be necessary in Switzerland. I had to specify not only the amount of letter-spacing but also the word spacing; if I did not do this, I infallibly got monstrously wide word spacing, which is for me the clearest proof of incompetence in the composing room. The shortcomings of English compositors – whose apprenticeship lasts a full seven years – are in sharp contrast with the opportunities offered by the splendid range of type-faces which have been available on English composing machines for more than twenty years. Fine type-faces, bad composition and appalling hand composition, are the characteristics of the average English printing house of today. The difference between the best English printing (e.g. Oliver Simon at the Curwen Press) and the average is very great - far greater than in Switzerland or the USA. It would be wrong to draw any inference from the one to the other, but unfortunately this fallacy is often committed when one thinks of English typography. While I was in England, I learned to appreciate the value of our own Further Education Courses and Trade Training Schemes in Switzerland.

As the designer responsible for the appearance of all Penguin books, I had to design specimen pages both for the reprints of books already published, and for new titles, as well as chapter openings and advertisement pages at the backs of books; covers had to be either specified typographically or designed entirely de novo, corrections for every book had to be examined typographically page by page, and many other tasks that were part of my job had to be attended to. This was such a gigantic task that I soon needed a full-time assistant. Only someone who has been concerned with all the minutiae and time-consuming attention to detail required of a publisher's typographer can begin to appreciate what was involved.

After my Composition Rules had been laid down and circulated, I moved on to the general appearance of Penguin books. They were then nearly all set in Times New Roman, a type outstandingly suitable for newspapers but much less so for books. Of the books I personally supervised, only about twenty per cent are still set in Times New Roman; the rest are now set in Baskerville, Bembo, Garamond and Caslon. In some of the King Penguin series, which resemble the illustrated Insel-Bücherei, I used more unusual type-faces, for example Pastonchi, Scotch Roman, Lutetia and Walbaum. These type-faces, mostly of classical origin, combined with the new composition rules, and a carefully considered overall re-styling, completely altered the appearance of Penguins.

Title-pages suffered from the heaviness of the Penguin symbol. This had gradually become more and more corrupted, and I had to find a new solution which would match up to the original design, which was good.

I redrew the Penguin in about eight different variations. For title-pages I designed some decorated swelled rules. The versos of title-pages, so often neglected by typographers, were a special concern of mine. That a solution can be found for even such a difficult problem as this, is shown by the illustration.

Finally, I had to work on designs for the covers of various series. I produced a successful new design for the covers of Pelican Books, the scientific and educational series, and a new design of mine for the main Penguin series, with a few alterations, is at the moment under discussion.

Up till now it has not been possible to alter the old flag-like division of Penguin covers: all I could do was to improve the proportions and replace the deformed symbol. Because the present standard Penguin cover is not entirely my own work, I do not reproduce it here. I do however show cover designs, which are entirely my own work, for The Centuries' Poetry, A Dictionary of Geography, The Penguin Shakespeare and Penguin Music Scores.

In addition, I had to oversee countless children's books, and besides their text pages to keep an eye on the typography of their covers, often an exhausting and sometimes a thankless task. From the middle of 1948 I had a young Dane, Erik Frederiksen, as my very congenial and hard-working assistant.

After a long struggle I finally won my battle for the correct direction of the paper, previously neglected, and for a slightly cream colour instead of the previous dirty grey.

Gradually the results of my work began to be noticeable.

In 29 months, I designed or prepared for press more than 500 books, mostly page by page, which must be nearly a world record. Eventually the work began to get easier, as the origination had been mostly done, and many things became a matter of routine.

Then, in September 1949, the English pound was heavily devalued, and I was compelled to return to Switzerland, a little earlier than I had expected. But I am glad to be able to say that my task at Penguins was already completed.

I am also glad that my work is being well taken care of by H. P. Schmoller, (1916-1985) a first-class book designer, and its fundamental lines can now hardly be altered. The firm of Penguins is assured that its books, produced as cheaply as possible in millions for the millions, are every bit as well set and designed as the most expensive in the country – indeed, better than most!

English Translation by Ruari McLean

APPENDIX 2: ON MASS-PRODUCING THE CLASSICS
Signature, No.3 (New Series), March, 1947

If an ordinary book deserves to be produced with the greatest possible care, then, certainly, so does a classic. The word 'classic' is perhaps too freely used nowadays, and is indeed applied to many more books than would have been the case fifty years ago. But all books whose value has been proved to be lasting deserve to be produced worthily: not only in spite of the fact that they have to be produced in such large numbers, but because of it. And faultless typography costs no more for a huge edition than for a limited one. Publishers indeed ought to take a special pride in lavishing their greatest typographical care on the largest editions of the classical authors.

Possessing the great works of literature in handy pocket size is one of the pleasures of life; and for many centuries the classics have been so produced. In the Middle Ages industrious monks copied out the Bible in tiny script on the thinnest parchment, of pocket size, to make as small a single volume as possible. As soon as printers learned how to cut small types, the first printed pocket editions appeared. But the editions which Aldus Manutius printed of his pocket volumes were not much greater than those of his normal books. Probably the first really large editions of pocket volumes were the famous Elzevirs, which as texts are as useful today as they ever were, besides being typographic masterpieces. It is not yet proved that we can today print such small formats with perfect legibility; modern publishers and readers seem surprisingly prejudiced against these small sizes.

The Didot pocket volumes must have been produced in very large editions, for they were printed from stereotyped plates. Their format, although very attractive, was rather larger than that of the Elzevirs; their typesetting was meticulous, of a standard of excellence since lost not only in France; their textual authority was a by-word. But from the mid-nineteenth century the quality of typesetting fell lower and lower. Spacing between words was increased excessively, and the arrangement of title-pages and headings was more and more neglected.

Sixty years ago in Germany, editions of the classics were unpleasing in appearance, and seemed designed rather to put readers off than to attract them. They were printed on ugly, shiny, ill-tinted yellow-grey or grey-white paper, in the thin, anaemic types of the late nineteenth century. The setting was careless, the type usually too small and not easily legible, the leading insufficient, and the pages overcrowded. Headings were set in particularly ugly types; title-pages lacked any typographical feeling. These feeble specimens of nineteenth-century typography were also of unhandy format, and bound in a way that today makes us shudder.

The Everyman Library and the World's Classics were among the earliest modern attempts to produce the classics in a more worthy form, turning to practical use the movement started by William Morris and his followers to reform book typography. To make them pocket editions, a new thin Bible paper was used, enabling a volume to run to six or seven hundred pages without becoming unwieldy. The Insel thin-paper editions, and the French 'Editions de la Pléiade' are faithful copies of English models.

These new series appealed immediately to the educated public, who were tired of the pretentious decoration and unnecessary size of the editions of classics then current, and found that these new and handsome-looking volumes were about half the size and weight of their predecessors. They have hardly been bettered since in their kind. In fact, little room has been left for improvement, except perhaps in the typography and the decoration of the binding.

The type used, Old Style, is now old-fashioned; and lettering on title-pages, even if by Eric Gill, does not harmonize so well with the rest of a printed book (just because the lettering is so perfect) as would a title-page carefully set in the same type used for the body of the book. The covers of these books are not entirely pleasing today, because they reveal too clearly the signs of the period of their origin.

The format (17.3 by 10.4 cm, 6 13/16 by 4 1/8 in.) corresponds exactly to the Golden Mean, and is undoubtedly the best format for pocket editions. It has been adopted with slight alterations for many similar series. All variations consisting of making the pages broader or narrower seem to me ugly and pointless. Format and type area cannot be protected by copyright, and no publisher need fear a lawsuit if he copies exactly the dimensions of a good page from another publisher. Perhaps in no other craft does it so often pay to follow tradition.

The aim of pocket editions is to get as much as possible into as small a space as possible, and narrow margins and cramped type areas can be forgiven, so long as the type used it not too small nor too widely spaced.

When these early thin-paper editions first appeared, Old Style was the best typeface available. But to use it nowadays as a standard face for a pocket edition would be wrong. Thanks largely to the efforts of Mr. Stanley Morison, we now have such a large range of fine types to choose from, that it is possible to find exactly the right face for nearly every kind of book.

The typographer who now has all these types to choose from must understand and appreciate the unique character of each. And as the complexity of book production and the number of specialized processes increase, so does the need, when a book is to be perfectly produced, for a typographer who can design every detail of size, setting, paper and binding; who can be, in fact, a true architect of the book. He must know every subtle effect and modulation to be gained by every possible variation in layout, in style of type, and in spacing. He must have a profound understanding of the nature of the type he is using, and he must be capable, not only of general direction, but of controlling every detail of the physical construction of a book. Only then will beautiful books be produced.

It is the close setting with the lines leaded that distinguishes a good modern edition from an old one. Close setting binds the words together in lines and greatly increases the legibility and beauty of a page. The typographer must use the accumulated experience of typographic history when giving instructions about chapter-openings, or paragraphing, or the layout of plays or poetry. Only the most careful and critical study of the best typography of the past will enable him to notice the details that make such a difference to the whole. The form of the running title, the folio numbering, and, not least, the proportions of the margins, are all questions of great importance.

The further specialization is carried, and the less the compositor's brain is given to do, the more essential does it become for the typographer to go over every page, almost line for line, before he passes it.

The choice of paper also demands the greatest care. White paper should be used when the type is heavily leaded and the type-face belongs to the vertical-stress family, for instance Bodoni, Walbaum or Didot. In all other circumstances, a slightly off-white is better. White paper is tiring to the eyes. Unfortunately, it seems that not a few printers and publishers think that the whiter a paper is, the better it is. This is an error, though not a new one. It seems to have originated with the contemporaries of the Didot and Bodoni, at a period when many papers used for cheap book-production really were too dark. The eye definitely finds it easier to read on slightly toned paper.

It is often necessary to produce a book in sheets of thirty-two pages, and this large number of pages can result in serious errors in folding which can be minimized only by using papers that are not too bulky. If the type-face to be used is one of the Venetian or Aldine group, then the paper surface must definitely be machine finished.

Since the paper for large editions is always specially made, the experienced book designer's stipulations about colour, surface and weight can easily be met. At a later stage, care must be taken to insist on the book being printed with the paper running the right way, i.e. with the laid lines parallel to the spine, and in the case of wove paper, the grain should likewise run parallel to the spine.

Even quite cheap paper can be distinctly improved by judicious tinting. The weight can also be adjusted, so that volumes of varying length can be produced in approximately uniform thickness.

The best binding for modern series of classics is whole cloth. The Birkhauser (Basle) series, for the design of which I am responsible, was originally launched in half-cloth, but the public did not find this form of binding wholly satisfactory; in consequence they now appear in whole cloth. The cloth should be neither too coarse nor too light, and should be proof against dust and fingermarks.

Whether gold is really best for printing the title on the spine and the front cover is difficult to decide. Possibly in ten years or so we will find to our shame that even our best gold leaf has oxidized. My own opinion is that either real gold should be used (for expensive editions) or that the cases should be made of smooth, not too dark, cloth, which can be printed on in colours by letterpress or offset, like the binding of Mr. Oliver Simon's *Introduction to Typography*. Coloured foil inks are transitory and often ugly, and should never be used in good quality productions. They are unsuitable for use on book materials, and wear off.

Whether books should be flexible or not depends entirely on their format. Only pocket editions should be flexible. It is flexibility which turns a pocket format into a genuine pocket edition. Books larger than Everyman or Penguin size should have stiff bindings, for in them flexibility is neither useful nor desirable. It goes without saying that all books, especially flexible books, should have slightly rounded spines, which prevent the middle pages losing shape after reading. Books with flat spines are an ugly and uncraftsman like invention, which no sound book designer would countenance; and they damage the pocket.

The pocket edition is symptomatic of the overcrowding and eternal house changing of our time, not least when it contains some text of lasting value. But it does not follow that all editions of the classics should be pocket size: one exception is the great critical editions. And, because a book is larger than pocket size, it need not be unwieldy: it can, and should, be correctly proportioned. neither too thick nor too heavy. All our books tend to be too heavy. One has to handle a Chinese book to discover how light paper may be.

Good proportions for trimmed page sizes are 3:5 and 5:8. The Birkhauser Classics are proportioned 5:8 (19.2 by 12 cm, 7 9/16 by 4 3/4 in.). A very beautiful edition of the works of Prosper Mérimée, printed by Jakob Hegner, has the 3:5 proportion (18.8 by 12.2 cm, 6 13/32 by 4 7/16 in.). When a book becomes too wide in proportion to its length, it will not lie easily in the hand: the law of leverage makes it more difficult to hold than a narrower book of the same weight. People read the classics in their leisure time, so that editions of the classics must be suitable for holding in the unsupported hand. Larger books, of what may be called 'table size', do not come within the scope of the present discussion. The typography of non-pocket editions is not subject to the laws of economy which apply to the pocket edition.

I find it consoling, in these days when civilization appears to be tottering, to think that the great tradition of European book-printing has been revived by a few faithful men and is now in our hands, to carry on and, even in the changed conditions of modern mass-production, to improve, if we go to our task with enough seriousness and sense of responsibility. Where could such qualities be more desirable than in the work of passing on the wisdom of the great poets and thinkers by means of books available to Everyman?

English Translation by Ruari McLean

Appendix 3: Letter written by Allen Lane to Oliver Simon 10th September 1946

I find it hard to know where to begin to thank you for the events of the last week: first of all for your suggestion of Tschichold, and secondly for being willing to give up so much of your time and to undertake a fairly arduous journey in order to effect the introduction and to sustain me with your advice. But above these what I value most is the recollection of the days of friendship, good conversation, and good food and drink: a combination which has not previously come my way.

Since my return I have had long conversations with my brother, and as a result I am happy to say that I am writing Tschichold today confirming our last conversation, and I am also starting negotiations through the proper channels with a view to obtaining the Bank of England sanction for the export of currency asked for by Tschichold.

As promised I am sending you herewith copies of our edition of the two Claudius books, *some Saki*, and the *GOOD SOLDIER SCHWEIK*. I am afraid that the production of some of these leaves much to be desired, but they are wartime jobs.

Yours sincerely,
(signed) Allen Lane

Appendix 4: Letter written by Raymond Hazell Esq. to Allen Lane November 24, 1947

Dear Allen,

Many thanks for lunch last Friday.

We shall be interested to hear in due course whether you feel that a certain amount of Mr. Tschichold's time could be lent in connection with typography and binding design for the new big 15 volume Encyclopedia.

It is difficult to say how much of his time this work would involve. In any event I do not think at any stage should his side of the work be very urgently pressed.

I have been wondering whether a further preliminary discussion could take place with him when dummies and suggested bindings could be shown, and perhaps as a result a better estimate of the amount of work involved could be assessed.

I think it is possible that visits to London by Mr. Tschichold could be reduced to perhaps only one or two. The rest of the work could be done by a representative of ours visiting him at Harmondsworth.

However, no doubt you will be good enough to think the matter over and let me know in due course what you feel.

Yours Sincerely,
(signed) Raymond Hazell

APPENDIX 5: LETTER WRITTEN BY ALLEN LANE TO RAYMOND HAZELL ESQ.

August 27, 1947

Dear Raymond,

Thank you for your letter of 25th inst. Referring to coloured edges on our Double Penguins. If you could give me even an approximate idea of cost, I would tell you immediately whether the idea was possible.

I certainly agree with Tchichold that it would be by far the most fool-proof method of enabling the booksellers' assistants to check the price.

Yours Sincerely,
Allen Lane

Appendix 6: Letter written by Allen Lane to Raymond Hazell Esq. and copies to E.F. (Erik Ellegaard Frederiksen), and R.L. (Richard Lane).

December 4, 1947

Dear Raymond,

I am sorry about the lunch on Monday, but I hope you understand. It was the only appointment I had in the whole day, and I was very anxious to get a clear run at my work here. As a matter of fact it was as well that we did cancel it as it would probably have taken me about five hours to get home afterwards in the fog.

About Tschichold, I have talked the matter over with him, and our feeling is that he has so much work on hand that he really can't spare the time for an extra job. I mentioned the possibility of his doing it in his spare time, but he said that with the present rate of income tax it was not really worth his while, and he made the additional point that his leisure was so precious to him that he didn't like contemplating making any inroads upon it.

On the question of libel I am taking up the matter as you suggest with our Insurance Company, and will write to you again in due course.

Yours,
Allen Lane

Appendix 7: Letter written to G. Bernard Shaw, Esq.

June 8, 1949

Dear Bernard Shaw,

Thank you very much for your card. We will now forge ahead with production both here and in America.

I yesterday saw Mr Stanley Morison, who is going to America next week, where he will be staying with the Donnelleys in Chicago, who as you may know are the largest high-quality printers in the United States, and both Morison and I agreed that they were the proper people to undertake such a large job.

You may remember that when I came to see you I showed you an advance proof of the cover of our re-designed Penguin Shakespeare. We now have advance copies from the printers, and I am sending you a couple herewith. I am also enclosing advance copies of the first Penguin Scores, of which we are commencing publication this month. Mr Tschichold our typographer, who designed these books throughout, is now engaged on preliminary work on the complete Shaw.

Please do not trouble to acknowledge this letter,

Yours Sincerely,

Appendix 8: Memo to Jan Tschichold, Erik Ellegaard Frederiksen, J.O., J.P., and A.S.B.G.

September 27, 1947

In future, A.L. would like the price on Pelican and Penguin covers to be centered under the bird device. Also the words 'complete and unabridged' should appear on Pelicans where appropriate as well as on Penguins.

A.L. would also like the titles of books advertised in end pages to be printed in a large type, say 12 point, so that they stand out more.

A.S.B.G.
ASGB/McQ

APPENDIX 9: LETTER WRITTEN BY JAN TSCHICHOLD TO ALFRED FAIRBANK

Sept. 15, 1946

Dear Fairbank,

First I have to apologize for not having answered you on your different sendings and especially on your letter of August 28. In the meantime the good wishes you sent me have been accomplished. Perhaps you already are informed that I shall move to England at the beginning of the next year, for to work for the Penguin Books and to supervise their physical appearance. I had the pleasure to see here fourteen days ago Allen Lane and Oliver Simon. At this occasion I also heard that you prepare a King Penguin about Calligraphy on which I am very glad.

Many thanks for the review you wrote about *Barbedor* and the *Schatzkammer der Schreibkunst*. A translation of the sentence you mention would be: Calligraphic exercises are able to harmonize the whole man, as scarcely another occupation does, and therefore it is commendable to everyone.

"*Schriftzeichnen* means Lettering, in difference to genuine Calligraphy which only can be produced with the broad-nipped pen. Every letterer should be able to conduct it because he only in this way could learn the right forms of letters.

When I wrote that there are not more than 20 active calligraphers in Europe and North America together I wished to be not to impolite and in any case to forget none of the unknown ones too. Of course I know there are much fewer than ten!

My article I prepared for the England number of *Graphis* has been postponed by the editor because the "actual" material already was to much. The article now shall be printed in the next number, and I hope I can send you the proofs before the printing.

I shall pay a visit of a week to Harmondsworth and London in November.

Perhaps I will have the opportunity to meet you then. In any case, in the first months of the new year I shall have much pleasure to make your personal acquaintance when I will live in England. I am very glad to move thereover.

With always good wishes,
Yours,
(signed) Jan Tschichold

Appendix 10: Rough notes of speech by Allen Lane at the opening of the Monotype Showrooms of the Typography and Production of Penguin Books on July 2, 1951

Thanks to the Monotype Corporation, Mrs. Beatrice Warde and Alan Pryce-Jones.

Exciting to see so comprehensive a display. Day to day lay-outs, specimens and proofs tend to blind one to the mass effect as the public sees it or could see it if such a show as this was available to them.

Interesting too to see how we have moved on since 1935.

The fundamentals are still the same. As good a collection of books as we can find in the best form we can devise.

There was nothing new about cheap additions or even sixpennies in 1935: Reader's Library, Hodders' Ninepennies, Collins several sixpennies. The only originality we had was a more sophisticated editorial policy and no pretence in production. We wanted a book one would be proud to own and be seen owning as no greater sacrifice than ten Players.

That was Edward Young's problem and he solved it so brilliantly that is has survived 15 years without essential change. He has gone from strength to strength but I don't think he has done a more satisfying job than this and certainly nothing which is likely to face him more whether he likes it or not.

How Penguins got their name – we thought of Phoenix and Dolphin, but were beaten to it by other publishers. Then a girl in the office said '*Why not Penguins*', and Penguins it was. No problem of colour in reproduction. Edward Young went off with a thickness dummy (we didn't have paper pads) to the Zoo on as hot a day as it is today, with 2d for his fare. He returned with sketches but all he could say was '*My god how those birds stink*'.

During the war the torch was carried on from hand to hand. John Overton's arrival straight from school and how much is owed to him. The end of austerity and the need for a typographer.

Charles Prentice suggested by Oliver Simon – started us on our upward trend. Had to leave because of ill-health.

Back to Oliver Simon for advice, who suggested Jan Tschichold. Flight in chartered aircraft to Basle, the most awful flight I have experienced. But nothing compared to storm which arose when Jan Tschichold arrived. Mild-mannered man with an inflexible character. Screams heard from Edinburgh to Ipswich and from Aylesbury to Bungay.

Fantastic industry – when he returned to Switzerland on the devaluation of the £ he told me he had designed 500 books in under three years. One of the best things he did was to suggest as his successor Hans Schmoller from the Curwen Press, who is building on the solid foundation laid by Tschichold with imagination and youthful zest during the last eighteen months has taken charge of all our typographical design.

By now the original Penguin had been joined in the aviary by Pelicans, Puffins of two kinds, Scores, Painters and Prints – indeed I don't have to tell you as you can see for yourself.

Schmoller and his department are now responsible for every bit of print which emanates from Harmondsworth – not only some 200 – 250 new books or new editions (a year?); but labels, invoices, show-cards, cheques, letter-headings, and even the 'In and Out' signs on the gates.

We have recently banned the use of the word integration at Harmondsworth so I'll say that we feel that one can't have one set of standards for editorial policy, another for production and another for showcards or exhibition stands. They have to form a whole and there the typographer is in full control. The result you can see.

In conclusion I don't think I need say I'm not even an amateur in typography myself but like the woman in the superb short story Somerset Maugham read as a speech at the Academy Banquet said of art 'I don't know anything about it but I know what I like'.

I have only to say thank you once again to all concerned with this exhibition and for the party into which I am about to plunge.

APPENDIX 11: MY TYPOGRAPHICAL THOUGHTS
Typographische Gedanken
Plus, no. 11, 1965

Jan Tschichold

Good typography is quiet – it does not shout.

Easily readable type and pleasant presentation are the two first requirements of good printing.

Asymmetry is used often today, very pleasingly. But the true shape of typography is symmetry.

Text set without indentation of paragraphs is not clear. Indentation helps the reader and makes the meaning permanently clear.

Typography's duty to the reader is to provide effortless communication of words and thought.

Only extremely well-set type is perfectly readable.

One of the highest virtues of good typography is obtrusive elegance.

It is not the duty of typography to create deliberate images of its own time. It must actually be its own time. It must express our own vision, in a pleasing way.

Good typography categorically does not depend on special and exceptional type-faces – that is the way of the novice.

It is readability, not modernity, that we ask from a type-face. Those who can read – and not everyone has learned to read in school can – do so in exactly the same way as those who could read in 1540.

English Translation by Ruari McLean

APPENDIX 12: ERIK ELLEGAARD FREDERIKSEN
Correspondence with Colin Banks

After some years at the Danish Royal Academy under Professor Gunnar Biilmann Petersen and some more time in his private studio, I felt the need to widen my experience. Petersen had taught letter design and some typography, but to my way of thinking I needed two teachers, if I was to avoid seeing things and problems with only one eye.

In 1948, at the age of 24, I went to London (with a return ticket) to get a job. I came with introductions: Beatrice Warde, though, was on her doorstep just off to America and Oliver Simon was not much help either.

I started the rounds of advertising agencies and suddenly one morning met a gentleman at Crawfords, behind a white telephone: Ashley Havinden. I knew his posters from *Graphis* and I think he was flattered that a young Dane knew his work.

"*This is not the place for you. I know where you are to go!*" and saying that he picked up his phone and talked to Jan Tchichold.

I already knew that Tschichold was at Penguins, but I had not on my own the courage to go and see him: he was my typographic king. His books on asymmetric typography had been translated into Danish; I had bought them at the Royal Academy at a time when I intended to study architecture.

An hour later I was facing a small, round, smiling man who recalled his visit to Copenhagen before the war with great pleasure. Danish Printers had received him with more enthusiasm than he had met anywhere else, and after examining my work he asked: "*Would you like to become my assistant?*" What a question! Formalities were soon settled with Allen Lane, Penguin Books' proprietor, and so started a period which became the typographic foundation of the rest of my life. It continued until Christmas 1949, 18 months in all, not a long period, but comprehensize. We were placed together in a very small room. Our desks were at right angles, so that he could see what I was doing, and — more important — I could watch him working.

I already had some training and could make some sort of layouts, but of course it took time to grow into his atmosphere. It was to my advantage that he had already worked at Penguins for about a year, so the first results had just begun to show up in finished books. Tschichold had altered the paper colour from grey to off-white; a great improvement. He had published the Penguin Composition Rules demanding tight word spacing, en-rules with word spaces and some other points of typography decency. The printers were furious: *"what foreigner could decide upon things like that, and breaking traditions,"* but they had to obey.

I started slowly, but soon I was taking over even complicated paste-ups of illustrated King Penguins. As we sat so close together I could ask him about difficult points. He was always willing, not only to answer the specific question, but to teach me the reasons, and fill in the background. He lent me books (Updike and others), and he taught me to write a calligraphic handwriting in the cancellaresca style. Of course, he did many things that I could just register and had at that time to take for granted. Only several years later did I realise the reasons for his solutions — they were always based on a historical background. As we were both paid by Penguins, he took his time to educate me. But don't think we were not occupied; at that time we published a book per working day! And although much work was standardised, we were always extremely busy. We enjoyed, however, not only the work but also each other's company. Tschichold felt a little foreign in England, and I am sure it helped that I was an alien too. He was like a father to me and invited me home for dinner on special occasions. He brought materials and books from his private files and library to go through with me, and invited me to stay in his flat in Switzerland for the vacations.

After some time at Penguins I worked more independently, but of course very much influenced by his points of view, for I had learned book typography only from him. But I found him always willing to listen to other suggestions on typographic style. The small Penguin emblem, for example, was redesigned by me under his guidance. I was the one to go to the Zoo to make sketches from nature to ensure that the bird stood properly on its feet! He was, however, very strict and rather narrow in his attitude. Asymmetric typography was used only once, for a book on modern painting that included many illustrations of different sizes. With this book I got a chance to learn his former principles. He developed a grid and a system to work within, which made the whole concept look easy and orderly. Otherwise we worked only in symmetry and with serifed roman letters, except for the covers. Tschichold was still trying energetically to disassocciate himself from his 'German' period.

His craftsmanship was of course great. I recall that Reynolds Stone had engraved the Shakespeare portrait in a medallion for the cover of the Penguin series, but Tschichold wanted to make the frame himself. This he did in scraper board in the original size. The lettering was made with a pin held in a pen-holder with string, He did not alter anything, letter-spacing, serifs, everything was correct in one attempt! For the cover of *Early Man* he dipped his finger in indian ink and wrote the headline with his finger-tip. But mostly he restricted himself to typographic solutions – because of time limits – and most of the books were pocket editions with a fixed cover style. Much of the work was routine and we let it be so, although every single page was carefully controlled. Only special editions and series were planned individually.

Tschichold could get very upset, but never with me. If I made a mistake he would cover me completely, he was the man responsible, not I. But if printers did not do their work properly he would shout: *"whom do they think I am? I am not somebody so-and-so, I am Jan Tschichold!"* I understood him very well, for all our work was done with utmost care and all the information was stated minutely on the layouts. We knew that we would never meet the printers personally as they were scattered round the whole of England, so we had to tell them what we wanted in writing. Only a few questions were answered by telephone and this sharpened our attention to the details of layout. Today I still work with many printers entirely through correspondence.

I remember that Dorothy Sayers had done a translation of Dante. The title-page carried a lot of information; many lines of differing importance. I worked on the title-page for several hours under Tschichold's guidance. The solution was, as always, as few sizes of type as possible, but separated by three or four asterisks. You should have seen Tschichold's face when we read on the proof from the translator *"Will you please de-bug this title-page!"* I was responsible only to Tschichold and never worked for anybody else in the firm, but I became very friendly with Allen Lane and he and his wife invited me several times to their home. Tschichold always spoke nicely about me, and helped me to get a higher salary, for I was a sort of apprentice. Allen Lane taught me, indirectly, how a firm like his could work socially. His calling on Tschichold in 1946-47 was part of a plan to give everyone the best opportunities and his choice of Tschichold proved to be the right one. Allen Lane always said that the money spent on Tschichold "paid itself back several times – it was a sort of advertising, a raising of the appearance which gave Penguins much favourable publicity." Books, he claimed, "were selected for their good printing."

What was Tschichold like in daily work? Rather silent, always a little worried, but with some sense of humour to clear away the worst calamities. His opinions were clearly stated. He knew exactly what he wanted and how to carry matters through in his own way: a rather German way and very different from the English, which often made him feel uncomfortable and lonely. Our one small room department became an island inhabited by two foreigners, and psychology was not his forté. I am sure his stay in England would have been happier had he only tried to understand better the special way of living, so contrary to strict German attitudes. Although he felt lonely, he very-seldom saw colleagues, and I do not know if he really wished to. Sometimes I guess he felt himself superior to most typographers, Oliver Simon and Stanley Morison excepted. At Penguins he was able to practice all his theories and apply his enormous knowledge and abilities to mass production of a previously unheard-of scale. Unfortunately, this offer came from a country alien to his former way of life. For the second time in his life he felt a refugee; no wonder that a foriegn colleague could sometimes be a sort of consolation to him. Method, efficiency, hard working, seriousness:

these were the ingredients of the long working days of this perfectionist.

After a year I felt that I should go and work somewhere else. In one's youth one must not stay too long in one place and do routine work, but long enough to gain all you can from your boss. So I went to see Milner Gray and arranged for a job with his Design Research Unit for the following January. But in October or November that year came devaluation of the pound. Tschichold asked for, but did not get, an increase in his salary, so we both left Penguins on the same day, a fortnight before Christmas 1949.

My job with Milner Gray did not turn out as I had hoped, and before my return to Denmark in April 1950 I went back to Penguins to help our successor, Hans Schmoller from Curwen Press, into his new job.

My stay with Tschichold stands for me as one of the brightest and most happy periods of my life. I was being taught by one of the foremost typographers in the world – and being paid for it. The teacher was a man who wanted to give away for nothing his great knowledge to a younger man; one, who, on his side, tried to live up to the demands of a master.

On the other hand, however, the impression Tschichold made on me was so deep that it was many years before I was able to stand on my own two feet. Tschichold was terribly restricting with specific personal rules and conventions. Many things just could not be done! Later I realised that the possibilities were endless. On the other hand, we should always start off by learning basic principles properly in order to know when to break them, for freedom can only be based on rules. Tschichold made me realise these rules, but, at the same time, prevented me from expressing my true temper.

Well, that's the price of a strong teacher, and I never regret this period of restriction. It is still there at the back of my mind, but over it the waves roll. Christopher Plantin has shown us in his printer's mark that the art of typography is a pendulum between the fixed and the variable.

A Selected List of Publications by Jan Tschichold

Many of Tschichold's articles published between 1925 and 1944, and also numerous translations of articles published after 1944 into danish, english, finnish, dutch, swedish and czech are not included.

Books

Die neue Typographie. Berlin 1928. Out of print.

Foto-auge. Photo-Eye (with Franz Roh). Stuttgart 1929. Out of print.

Eine Stunde Druckgestaltung. An Hour of Print Design, Stuttgart 1930. Out of print.

Schriftschreiben für Setzer. Lettering for Compositors, Frankfurt am Main 1931. Out of print.

Typographische Entwurfstechnik. The Technique of Drawing Layouts, Stuttgart 1932. Out of print. Translated into English by Ruari McLean, *How To Draw Layouts*, limited edition of 150 copies by Merchiston Publishing, Napier University in Edinburgh, 1991.

Typographische Gestaltung. Typographic Design, Benno Schwabe, Basle, 1935.

Funktionel Typografi: København 1937. Out of print.

Typografisk gestaltning. Stockholm 1937. Out of print.

Typografische Vormgeving. Amsterdam 1938. Out of print.

Der frühe chinesische Farbendruk, Early Chinese Color Printing, Holbein-Verlag, Basle, 1940 and 1951. Also in French and English. Out of print.

Chinesische Farbendrucke aus dem Lehrbuch des Senfkorngartens. Basel 1941 and 1951. Also in English. Out of print.

Schriftkunde, Schreibübungen und Skizzieren für Setzer. Basel, 1942.

Der Holzschneider und Bilddrucker Hu Cheng-yen. Basel 1943 and 1951. Also in English. Out of print.

Chinesische Farbendrucke der Gegenwart. Basel 1944 and 1951. Also in English. Out of print.

Chinesisches Gedichtpapier vom Meister der Zehnbambushalle. Basel 1947. Also in English. Out of print.

Papiergotter aus Peking. Basel: Basler Druck- and Verlagsanstalt, 1951. Private edition; not available through the book trade.

Geschichte der Schrift in Bildern. An Illustrated History of Writing and Lettering. Holbein-Verlag, Basel 1941, 1946, 1951. Fourth edn.: Hamburg: Hauswedell, 1961.

An Illustrated History of Lettering and Writing. London 1947. Out of print.

Gute Schriftformen. Good Letter Forms, Basel: Lehrmittelverlag des erziehungsdepartements, 1941/42, 1943/44, 1945/46. Out of print.

Schatzkammer der Schreibkunst. A Treasury of Calligraphy, Basel: Birkhauser, 1945.

God och dålig typografi. Goteborg. Wezata, 1947.

Letterkennis. Mijdrecht: Stichting Graphilec, 1948. (Typography not by the author.)

Was jedermann vom Buchdruck wissen sollte. Basel: Birkhauser, 1949.

About Calligraphy, Typography and Letterspacing. Southampton: Southern College of Art, 1951. Previously printed in Printing Review.

Wat iederen van drukwerk behoort te weten. Amsterdam: Allert de Lange, 1951.

Vad var och en bör reta om boktryk. Stockholm: Grafiska Konstanstalten Tryckeri. AB, 1952. Out of print.

Hvad enhver bor vide om bogtryk. København: F.E. Bording AS, 1952.

I bogens tjeneste. København: Forening for Boghaandvaek, 1951.

Im dienste des buches. Designing Books, St. Gallen: SGM-Bücherei, 1951. Out of print.

Designing Books. New York: Wittenborn, Schultz, Inc., 1951.

Schriftkunde, Schreibübungen und Skizzieren fur Setzer, Lettering and Layout for Compositors, Benno Schwabe, Basel 1942. Second edn.: Berlin 1951. Out of print.

Meisterbuch der Schrift. Treasury of Alphabets and Lettering, Ravensburg: Otto Maier, 1952. Second edn. 1965.

Treasury of Alphabets and Lettering. (English edition of the previous title.) New York: Reinhold Publishing Corporation, 1966.

Beschreibendes Verzeichnis von einhundertzwanzig Blättern verzierten chinesischen Briefpapiers der jüngsten Zeit aus der sammlung Jan Tschichold. Basel: Gewerbemuseum, 1953.

Formenwandlungen der Et-Zeichen. Frankfurt am Main: D. Stempel, 1954.Not available through the book trade.

Bokens Proportioner. Göteborg: Wezäta, 1955.

De Proporties van het boek. Amsterdam: Intergrafia, 1955.

Kinesisk bogtryk. Privately printed. København: Viggo Borch, 1957.

Ts' ai Lun, papirets opfinder. Privately printed. København: Viggo Borch, 1957.

Schonste liebe mich, German Baroque Love Poems, Heidelberg, 1957.

Der chinesische und der japanische mehrfarbige Holztafeldruck, technisch, Privately printed. Basel, 1959.

Erfreuliche Drucksachen durch gute Typographie. 'Enjoyable printed matter by means of good typography', Verlag, Ravensburg: Otto Maier, 1960.

Zur Typographie der Gegenwart. Privately printed. Bern: The Monotype Corporation Ltd., 1960.

Vues cavalières sur le modernisme en tyographie. Privately printed. Bern: The Monotype Corporation Ltd, 1961.

Willkürfreie Maßverhältnisse der Buchseite und des Satzspiegels. Privately printed. Basel: Bucherer Kurrus, 1962.

La technique de l'estampe polychrome, en Chine et au Japon. Privately printed. Basel: Bucherer Kurrus, 1962.

[Translation of.] T .J. Cobden-Sanderson: *Das Ideale Buch oder Schöne Buch.* Deutsch von Jan Tschichold. Privately printed. Basel: Bucherer, Kurrus, 1963.

Ändamålsenliga och vackra trychsaker genom god typograie. Stockholm: Bonniers, 1965.

Asymmetric Typography. Translated by Ruari McLean. (English translation of *Typographische Gestaltung*.) New York: Reinhold Publishing Corporation, and London: Faber & Faber, 1967.

Die Bildersammlung der Zehnbambushalle. Chinese Color Prints from the Ten Bamboo Studio, With twenty-four colored full size copies of the earliest proofs from the masterpiece of Chinese colour printing of the Ming dynasty. Eugen Rentsch, Verlag, Erlenback-Zürich, Switzerland and Stuttgart: 1970. (Gold medal of the International Book Art Exhibition, Leipzig 1971. The work received the further distinction of being judged one of the twenty-five finest books in Switzerland in 1970 and as one of the thirty-five finest books of the world in 1969/70 by the jury of the Second Biennial Israel Museum International Art Book Prize.)

Das Alphabet des Damianus Moyllus, Parma um 1483. Privately printed. Basel: Bucherer, Kurrus, 1971.

Der chinesische Stempel: Ursprung des Buchdrucks. Privately printed. Basel: Bucherer Kurrus, 1971.

Schriftkunst. Kalender für 1975. 'Das Kabinett.' Dresden: VEB Verlag'der Kunst, 1974.

Ausgewählte Aufsatze über Fragen der Gestalt des Buches und der Typographie. – Basel: Birkhauser, 1975.

Die neue Typographie, Facsimile reprint of 1928 edition, with essays on the book's history by Werner Doede, Jan Tschichold and Gerd Fleischmann, Berlin, 1987.

BOOKS EDITED BY JAN TSCHICHOLD

Chinesisches Novellenbuch. Deutsch von Eduard Grisebach. Basel: Birkhäuser, 1945.

Hafis. Eine Sammlung persischer Gedichte von George Friedrich Daumer. Basel: Birkhäuser, 1945.

Louis Barbedor: *Les Ecritures Financiere, et Italienne-Bastarde dans leur naturel* (Paris, 1647). New impression. The identity of the editor is not stated in the text and is appears only on the book jacket. Basle, 1946. Out of print.

Laurence Sterne: *Yoricks empfindsame Reise durch Frankreich und Italien.* With etchings by H.F. Füger and C.G. Geyser. Basel: Birkhäuser, 1951.

Schönste liebe mich. Heidelberg: Lambert Schneider, 1957.

John Seddon: *The Penman's Paradise* (London, c. 1695). New impression. Stuttgart-Bad Cannstatt: Cantz, 1966. Out of print.

Ein Buchstabenbuch von Pierre le Bé (Paris 1601). New impression. Stuttgart-Bad Cannstatt: Cantz, 1974.

Das Schreibbuch des Vespasiano Amphiareo (Venedig, 1554). New impression. Stuttgart-Bad Cannstatt: Cantz, 1975.

ARTICLES

'Die neue Gestaltung.''Elementare Typographie.'' — *Typographische Mitteilungen,* October, Leipzig, 1925.

In the *Graphische Berufsschule,* a periodical of the Graphische Berufsschule of Munich, appeared the following articles by Jan Tschichold.

Nr. 1, 1928: 'Der Geschäftsbrief nach DIN 676';
Nr. 2, 1928: 'Japanische Typographie', 'Japanische Flaggen und Zeichen';
Nr. 3, 1928: 'Die genormte Geschäftspostkarte', 'Normung der Zeitschriften';
Nr. 3/4, 1930/31: 'Die wichtigsten geschichtlichen Druckschriften', 'Einige zweckmäßige Regeln für den Akzidenzsatz in neuer Typographie', 'Wie stellt man Negativzeilen her?';
Nr. 1/2, 1931/32: 'Die Rasterfolien, ein neues Hilfsmittel für Entwerfer';
Nr. 3, 1931/32: 'Vorgotische Buchmalerein'; 'Neue Formen der statistischen Darstellung', 'Zu Photos von Franz Roh, alten Briefmarken, frühen Guillochemustern und Briefmarken von Piet Zwart'.

'noch eine neue schrift, beitrag zur frage der ökonomie der schrift.'' — *Typographische Mitteilungen,* –March, Berlin, 1930.

'Die Entwicklung der neuen Typographie im In- und Auslande.'' — *Klimschs Druckerei-Anzeiger,* – 57, 1801-3 (Frankfurt am Main, 1930).

'Qu'est-ce que la nouvelle typographie et que veut-elle?'' — *Arts et métiers graphiques,* numéro 19, 46-52 (Paris, 1930).

'das neue plakat.' Catalogue of the exhibition''Neue Werbegraphik', held in the Gewerbemuseum, Basle, March to April 1930; 3-9.

'Das neue Plakat." — *Buch- und Werbekunst,* 7, 233-236 and IX-XVI (Leipzig, 1930).

'New Life in Print." — *Commercial Art,* The Studio, (London), July 1930, 2-20.

'The Composite Photograph and its Place in Advertising." — *Commercial Art,* December 1930, 237-49.

'Display that has Dynamic Force." — *Commercial Art,* January 1931, 21-26.

'Advertising the German Store." — *Commercial Art,* April 1931, 168-70.

'New Paths in Poster Work." — *Commercial Art,* June 1931, 242-47.

'Statistics in Pictures," — *Commercial Art,* September 1931, 113-17.

'The Constructivist El Lissitzky." — Commercial Art, October 1931, 149-50.

'Der Konstruktivist El Lissitzky." — *Graphische Revue,* 33, heft 4 (Wien, 1931).

'über el lissitzky." — *Imprimatur 111,* 97-112 (Hamburg: Gesellschaft der Bücherfreunde, 1932).

'Grundfragen typographischer Gestaltung." — *Typographische Monatsblätter,* 1, 157-58 (Zürich, 1933).

'Der Satz des Buches." — *Typographische Monatsblätter,* 1, 321-28 (Zürich, 1933).

'Die Elementarschrift in den Schulen." — *Typographische Monatsblätter,* 1, 369-71 (Zürich, 1933).

Collector (Jan Tschichold): 'Das russische Kinderbuch von heute." — *Typographische Monatsblätter,* 1, 409-11 (Zürich, 1933).

'Japanische Typographie." — *Typographische Monatsblätter*, 2, 126 (Zürich, 1934).

'Für die Hulliger-Schrift." — *Typographische Monatsblätter*, 1, 434-36 (Zürich, 1933).

'Mechanographik vor hundert Jahren. Guillochen, ein vergessenes graphisches Verfahren des 19. Jahrhunderts." — *Typographische Monatsblätter*, 2, 183-84 (Zürich, 1934).

'Die Anordnung des Schriftsatzes im Flächenraum." — *Typographische Monatsblätter*, 2, 214-19 (Zürich, 1934).

'Der Lehrling und die moderne Satzweise." — *Typographische Monatsblätter*, 2, 241-42 (Zürich, 1934).

'Europäische Schriften aus zweitausend Jahren." — *Typographische Monatsblätter*, 2, 349-80 (Zürich, 1934).

'Schriftmischungen." — *Typographische Monatsblätter*, 3, 32-37 (Zürich, 1935).

'Vom deutschen Holzschnitt des fünfzehnten Jahrhunderts.' — *Typographische Monatsblätter*, 3, 69-73 (without the author's name) (Zürich, 1935).

'Vom richtigen Satz auf Mittelachse, — *Typographische Monatsblätter*, 3, 113-18 (Zürich, 1935).

'Die gegenstandslose Malerei und ihre Beziehungen zur Typographie der Gegenwart." — *Typographische Monatsblätter*, 3, 181-87 (Zürich, 1935).

'On Ben Nicholson's Reliefs."*Axis*, April (London, 1935).

'These are the fundamental ideas of my typography." — *Typographical Work of Jan Tschichold*. London: Lund Humphries, 1935. (Eight-page pamphlet.)

'Neue Formen der statistischen Darstellung." — *Typographische Monatsblätter*, 4, 37-38 (without the author's name) (Zürich, 1936).

'Vom Basler Frühdruck." — *Typographische Monatsblätter*, 4, 149-52 (without the author's name) (Zürich, 1936).

'Die schweizerische Briefbogennorm." — *Typographische Monatsblätter*, 4, 156-64 (Zürich, 1936).

'Abstract Painting and the New Typography." — *Industrial Arts, 1*, 157-64 (London, 1936).

'Type Mixtures." — *Typography*, 3, 2-7 (London, 1937).

'The New Typography." — *Circle*. Editors J. L. Martin, Ben Nicholson, N. Gabo.London: Faber & Faber, 1937 (Reprinted, 1971).

'Satzregeln des Verlegers für den Drucker." — *Schweizer Reklame und Schweizer Graphische Mitteilungen*, – June, St. Gallen, 1937.

'Tafeln in Büchern and Zeitschriften." — *Schweizer Reklame und Schweizer Graphische Mitteilungen*, July, St. Gallen, 1937.

'Vom Papier and seiner Erfindung." — *Schweizer Reklame und Schweizer Graphische Mitteilungen*, August, St. Gallen, 1937.

'Vom guter und schlechter Typographie." — *Schweizer Reklame und Schweizer Graphische Mitteilungen*, October, December 1937 and February 1938. St. Gallen.

'Sinn und Form der Schriftproben von Druckereien." — *Schweizer Reklame und Schweizer Graphische Mitteilungen*, August, St. Gallen, 1938.

'Unsere Arbeit am Buche." — *Schweizer Reklame und Schweizer Graphische Mitteilungen,* May and July, St. Gallen, 1939.

'Gebrochene Schriften als, Auszeichnung zur Antiqua."– *Schweizer Reklame und 'Schweizer Graphische Mitteilungen,* November, St. Gallen, 1939.

'Der sogenannte Naturselbstdruck." — *Schweizer Reklame und Schweizer Graphische Mitteilungen,* December, St. Gallen, 1939.

'Sinn und Mißbrauch des Büttenpapiers and seines Namens."– *Schweizer Reklame und Schweizer Grapbiscbe Mitteilungen,* April, St. Gallen, 1940.

'Schriftübungen für Setzer und verwandte Berufe 1:" — *Schweizer Reklame und Schweizer Graphische Mitteilungen,* May, St. Gallen, 1940. nummern august, september 1940 und januar 1941.

'Titelblätter des 16. Jahrhunderts aus der Offizin Froschauer."– Beilage zur juni-julinummer, *Schweizer Reklame und Schweizer Grapbiscbe Mitteilungen,* St. Gallen, 1940.

'Herkunft und Form des ß in der Fraktur und der Antiqua." — *Schweizer Reklame und Schweizer Graphische Mitteilungen,* June-July, St. Gallen, 1940.

'Proportionen in unsymmetrischer Typographie." — *Typographische Monatsblätter,* 7, 65-67 (Zürich,1940).

'Die typographische Einrichtung von Tafelwerken." — *Typographische Monatsblätter,* 7, 106-8 (Zürich, 1940).

'Ursprung und Form der Zahlzeichen." — *Typographische Monatsblätter,* 7, 261-64 (Zürich, 1940).

'Vom Durchschuß." — *Schweizer Reklame und Schweizer Graphische Mitteilungen,* August, St. Gallen, 1940.

'Schreiben und Drucken." — *Schweizer Reklame und Schweizer Graphische Mitteilungen,* October, St. Gallen, 1940.

'Daten der chinesischen Erfindungen für das Buchdruckgewerbe." — *Schweizer Reklame und Schweizer Graphische Mitteilungen,* April, St. Gallen, 1941.

'Inserate in Zeitschriften."– Beilage, *Schweizer Reklame und Schweizer Graphische Mitteilungen,* August-September, St. Gallen, 1941.

'Wie muß ein Buch beschaffen sein . . .' (quotation from Taubel's Lehrbuch der Buchdruckerkunst, Wien, 1809.) — *Schweizer Reklame und Schweizer Graphische Mitteilungen,* July-August, St. Gallen, 1942.

'Die zehn schönsten Bücher des Jahres. Eine Anregung.' [Plea for the founding of an annual selection of the best books produced in Switzerland.] — *Der Schweizer Buchhandel,* 1, 393 (Zürich, 1943).

'Louis Barbedor, ein französischer Meister der Schreibkunst." — *Graphis, 1,* 218-26 (Zürich, 1944).

'Bonne et mauvaise typographie."– Von guter und schlechter Typographies."– *Publicité et arts graphiques, 1944-45,* 57-68 (Genève: Collet, 1945).

'Vom i-Punkt."'Der Ursprung einiger Zahlennamen." — *Schweizer Graphische Mitteilungen,* October, St. Gallen, 1945.

'Das schöne Schweizerbuch." — *Echo,* 25, 28-29, March (Bern, 1945).

'Einzüge." — *Schweizer Graphische Mitteilungen,* February, St. Gallen, 1946.

'Graphik und Buchkunst." — *Typographische Monatsblätter,* *14,* 263 (Zurich, 1946).

'Spanische Schreibvorlagen des 16. Jahrhunderts." — *Graphis*, 2, 79-86 (Zürich,1946).

'Alfred Fairbank, ein englishcher Kalligraph und Schreiblehrer." — *Graphis*, 2, 462-67 (Zürich, 1946).

'Rückentitel." — *Schweizer Graphische Mitteilungen*, March, St. Gallen, 1946.

'Enger Satz und Trennregeln."'Schlechter und guter Satz." — *Schweizer Graphische Mitteilungen*, April, St. Gallen, 1946.

'Glaube and Wirklichkeit, Belief and Reality." — Schweizer Graphische Mitteilungen, June, St. Gallen, 1946.

'Schutzumschlag and Streifband." — *Schweizer Graphische Mitteilungen*, July, St. Gallen, 1946.

'Die Maßverhältnisse der Buchseite, der Schriftläche und der Ränder." — *Schweizer Graphische Mitteilungen*, August, St. Gallen, 1946.

'Von der Schreibbinse zur Goldfüllfeder." — *Schweizer Graphische Mitteilungen*, September, St. Gallen, 1946.

'Die typographische Planung von Tafelwerken." — *Schweizer Graphische Mitteilungen*, October, St. Gallen, 1946.

'Bemerkungen zur Auswahl der schönsten Schweizer Bücher." — *Schweizer Graphische Mitteilungen*, November, St. Gallen, 1946.

'Auszeichnungen im glatten Satz." — *Schweizer Graphische Mitteilungen*, January, St. Gallen, 1947.

'Bogensignaturen und Bogenrücken-Signaturen." — *Schweizer Graphische Mitteilungen*, February, St. Gallen, 1947.

'Vom chinesischen Buch- and Druckwesen." — *Schweizer Graphische Mitteilungen,* March, St. Gallen, 1947.

'Die Auszeichnung von Überschriften."'Richtige Satzarten von Überschriften."— *Schweizer Graphische Mitteilungen,* April, St. Gallen, 1947.

'On mass-producing the classics." — *Signature,* New series number 3, March, 27-32 (London, 1947).

Penguin Composition Rules. [4 pages.] Penguin Books Ltd, Harmondsworth [1947]. (Not available through the book trade.)

'Herstellung von Klassikern in großen Auflagen." — *Schweizer Graphische Mitteilungen,* June, St. Gallen, 1947.

'Chinesische Volksholzschnitte." — *Schweizer Graphische Mitteilungen,* July, St. Gallen, 1947.

'Le caractère d'imprimerie dans l'imprimerie publicitaire – Über den Gebrauch von Buchdrucklettern in Werbedrucksachen." — *Publicité et arts graphiques, 1946-47,* 69-74 (Genéve: Collet, 1947).

'Kann Typographie von der bildenden Kunst oder von gesellschaftlichen Umständen beeinflußt werden?" — *Der Schweizer Buchhandel,* heft 16, Bern, 1948.

'Clay in the Potter's Hand." — *The Penrose Annual,* volume XLIII, 1949.

'Ton in des Töpfers Hand."– *Schweizer Graphische Mitteilungen,* February, St. Gallen, 1949. – Stultifera Navis, 6, 16-7 (Basel, 1949).

'Wirken sich gesellschaftliche oder politische Umstande in der Typographic aus?"— *Schweizer Graphische Mitteilungen,* June, St. Gallen, 1948.

'Einige Arbeiten von Jan Tschichold.' Beilage, *Schweizer Graphische Mitteilungen,* August, St. Gallen, 1949.

'Bildreproduktionen im Buch und an der Wand."— *Schweizer Graphische Mitteilungen,* September, St. Gallen, 1949.

'Zur Problematik der Reproduktion von Kunstwerken." — *Der Schweizer Buchhandel,* heft 11, Bern, 1949.

'Das Buchmuseum im Hause." — *Schweizer Graphische Mitteilungen,* March, St. Gallen, 1950.

'Meine Reform der Penguin Books." — *Schweizer Graphische Mitteilungen,* June, St. Gallen, 1950.

'A propos de l'emploi de caractères d'imprimerie dans la publicité." — *Revue suisse de l'imprimerie,* July-August, St-Gall, 1950.

'Wie Probeseiten aussehen müssen." — *Schweizer Graphische Mitteilungen,* October, St. Gallen,1950.

'Warum Absatzanfänge eingezogen werden müssen." — *Schweizer Graphische Mitteilungen,* November, St. Gallen, 1950.

'Die Garamond."– Beilage, *Schweizer Graphische Mitteilungen,* December, St. Gallen, 1950.

'Typographie einer Dünndruckausgabe im Taschenformat." — *Das Druckgewerbe,* heft 24, Berlin, 1950.

'Studie über die "beste" Satzbreite." — *Schweizer Graphische Mitteilungen,* February, St. Gallen, 1951.

'Typographie einer Liebhaberausgabe von sehr kleinem Format." — *Schweizer Graphische Mitteilungen,* June, St. Gallen, 1951.

'Typographie einer Liebhaberausgabe von sehr kleinem Format." — *Der Druckspiegel,* heft 11, Stuttgart, 1951.

'Erstrebenswere Eigenschaften zukünftiger Typographie." — *Der Polygraph,* 4, 312-13 (Frankfurt am Main, 1951).

'Symbolische Typographie." — *Der Polygraph,* 4, 576-77 (Frankfurt am Main, 1951).

'Det kinesiska brev - och diktpapperets historia.' *Svensk Grafisk Arsbok,* 1951, 61-77 (Stockholm, 1951).

'Weißes oder getöntes Werkdruckpapier?" — *Schweizer Graphische Mitteilungen,* March, St. Gallen, 1951.

'Über Kalligraphie, Typographie, Ausschluß und Sperren." — *Schweizer Graphische Mitteilungen,* April, St. Gallen, 1951.

'Klassifizierung der von uns gebrauchten Buchdruckschriften." — *Schweizer Reklame,* special number, May 1951 (Zürich, 1951).

'Was bei der Anschaffung neuer Schriften zu bedenken ist." — *Schweizer Reklame,* special number, May 1951 (Zürich, 1951).

'Hurenkinder und Anfangszeilen am Fuß von Buchseiten." — *Schweizer Graphische Mitteilungen,* November, St. Gallen, 1951.

'Vom chinesischen Buch- und Druckwesen." — *Form und Technik,* 3, 251-58 (Stuttgart, 1952).

'Alte Fehler aufgewärmt– Gerader Rücken, Kastenband." — *Typographische Monatsblatter,* October, St. Gallen, 1952. — *Der Druckspiegel,* 5, 261-262 (Stuttgart, 1957) and 6, 339-340 (Stuttgart, 1958).

'Über Typographie." — *Typographische Monatsblätter,* January, St. Gallen, 1951.

'Die Leserlichkeit verschiedener Schriftschnitte auf verschiedenen Papieroberflächen in Buchdruck, Offsetdruck and Tiefdruck." — *Kupferschmid-Blätter,* heft 10, seite 1-40 (Basel, 1953). Werner Kupferschmid & Co., Basel (Also published in French.)

'Wie der chinesische Holzschnittdrucker die Farben einpaßt.' — *Börsenblatt für der deutschen Buchhandel,* Frankfurter ausgabe, jahrgang 9, 341-42 (nr. 56, 14. jun 1953). — *Form und Technik,* Stuttgart, 8, 301-2 (nr. 7, August 1953).

'Color Registering in Chinese Woodblock Prints." — *Printing & Graphic Arts,* Lunenburg, Vermont, 2, 1-4 (1954).

'Der Erfinder des Papiers, Ts'ai Lun, in einer alten chinesischen Darstellung.' Ihren Geschäftsfreunden und Liebhabern schöner Papiere überreicht von der Zürcher Papierfabrik an der Sihl, Neujahr 1955. (With a color print.)

'Neujahrswünsche." — *Der Druckspiegel, 12,* 689-693 (Stuttgart, 1955).

'Die Proportionen des Buches." — *Der Druckspiegel, 10,* heft 1-3 (Stuttgart, 1955).

'Schrift als Kunst." — *Börsenblatt für den deutschen Buchhandel, 12,* 851-52 (Frankfurt am Main, 1956).

'Zur Typographie der Gegenwart." — *Börsenblatt für den deutschen Buchhandel, 13,* 1487-90 (Frankfurt am Main, 1957).

'Die Herstellung eines mehrfarbigen Holztafeldruckes in China." — *Typographische Monatsblätter,* April, St. Gallen, 1956.

'Konsequenzen des Drittelsatzes." — *Der Druckspiegel, 7,* 398 (Stuttgart, 1956).

'Rückentitel sind unentbehrlich." — *Der Druckspiegel, 1,* 22 (Stuttgart, 1957).

'Die Namen der Schriftgrade." — *Typographische Monatsblätter,* November, St. Gallen, 1957. (Seite 696).

'Auslassungspunkte." — *Typographische Monatsblätter,* October, St. Gallen, 1957. (Seite 614).

'Kann Typographie von der bildenden Kunst oder von gesellschaftlichen Umständen beeinflußt werden?' — *Typographische Monatsblätter,* August, St. Gallen, 1958.

'Geschichte des chinesischen Brief- und Gedichtpapiers." — *Philobiblon,* 2, 31-56 (Hamburg: Hauswedell, 1958).

'Fingerabdruck und Stempel, chinesische Ahnen des Hochdrucks." — *Börsenblatt für den deutschen Buchhandel,* 14, 625-26 (Frankfurt am Main, 1958).

'Ursprung und Formwandel unserer Lautzeichen." — *Börsenblatt für den deutschen Buchhandel, 14,* 803-5 (Frankfurt am Main, 1958).

'Das traditionelle Titelblatt, typographisch." — *Börsenblatt für den deutschen Buchhandel, 14,* 1378-82 (Frankfurt am Main, 1958).

'Graphik und Buchkunst." — *Der Druckspiegel, 2,* 126-128 (Stuttgart, 1958).

'Der chinesische Schutzgott der Drucker und Buchhändler." — *Der Druckspiegel, 6,* 305 (Stuttgart, 1958).

'Die Herstellung eines mehrfarbigen Holztafeldruckes in Japan." — *Typographische Monatsblätter,* October, St. Gallen, 1959.

'Chinesische Steinabreibungen." — *Börsenblatt für den deutschen Buchhandel, 16,* 1265-1267 (Frankfurt am Main, 1960).

'Der älteste erhaltene Bilddruck, China, 868 n. Chr.' (With a reproduction of the title-page woodcut of the Diamond-Sutra in larger size.) Basel: Clichés Schwitter, 1961.

'Gute Typographie in Gefahr." — *Börsenblatt für den deutschen Buchhandel,* Frankfurter ausgabe, 18, 1840-50 (1962). — *Der Druckspiegel,* 17, 754-67 (Stuttgart, 1962).

'Einst und jetzt." — *Linotype Post,* November, Berlin and Frankfurt am Main, 1962.

'Über Spitzenbildchen des achtzehnten Jahrhunderts. Notizen eines Sammlers.' — *Börsenblatt für den deutschen Buchhandel, 16,* 2080-85 Frankfurt am Main, 1960) and (with minor corrections and with six illustrations instead of one) in *Schweizerschen Gutenbergmuseum,* 49, 145-56 (Bern, 1963).

'Ein einfacher Weg, sich den Anblick häßlicher Schutzumschläge und Rückentitel zu ersparen." — *Schweizerisches Gutenbergmuseum,* 49, 169-171 (Bern, 1963).

'Neujahrswünsche aus vergangenen Zeiten." — *Roche-Zeitung,* 1963/4, 28-36 (Basel: F. Hoffmann-La Roche, 1963).

'Schrift, Papier, Druck." — *Roche-Zeitung,* 1963/2, 23-32. (Basel: F. Hoffmann-La Roche, 1963).

'Wilkürfreie Maßverhältnisse der Buchseite und des Satzspiegels."– The original edition of this text appeared privately at Basle in 1962. As well as having been published seven times in German, three times in French, twice in Dutch, it has also appeared in Danish, Norwegian, Finnish, Italian and Hungarian. A German reprint appeared in *Typographische Monatsblätter,* February 1964. The only authorized French translation is: 'Proportions rationnelles du format du livre et de la page imprimée."
— *Revue suisse de l'Imprimerie,* 4 (St Gall: Zollikofer) 1964.
A complete English translation entitled. 'Non-arbitrary proportions of page and type area' appeared in *Print in Britain* (London), September 1963.

'Rapporti tra formato carta e composizione di un libro." — *Graphicus,* 44, 13-20. (Torino, 1963).

'Kursiv, Kapitälchen und Anführungen im Textsatz des Buches und in wissenschaftlichen Zeitschriften." — *Börsenblatt für den deutschen Buchhandel, 20,* 1213-18 (Frankfurt am Main, 1964).

'Quousque tandem." — *Print,* XVIII, 16-17 (New York, 1964).

'Vietnamische Volksgraphik." — *Schweizerisches Gutenbergmuseum, 50,* 54-58 (Bern, 1964).

'Lithographierte Geschäftskarten des neunzehnten Jahrhunderts." — *Schweizerisches Gutenbergmuseum, 51,*–25-27 (Bern, 1965).

'Das älteste gedruckte Plakat eines seßhaften Händlers: Paris, um 1560.' [Discovered by Jan Tschichold.] Large portfolio with two original size reproductions and text. Basel: F. Schwitter AG, 1965.

'Tschicholds typographiske tanker . . ." — *Plus,* no. 11, 8-10 (København, 1965).

'Symmetrische oder asymmetrische Typographie?" — *Börsenblatt für den deutschen Buchhandel, 21,* 1581-82 (Frankfurt am Main, 1965).

'Die Bedeutung der Tradition für die Typographie." — *Deutscher Drucker,*
January, Stuttgart, 1966.

'Eine noch erhaltene gotische Holztype aus Christoph Plantins Offizin, um 1570.' Mit den besten Wünschen zum Jahreswechsel dargeboten von Bucherer, Kurrus & Co., Papiere en gros, Basel [1966].

'Herstellung und Druck von Einzellettern aus Holz in China, 1776." — *Schweizerisches Gutenbergmuseum, 52,* 116-128 (Bern, 1966).

'Folkegrafik fra Vietnam." — *Plus,* no. 18, 16-19 (København, 1967).

'Leben und Bedeutung des Schriftschneiders Jacob Sabon." — *Linotype-Post,* May, Frankfurt am Main, 1967. (Also issued as a separate item by the firms of D. Stempel AG and Linotype GmbH, Frankfurt/Main.)

'Clay in the Potter's Hand." — *Homage to the Book.* New York: Westvaco, 1968.

'Die Bedeutung der Tradition für den Entwurf neuer Schriften." — *Deutscher Drucker,* 26 June, Stuttgart, 1969.

'En sehr seltener Ku-su-Druck aus dem Jahre 1740." — *Druck, Archiv für Drucktechnik, 106,* 818-19. D-6056 Heusenstamm, 1969.

'Typographische Möglichkeiten im Zeitalter des Computer' 56-59. Prague: Typografia, 1970.

'Vorzüge und Mängel älterer and heutiger Typographie." — *Der Druckspiegel,* February, Stuttgart, 1970.

'Flöhe ins Ohr." — *Von den Möglichkeiten und den Notwendigkeiten künftiger Buchgestaltung.* Hamburg: Christians, 1970.

'Snatschenije tradizii w tipografskom iskusstwe." — *Iskusstwo knigi '65/66,* 120-128. Moscow: Isdatelstwo Kniga, 1970.

'Werke und Aufsätze von El Lissitzky." — *Typographische Monatsblatter,* December 1970, 1-24. (Also issued as a separate item by Gerhardt Verlag, D-1 Berlin 31, Jenaer straße 7, 1971.)

'El Lissitzky.' *Typographische beilage zum Druckspiegel,* juni 1971, zusammengestellt von Jan Tschichold (Stuttgart, 1971).

'Buchherstellung als kunst." — *Typographie und Bibliophilie.* Vorträge über die Kunst des Buchdrucks aus zwei jahrhunderten. Hamburg: Maximilian-Gesellschaft, 1971.

'Die Drucktechnik des japanischen Farbenholzschnittes ist nicht chinesischen Ursprungs."'Fourniers Geschäftskarte, 1752."'Kursiv, Kapitälchen und Anführungszeichen im Textsatz des Buches und in wissenschaftlichen Zeitschriften.' 'Chinesisches'"Reispapier": eine falsche Bezeichnung." — *Satz und Druck*, ausgabe 4/71. Radolfzell: Ernst Uhl, 1971.

'Das älteste gedruckte Bildplakat, Antwerpen, 1491." — *Druck Print, 109*, 240-241. D-6056 Heusenstamm, 1972.

'Eine schöne Handschrift aus der Glanzzeit der böhmischen Buchkunst." 'Fourniers Geschaftskarte, 1752." — *Typographische Monatsblatter,* April, 320-22 (St. Gallen, 1972).

'Illustration und Typographie." — *Die Buchillustration in Deutschland, Österreich und der Schweiz seit, 1945,* Band 111, 1-9. Neu-Isenburg: Tießen, 1972.

'Die älteste Schriftprobe: Erhard Ratdolts Index Characterum, Augsburg, 1486.'– Basel: Clichés Schwitter, 1972.

'Die beiden ältesten gedruckten bildlichen Händlerplakate." — *Satz und Druck,* ausgabe 4/72. Randolfzell: Ernst Uhl, 1972.

'Vietnamische Volksgraphik.' [Altered reprint.] — *Satz und Druck,* ausgabe 2/73. Radolfzell: Ernst Uhf, 1973.

'Wie das Buch foto-auge (1929) entstand." — *Kaldewey-Katalog 20*, (Hamburg, o.j. [1974].)

Works published in English Translation

Early Chinese Color Printing, London and New York, 1940.

An Illustrated History of Lettering and Writing, London 1947.

About Calligraphy, Typography and Letterspacing, Southhampton College of Art, 1951.

Designing Books, Joyce Wittenborn, New York, 1951.

Chinese Color Printing of the present day, London and New York, 1953.

Contemporary Typography, The New Laboratory Press, Pittsburgh, 1961.

Treasury of Alphabets and Lettering, New York, 1966.

John Seddon: The Penman's Paradise, Cantz, Stuttgart, 1966.

Asymmetric Typography, London and New York, 1967.

Chinese Color Prints from the Ten Bamboo Studio, London and New York, 1972.

How To Draw Layouts, Translated into English by Ruari McLean, limited edition of 150 copies by Merchiston Publishing, Napier University in Edinburgh, 1991.

The Form of the Book: Essays on the Morality of Good Design, Hartley & Marks, 1996.

The New Typography: A Handbook for Modern Designers, Ruari McLean, University of California Press, 1998.

Texts translated by Jan Tschichold

From English:

T.J. Cobden-Sanderson: *Das Ideale Buch oder Schöne Buch*. Deutsch von Jan Tschichold. Privately printed. Basel: Bucherer, Kurrus, 1963.

From French:

Paul Valery: Die beiden Eigenschaften eines Buches — Typographie und Bibliophilie. Vortrage über die Kunst des Buchdrucks aus zwei Jahrhunderten. Hamburg: Maximilian-Gesellschaft, 1971.

From Italian:
Das Alphabet des Damianus Moyllus, Parma um 1483. Privately printed. Basel: Bucherer, Kurrus, 1971.

Works on Jan Tschichold

Robert Harling: 'What is this'"Functional" Typography? The Work of Jan Tschichold:' — *Printing*, January, 4 (London, 1936). 'The man is different.'

B.E. [Bertram Evans]: 'Printing Art.' — *Industrial Arts*, 1, 155-56 (London, 1936).

Robert Forster: 'Jan Tschichold, Go-Winner for '54 of the AIGA Gold Medal.' — *Publishers' Weekly*, *166*, 2222-24 (New York, 1954) .

Paul Standard: 'Jan Tschichold: AIGA Medalist for 1954' — *Productionwise*, vol. 3, no. 5, 38-42 (New York, 1954).

Frederiksen, Ellegard Erik: *Penguin-bogerne og deres typografi.* (Denmark, 1956).

Mildred Constantine: 'Jan Tschichold – Master Typographer.'– Noel Martin: 'Tschichold's Position Today." — *Modern Graphic Design Number Two: The Typography of Jan Tschichold.* — Cincinnati: Th. J.W. Ford Company, 1957.

Max Caflisch: 'Jan Tschichold zum sechzigsten Geburtstag. Eine Würdigung seines Schaffens.' *Schweiz Gutenbergmuseum*, *48*, 87-91 (Bern, 1962).

Max Caflish: 'Jan Tschichold zur Vollendung seines 60. Geburtstages.' — *Schweizer Reklame*, heft 12, 535-38, Zürich, 1962.

Max Caflish: 'Jan Tschichold, an evaluation of his work to mark his sixtieth birthday.' — *Book Design and Production*, 5, 110-12 (London, 1962).

Georg Kurt Schauer: 'Ein kritischer Liebhaber.' — *Börsenblatt für den deutschen Buchhandel*, 18, 578 (Frankfurt am Main, 1962).

Georg Kurt Schauer: 'Typographie der Mitte.'– In G.K. Schauer, *Deutsche Buchkunst 1890 bis 1960*, seite 241-45. Hamburg: Maximilian-Gesellschaft, 1963.

Kurt Weidemann: 'Über die Arbeit von Jan Tschichold.' — *Landesgewerbeamt-Ausstellungsreihe Dokumentation der Grafik, Katalog 1-1963*. Stuttgart, Landesgewerbeamt Baden-Württemberg, 1963.

Kurt Weidemann: 'Jan Tschichold.' *Print in Britain, 11*, 24-29 (London, 1963).

[Paul Standard:] 'Heritage Session Cites Noted Work of Jan Tschichold.' — *Printing News*, LXXVII no. 25 (New York, 1966).

Paul Standard: 'Jan Tschichold: Proponent of Asymmetry and Tradition.' — *Publishers' Weekly, 191*, no. 18, 89-94 (New York, 1967).

Jost Hochuli: 'Sabon-Antiqua, eine neue Schrift nach Entwürfen von Jan Tschichold.' — *Typographische Monatsblätter 88*, 113-28 (St. Gallen, 1969).

Paul Rand 'Jan Tschichold: The New Typography.' *Print* (in a special issue on the 'Great Graphic Designers of the 20th Century'), XXIII, 45-49 121 (New York, 1969).

Herbert Spencer: 'Jan Tschichold.' — *Pioneers of modern typography*. London, 1969.

Willi Rotzler: 'Buchkunst in der Schweiz.' — *Schweizerisches Gutenbergmuseum*, 56, 1-65 (Bern, 1970).

Ruari McLean: 'Jan Tschichold.' — *Penrose Annual 1970*, volume 63, 88-104. London: Lund Humphries, 1970.

Werner Doede: 'Jan Tschichold zum siebzigsten Geburtstag.' — *Linotype Post*, heft 74 (Frankfurt am Main, 1972).

Georg Kurt Schauer: 'Meister und Mittler. Zum 70. Geburtstag von Jan Tschichold.' — *Philobiblon 16*, 79-91 (Hamburg: Hauswedell, 1972).

Georg Kurt Schauer: 'Die Funktion des Lehrers.' — *Der Polygraph, 25,* heft 7, 5 April (Frankfurt am Main, 1972).

Kurt Weidemann: 'Wo das Werk den Meister lobt.' — *Deutscher Drucker, 8,* heft 13 (Stuttgart, 1972).

Hans Peter Willberg: 'Dieser Mann macht uns zu schaffen. Zum siebzigsten Geburtstag von Jan Tschichold.' — *Der Druckspiegel,* March, 33-38 (Stuttgart, 1972).

Berthold Hack: 'Jan Tschichold als solcher.' — *Börsenblatt für den Deutschen Buchhandel,* 28, 602 (Frankfurt am Main, 1972).

Georg Ramseger: 'Der große Alte von Berzona.' — *National-Zeitung Basel,* nr. 152, seite 5 (Basel, 1972).

Erich Pfeiffer-Belli: 'JanTschichold 70.' — *Süddeutsche Zeitung,* nr. 76, seite 35 (München, 1972).

Fredric Baggi: 'Jan Tschichold – 70-årig bokskapare.' — *Grafiskt Forum,* nr. 4, 24-25 (Stockholm, 1972).

Albert Kapr: 'Jan Tschichold zum Siebzigsten.' — *Papier und Druck, 21,* 62-64 (Leipzig, 1972).

Rene Murat: 'Sedmdesátiny Jana Tschicholda.' — *Typografia, 75,* 430-433 (Praha, 1972).

Reminiscor (i.e. Jan Tschichold): 'Jan Tschichold: Praeceptor typographiae.' — *Typographische Monatsblätter,* 91, 287-322 (St. Gallen, 1971).

Erhard Frommehold: 'Jan Tschichold in Dresden.' — *Börsenblatt für den Deutschen Buchhandel,* Leipzig 1973- 140 (30) s. 552.

Hilmar Frank: 'Zum Tode von Jan Tschichold.' — *Mitteilungen der Akad. der Künste,* 12 (1974) h. 6, s. 19.

Erhard Frommhold: 'Zum Tode Jan Tschicholds.' — *Papier und Druck*, 23, 190-192 (Leipzig, 1974).

'Obituary. Herr Jan Tschichold: Influential typographer.' — *The Times*, 19 August 1974.

Georg Ramseger: 'Streng gegen die modischen Gags. Jan Tschichold, der große Typograph ist gestorben.' — *National-Zeitung Basel*, nr. 258, 19 August 1974.

Georg Ramseger: 'Kein Tummelplatz für Experimente.' — *St. Galler Tagblatt*, 22 August 1974.

H.P. Willberg: 'Jan Tschichold. Apologet der klassischen Typographie.' — *Börsenblatt für den Deutschen Buchhandel*, 72, 1392 (Frankfurt am Main, 1974.)

Philipp Luidl, ed.: *Jan Tschichold*, (Munich, 1976).

Ruari McLean: *Jan Tschichold. Typographer.* Boston: David R. Godine, Publisher, Inc., 1975. London: Lund Humphries, 1975. *Leben und Werk des Typographen Jan Tschichold*. Introduction by Werner Klemke, Dresden: VEB Verlag der Kunst, 1977.

Philipp Luidl: *Jan Tschichold Typographer and Type Designer: 1902-1974*, (Edinburgh, 1982).

Ruari McLean: *Jan Tschichold: A Life in Typography*. Princeton Architectural Press, (December 1997).

Print, European Design Annual, Bird in Hand, Jan Tschichold: Penguin Books by Richard B. Doubleday, New York, May/June 2005.

Bibliography

Atterbury, S. Rowley. *The Contributors,* Being the paper talk delivered to the Wynkyn de Worde Society at Stationerys' Hall on 16th May 1974. [With a Note by Sir Francis Meynell.] Westerham, Kent: Westerham Press Limited, 1974.

Aynsley, Jeremy. *Graphic Design in Germany 1890 — 1945*. London: Thames & Hudson Ltd, 2000.

Bartram, Alan. *Making Books. Design in British Publishing Since 1945*. London and New Castle, Delaware The British Library and Oak Knoll Press, 1999.

Bringhurst, Robert, Hadeler, Hajo. *The Form of the Book, Essays on the morality of good design*. London: Lund Humphries, 1991.

Brockmann, Josef Müller. *A History of Visual Communication*. New York: Hastings House, 1971.

Droste, Magdalena. *Bauhaus 1919 — 1933*. Berlin: Bauhaus — Archiv Museum für Gestaltung, Taschen, 1998.

Fifty Penguin Years at the Royal Festival Hall — This book has been published to accompany the exhibition Fifty Penguin Years, London, 21 September — 27 October, 1985. Published by Penguin Books Ltd., 1985.

Feather, John. *A History of British Publishing*. Routledge and Taylor & Francis Ltd., 1988.

Flower, Desmond. *The Paperback, Its Past, Present and Future*. Arborfield Products Ltd., 1959.

Frederiksen, Ellegard Erik. *Penguin — bogerne og deres typografi*. Danish, 1956.

Hare, Steve. *Penguin Portrait, Allen Lane and the Penguin Editors 1935 — 1970*. Harmondsworth, Middlesex, England: Penguin Books Ltd., 1995.

Hochuli, Jost & Kinross, Robin. *Designing Books: Practice and Theory*. London: Hyphen Press, 1996.

Hochuli, Jost. *Jan Tschichold, Typographer and Type Designer, 1902 — 1974*. The English translation of the catalogue is by Ruari McLean, W.A. Kelly and Bernard Wolpe. Edinburgh: National Library of Scotland, 1982.

Lane, Sir Allen, *Penguins Progress 1935 — 1960*, Published on the occasion of the Silver Jubilee of Penguin Books, Harmondsworth, Great Britain: Penguin Books Ltd., 1960.

McLean, Ruari. *How Typography Happens*. New Castle, Delaware: The British Library & Oak Knoll Press, 2000.

McLean, Ruari. *Jan Tschichold: Typographer*. Boston: David R. Godine, Publisher, 1975.

McLean, Ruari. *True To Type: A Typographical Autobiography*. New Castle, DE: Oak Knoll Press, London: Werner Shaw, 2000.

Meggs, Philip B. *A History of Graphic Design. 3rd ed.* New York: John Wiley & Sons, Inc., 1998.

The Monotype Recorder. New Series Number 6, Hans Schmoller Typographer, His Life and Work, edited by Gerald Cinamon April, 1987.

Penguin (Firm). *Penguins: A Retrospect: 1935 — 1951*. (Harmondsworth, Middlesex, England: Penguin Books Ltd., 1951), Pamphlet.

Penguins Progress, Number 5. Mass Production and the Art of the Book by Oliver Simon, September 1947.

Penrose Annual, A Review of the Graphic Arts. Volume 40, Penguins and Pelicans by Allen Lane, 1938.

Penrose Annual, A Review of the Graphic Arts. Volume 43, The King Penguins by Eric Newton, 1949.

Penrose Annual, A Review of the Graphic Arts. Volume 47, Reprints: Aldine and After by Hans Schmoller, New York: Visual Communications Books, Hastings House 1953.

Penrose Annual, A Review of the Graphic Arts. Volume 46, Penguins Books — Style and Mass Production by Lynton Lamb, 1952.

Penrose Annual, A Review of the Graphic Arts. Volume 51, A century for Picture Puffin Books by Noel Carrington, 1957.

Penrose Annual, A Review of the Graphic Arts. Volume 51, The Penguin Look and 'Monotype' faces, 1957.

Penrose Annual, A Review of the Graphic Arts. Volume 62, The impact of Stanley Morison by John Dreyfus, 1969.

Penrose Annual, A Review of the Graphic Arts. Volume 62, A checklist of Penrose articles 1895 — 1968 by John Taylor, 1969.

Powers, Alan. *Front Cover, Great Book Jacket and Cover Design.* London: Octopus Publishing Group Ltd., 2001.

Print, Bird in Hand, Jan Tschichold: Penguin Books by Richard Doubleday, New York, May/June 2005.

Print XVIII, No. 1, America's graphic design magazine, Jan Tschichold lecture to The Type Director's Club, New York, April 18, 1959. New Haven, Connecticut: W.E. Rudge Inc., New York, 1964.

Print in Britain, Issue 6. Style and Legibility: The Penguin Composition Rules, reprinted by kind permission of Penguin Books Ltd, October 1953.

Printing Review, Number 72, Penguin Panorama, A historical and typographical study of the publications of Penguin books, In honour of their twenty — first birthday by P.G. Burbidge and L.A. Gray, 1956.

Roh, Franz, *Jan Tschichold. "Mechanism and Expression."* Seventy — six photos of the period. Germany: 1929.

Schmoller, Hans, *Two Titans Mardersteig and Tschichold, A Study in Contrasts,* New York: 1990.

Signature, New Series Number 3, On mass-producing the classics by Jan Tschichold, London, March, 1947.

Tschichold, Jan. *Asymmetric Typography.* Basel: 1935; Toronto, New York & London: Reinhold Publishing Corp., 1967.

Tschichold, Jan. *Designing Books.* New York: Wittenborn, Shultz, Inc., 1951.

Tschichold, Jan. "Die neue Typographie." *Print Magazine.* 1959; submitted statement. New York: Vol. 18, No. 1, 1964.

Tschichold, Jan. *Leben und Werk des Typographen.* Introduction by Werner Klemke, Dresden 1977.

Tschichold, Jan. *Schweizer Graphische Mitteilungen,* No. 6, translated by Ruari McLean, Basle: 1950.

Tschichold, Jan. *Signature,* No. 3 (New Series), On mass — producing the classics, March, London, 1947.

Williams, Sir William Emrys. *The Penguin Story MCMXXXV MCMLVI.* Harmondsworth, Middlesex, England: Penguin Books Ltd., 1956.